THE
'EṢÂ

THE

G-d's Rescue Plan for Humanity

THE LOVING-KINDNESS OF G-D | VOLUME THREE

MARK STOUFFER

Note: in some cases, the verse numbers in the Tanakh are different from those in the Christian Bible. In this book, when such verses are cited, the verse numbers from the Tanakh are displayed in parentheses after the verse numbers from the Christian Bible.

The term "G-d" means God, and the term "L-rd," means Lord. I have chosen to use the hyphenated forms of these words out of respect to Jewish readers, as some Jewish authors spell these words with hyphens.

The term "Bible" is used in this book to refer to the Christian Bible, which includes the Tanakh and the New Testament.

For the sake of simplicity, I use the term "Jews" to refer to Abraham's descendants throughout their history, even though they should technically be referred to as either "Hebrews" or "Israelites" at certain points in their history.

Cover design and interior formatting by Rachael Ritchey

PERMISSIONS

Scripture quotations taken from the (NASB®) New American Standard Bible®, Copyright © 1960, 1971, 1977 by The Lockman Foundation. Used by permission. All rights reserved. lockman.org

Church History in Plain Language, Bruce L. Shelley. Published by Thomas Nelson Publishers, Copyright © 1982, 1995 ISBN: 0849938619 (PB). pp. 188, 211-212.

Let's Get Biblical, New Expanded Edition, Volumes 1-2, Rabbi Tovia Singer. Published by Outreach Judaism, Copyright © 2014 ISBNs: 9780996091305 (PB V1) and 9780996091312 (PB V2). pp. 1:4, 2:82-83.

Pontifex Maximus, Christopher Lascelles. Published by Crux Publishing Ltd., Copyright © 2017 ISBN: 9781909979451 (PB). pp. 103.

Saints and Sinners: A History of the Popes, Eamon Duffy. Published by Yale University Press, Copyright © 1997, 2006, 2014 ISBN: 9780300206128 (PB). pp. 94, 114-115, 233-234.

The Pope at War, David I Kertzer. Published by Random House, Copyright © 2022 ISBN: 9780812989960 (PB). pp. 215-216, 239-243.

Wanderings: Chaim's History of the Jews, Chaim Potok. Published by The Ballantine Publishing Group, Copyright © 1978 ISBN: 0449215822 (PB). pp. 413, 415-416.

"Remember the former things long past, for I am G-d, and there is no other; I am G-d, and there is no one like Me, declaring the end from the beginning, and from ancient times things which have not been done, saying, 'My purpose will be established, and I will accomplish all My good pleasure.'…"
(Isa. 46:9–10)

G-d has long-term plan for humanity. Unfortunately, we are too self-absorbed today to examine what He has done in history or to consider the future. Yet, the prophets have foretold of the day when He will set us free from all that is broken in this world.

CONTENTS

Acknowledgments xi

Preface.. xiii

part five
The Plan of G-d

Chapter 1   Eve's Sin; G-d's Plan 3

Chapter 2   The Tower of Babel 14

Chapter 3   G-d's Promises to Abraham...................... 20

Chapter 4   Moses and the Law.................................30

Chapter 5   Jewish History from Moses to the
Babylonian Exile 50

Chapter 6   Malachi 79

Chapter 7   The Sabbath 91

Chapter 8   The Incarnation 109

Chapter 9   70 CE 119

Chapter 10   G-d Loves Gentiles Too 135

Chapter 11   A Two-Stage Plan 148

Chapter 12   The First Century CE............................. 153

Chapter 13   The Christian Age.................................. 173

Chapter 14   Christianity in the Modern Age 205

Chapter 15   The Regathering of the Jews 223

Chapter 16   The 70th Week 234

Chapter 17   Daniel 9:24.................................256

Chapter 18   The Magnificent Plan of G-d 273

Index 287

ACKNOWLEDGMENTS

Thanks to all who have helped me in the production of this book. I appreciate you!

Thank you Todd Friedberg, Ken Barker, Rich Smith, Dan Scott, and Noushi for fact-checking all of the chapters.

Thank you Andrea Baugher for editing this book. You made it better. I was surprised by how good you are at catching mistakes.

Thank you Todd for the final review. It was needed.

Thanks once again to Rachael Ritchey for the great cover and formatting. You are such a joy to work with.

Thank you J. R. Klein for helping with the pronunciation of the Hebrew words and for your cultural check of the final chapter.

Thanks to Dennis Kambury for narrating this book. Your talent makes my writing better.

Thank you to all the people on the launch team. Your hard work is necessary for this book to get off the ground. Thank you, Joyce Aubuchon, Haven Barker, Victoria Bonner, Angela Breaux, Edison, Todd Friedberg, Ken Harrah, Scott Herrmann, John Hoban, Hannah Keyes, Tony Khoury, Anya Mundew, Mike Mundew, Dave Powers, Hassan Saadat, Patrick Schumer, Dan Scott, Chuck Sheridan, Chip Shillington, Dave Stouffer, Jim Swearingen, Lisa Thomas, Al Tucker, Andy Watkinson, Rebecca White, and Susan Williams.

Thank you Ben Gibbons for sharing with me your experience with the Catholic Church.

Thank you to everyone in my Home Church for praying for G-d to use this book. Thanks also to the people on the launch team for all of your prayers. Every prayer is invaluable.

Thank you Noushi for promoting all of my books and for your unwavering support.

Finally, thank you G-d for including me in the writing of your book. How exciting it has been to watch you get the first two books into the hands of people who connect with them.

PREFACE

I am a Christian layperson, and I love G-d and the Bible. I am writing this book to Jewish laypeople who want to know the truth about Jesus. Of course, many Jewish people have already made up their minds about Jesus, and they are not interested in Him. If you are in that group, this book is not for you. But, if you have some level of curiosity about Jesus, then I encourage you to read on.

This book is the third volume in a series of four. In the first book, we considered if the sacrificial system in the Tanakh foreshadowed Jesus' death on the cross. We also looked at the lives of a series of heroes from the Tanakh. Then we asked if the events in their lives that were similar to events in Jesus' life were placed in the Tanakh on purpose to foreshadow Jesus. In the second book, we examined the messianic prophecies of the Tanakh to see how well Jesus fulfilled them.

In this book, we will study the plan of G-d presented in the Tanakh and the New Testament. For, G-d has a plan to deliver mankind from the curses we have been living under since the dawn of history, when our foreparents rebelled in the Garden of Eden. These curses include separation from G-d, the suffering that goes on in this broken world, and death. G-d's plan has included using His people, the Jews, to reveal Himself to the world by blessing them and giving them the Law and the Tanakh. G-d's plan also includes sending a deliverer, born of the Jews, to pay the price of justice for our moral guilt. Jesus of Nazareth claimed to be the Messiah.

In His famous speech, the Olivet Discourse, Jesus stated that He will return at the end of time to carry out the remainder of G-d's plan. Namely, He will deliver the Jews from a violent, anti-Semitic world.

Hence, according to Jesus, there are two comings of the Messiah. Indeed, it is necessary for there to be two comings with a substantial gap of time between them in order for everyone on earth to have a chance to hear about Jesus and receive forgiveness for their sins.

Evil is on the rise today. One day, this evil will reach a point of no return, and Jesus will return. We will study the prophecies of the end times, including Daniel Chapter 9. In Dan. 9:24, Daniel lists the six outcomes of G-d's long-term plan, which He will accomplish at the end of history. These outcomes are G-d-sized. Indeed, it is hard for us to conceive how good it will be in that day.

Thank you G-d.

part five

THE PLAN
OF G-D

1

EVE'S SIN; G-D'S PLAN

G-d's enemy picked his moment and approached Eve when she was not with G-d. Then he whispered words of rebellion to Eve. His accusations against G-d's character were not true, but they sounded reasonable. In their exchange, Satan may have embodied a snake. That is the common understanding of this passage, and it is entirely possible. Or, the writer of Genesis may have merely called him a snake metaphorically. In other words, Satan approached her stealthily, and his words were venomous and lethal.

Here is the passage:

> Now the serpent was more crafty than any beast of the field which the L-rd G-d had made. And he said to the woman, "Indeed, has G-d said, 'You shall not eat from any tree of the garden'?" And the woman said to the serpent, "From the fruit of the trees of the garden we may eat; but from the fruit of the tree which is in the middle of the garden, G-d has said, 'You shall not eat from it or touch it, lest you die.'"

And the serpent said to the woman, "You surely shall not die! For G-d knows that in the day you eat from it your eyes will be opened, and you will be like G-d, knowing good and evil." When the woman saw that the tree was good for food, and that it was a delight to the eyes, and that the tree was desirable to make one wise, she took from its fruit and ate; and she gave also to her husband with her, and he ate. Then the eyes of both of them were opened, and they knew that they were naked; and they sewed fig leaves together and made themselves loin coverings.

And they heard the sound of the L-rd G-d walking in the garden in the cool of the day, and the man and his wife hid themselves from the presence of the L-rd G-d among the trees of the garden. Then the L-rd G-d called to the man, and said to him, "Where are you?" And he said, "I heard the sound of Thee in the garden, and I was afraid because I was naked; so I hid myself." And He said, "Who told you that you were naked? Have you eaten from the tree of which I commanded you not to eat?" And the man said, "The woman whom Thou gavest to be with me, she gave me from the tree, and I ate." Then the L-rd G-d said to the woman "What is this you have done?" And the woman said, "The serpent deceived me, and I ate." And the L-rd G-d said to the serpent, "Because you have done this, cursed are you more than all cattle, and more than every beast of the field; on your belly shall you go, and dust shall you eat all the days of your life; and I will put enmity between you and the woman, and between your seed and her seed; He shall bruise you on the head, and you shall bruise him on the heel." To the woman He said, "I will greatly multiply your pain in childbirth, in pain you shall bring forth children; yet your desire shall be for your husband, and he shall rule over you." Then to Adam He said, "Because you have listened to the voice of your wife, and have eaten from the tree about which I commanded you, saying, 'You shall not eat from it'; cursed is the ground because of you; in toil you shall eat of it all the days of your life. Both thorns and thistles it shall grow for you; and you shall eat the plants of the field; by the sweat of your face you shall eat bread, till you return to the ground, because from it you were taken; for you are dust, and to dust you shall return." Now the man called his wife's name Eve, because she was the mother of all the living. And the L-rd G-d made garments of skin for Adam and his wife, and clothed them.[1]

In Eve's dialogue with the serpent, she misquoted G-d. Evidently, she had not been paying attention very closely to G-d's words or His character. But Eve did hear Satan's words. Upon absorbing Satan's assault on G-d's character, she did not pause to consider the truthfulness of his claims. She did not discuss it with Adam, nor did she go to G-d to talk it over with Him. She just took the plunge and did the one thing G-d had instructed her and her husband not to do. She ate the forbidden fruit. Then she handed the fruit to Adam, and he joined her!

Satan questioned G-d's honesty, but Satan is the one who is a liar. G-d had told Adam and Eve that they could eat the fruit of any tree in the garden except one. If they ate from that specific tree, that would constitute their choice to sever their relationship with G-d, and they would die for their unfaithful act toward Him. Indeed, every word from G-d was true. In

---

[1] Gen. 3:1-21.

addition, Satan accused G-d of holding them down. Satan told them that if they ate the fruit from the one tree, they would become like G-d, knowing good and evil. That was a lie too, for G-d had created them in His image, and they were already like Him.[2] Furthermore, the implication that G-d is one who holds out on us was false. The truth is that G-d had provided for their every need. First and foremost, they had a relationship with Him, and they experienced His love personally. Beyond that, He provided them with a perfect environment in which to live, wonderful food to enjoy, and each other as spouses. In addition, G-d gave Adam and Eve a purpose and free will. They were literally in paradise! Yet, Satan spoke to Eve and subtly leveled these charges against G-d's character. Satan was partially right in that, before this time, Adam and Eve knew nothing of evil. They were innocent, and they only knew good. Satan's words seemed to make sense to Eve, and she fell into his trap.

These lies are the first ones ever told to human beings against G-d's character. There have been many told since that day. Today, G-d's name has been so muddied that many people disdain Him and prefer not to even think about Him.

One of G-d's attributes is justice, which He administered in this event. Previously, Adam was a gardener, and fruit trees would spring up wherever he planted them. Their fruit was delicious as well as nutritious. Unfortunately, Adam did not appreciate how good G-d's provision was. Therefore, after he rebelled, he was no longer a gardener in paradise, but rather he became a farmer who had to contend with weeds, insects, and sporadic rainfall. He had to work from sunup to sundown in order to produce a meager harvest. So too, Eve had been given the honor of bearing children, but no longer would giving birth be a special moment to look forward to for nine months. Rather, delivering babies became painful and even dangerous. Of course, eventually, Adam and Eve died, just as G-d said they would.

---

[2] Gen. 1:26-27.

One may ask, how is this fair? After all, they did not know what evil was. Yet, they did know what good was. They knew G-d and how good He is. In fact, unlike us today, they were not confused at all about G-d's goodness. Hence, they should not have cast Him aside so easily, but they did. They made a free will choice to rebel, and for that, they were held responsible.

However, as grave as their death sentence was, in a sense, it was for our good. In our current state, we are unfit to enter G-d's presence. Simply put, Adam and Eve could not take it back. They rebelled, and justice was required. Had they not been sentenced to die, perhaps they would have lived in this broken world, separated from G-d, forever. The world they and their offspring would have ultimately created in their morally compromised state would have been hellish, and we would all be stuck in it for eternity. But G-d had a better plan.

Needless to say, G-d was not caught off guard by their monumental mistake. He saw it coming, and He had a plan ready when the moment came. He presented the outline of that plan to Adam and Eve in their dialogue.

Interestingly, the rescue of humanity would be accomplished by a savior whom G-d said would be born of Eve's seed. According to author Francis Schaeffer, "The reference to "her seed" is peculiar in Semitic languages because the male is considered the one who has the seed."[3] Indeed, two chapters later in Genesis, a genealogy is given dating back to Adam, and only the fathers are named. However, we do see a passage in the New Testament in which the phraseology is similar to that of Genesis Chapter 3. In Matthew Chapter 1, Jesus' lineage is given in which all of His ancestors are said to be born of their fathers. But when it comes to Jesus, He is said to be born of His mother, Mary.[4] Furthermore, in an effort to make sure his words were completely clear, Matthew declared that Mary was a virgin who conceived Jesus by the power of the Holy Spirit.[5] Matthew also

---

[3] Francis A. Schaeffer, *Genesis in Space and Time* (Downers Grove, Illinois: InterVarsity Press, 1972) 103.

[4] Mt. 1:1:1-16.

[5] Mt. 1:20-23.

called Jesus the "Messiah" in this passage. Could it be that G-d was speaking of Jesus in His conversation with Adam and Eve? In other words, He had a plan to offer them redemption from the consequences of their choice, but it would take a very long time for the savior to come.

The next thing G-d said in their conversation was that this descendant would bruise Satan on the head despite being bruised by Satan on the heel. This statement is cryptic, and yet it fits what happened to Jesus when He visited us 2,000 years ago. At the beginning of His public ministry, He withdrew to the desert and underwent a forty-day fast.[6] To be clear, Jesus drank water, for otherwise He would have perished. But undoubtedly, He was in a very hungry and very weakened state when Satan approached Him. In fact, Satan approached Jesus similarly to the way he approached Eve. First, Satan tempted Jesus to misuse His power to produce bread in a moment in which it seemed warranted to do so. In Satan's second spiritual challenge, he attempted to get Jesus to test G-d. Finally, in his third challenge, Satan offered Jesus rulership over the entire world if Jesus would only bow to him. Satan even quoted the Tanakh to Jesus, but just as he did in the Garden, he subtly twisted it. As opposed to Eve, however, Jesus quoted scripture accurately back to him. Then Satan departed, as he could not tempt Jesus to transgress G-d's commands.

But Satan is patient. He watched as Jesus would go on to incur the ire of the Jewish religious leaders over the next three to three and a half years. Indeed, their hatred grew, and eventually they were seeking Jesus' death. Satan saw his moment, and he intervened in history again. This time he tempted one of Jesus' disciples, Judas, with money and led him to betray Jesus.[7] Judas brought the soldiers to Jesus, and He was arrested. Within twenty-four hours, He was dead.

Certainly, Satan knew of G-d's words that he (Satan) would bruise Eve's seed on the heel, and her seed would bruise him on the head. After all, those words were spoken to him. Perhaps

---

[6] Mt. 4:1-11.

[7] Jn. 13:27.

Satan thought he could circumvent this prediction by assisting in the killing of Jesus. But alas, Jesus was resurrected—His death was only temporary. Satan did not see that coming. This setback was only a bruise on Jesus' heel. It was violent and deadly, but it did not last. For unlike Adam and Eve, Jesus never rebelled, and He was not under a death sentence. He died voluntarily. In so doing, Jesus paid the price for the sins of mankind. Hence, in this contest between righteousness and evil, Jesus defeated Satan in that He undid the eternal sentences of banishment from G-d's presence hanging over Adam, Eve, and every person ever since.[8]

It should also be noted that although there was no autopsy report following Jesus' crucifixion, it is certainly plausible that the lower spike punctured one or both of Jesus' heels as it was driven through His feet into the cross.

Surely, Jesus' birth, crucifixion, and resurrection fulfill this prophecy in Genesis Chapter 3. As well, His sacrificial death makes perfect sense in light of this event in which G-d gave sentences to Adam, Eve, and Satan and also set in motion a plan that would one day provide mankind with a pathway to redemption. Furthermore, just as Adam and Eve had free will to either stay in a love relationship with G-d or cast Him aside, so too it would be the same for human beings in the future. It would come down to a simple, free will choice to either receive Jesus' payment of justice on their behalf so that they could come back into a love relationship with G-d—or turn it down.

Of course, when G-d spoke these words, it would have been impossible for the three offenders to foresee Jesus coming to earth and dying on a cross. This prophecy did not explicitly lay out the first coming of Christ. Rather, these words were cryptic and scant. This was purposeful by G-d. Later on, more details would be added by the Jewish prophets. We will explore G-d's reasons for the initial lack of clarity and detail in Volume 4. But enough detail was provided to Adam and Eve in this conversation for them to know that the story was not over, and

---

[8] Heb. 2:14-15.

that, in the future, one of their descendants would have dealings with this deceiver. Only the next time, their descendant would foil this snake who led them into a trap.

Snakes were cursed for all of time from this moment on. Prior to this conversation, snakes might have had legs and walked, or maybe they had wings and flew through the air like skinny dragons. But never again would they move about in either of these ways. From this point on, they were condemned to slither along the filthy ground, humiliated. They would forever be forced to hide for fear of being trampled. They are repulsive to most humans, and we innately recoil at the sight of them. They are symbolic of Satan and his poisonous words. He also seeks to remain hidden from sight, for Satan is crafty, and he is always working to bring about the destruction both of individuals and humanity as a whole.

So, both Satan and snakes were cursed. Satan's punishment lay in the future, and it consisted of being bruised on the head, implying a mortal sentence. There were reasons for the delay in Satan's sentence. He had made accusations against G-d's character, and G-d could not simply mete out justice to him in that moment. Then Satan's lies could not be irrefutably rebutted. But one day, Satan's demise will come, and it will be eternal. Satan was dealt a legal blow at Jesus' first coming, in which his participation in Jesus' murder stands in stark contrast to Jesus' innocence. Following the crucifixion, Satan's ability to influence and hold sway over those who have chosen to come back into a relationship with G-d was neutered. According to the New Testament, the final blow will be dealt to Satan at the end of time, after Satan incites yet another world war. At that point, G-d will end Satan's reign of sin and destruction by casting him into hell once and for all.[9]

There is another element from Genesis Chapter 3 that also foreshadows G-d's plan of salvation for the human race. It is also lacking in detail. This element is in verse 21, which says, "the L-rd G-d made garments of skin for Adam and his wife, and

---

[9] Rev. 20:7-10.

clothed them." G-d used animal skins to make their clothes. This implies that an animal's life was taken. Here we see a foreshadowing of the Jewish sacrificial system, with the message being that we human beings are in need of another to be sacrificed in our place in order to cover our shame. Undoubtedly, the makeshift loincloths Adam and Eve fashioned out of fig leaves were flimsy and inadequate. They needed G-d's help with their first set of clothes. This element of the story also shows that G-d still cared about their needs. There was reason for them to hope that one day G-d would restore them and make everything right.

Still today, fig leaves are synonymous with our attempts to cover up our mistakes. Indeed, we love to point out when other people's excuses are inadequate, and we call them "fig leaves." This term has even taken on a comical tone. But in Genesis 3, there was nothing humorous about the sin of these two or about the consequences they would face. The point is that though we may try to cover our shame, our attempts are woefully inadequate. We are incapable of making up for our moral failures and earning our way back into G-d's presence. But G-d has a plan to take care of our need for salvation.

*   *   *   *   *

Genesis Chapter 3 is very concise and somewhat cryptic, and yet it sets the stage for the rest of the Bible. In fact, it is an outline of G-d's rescue plan for humanity. It reveals the origin of our problems, the nature of the spiritual battle that rages in the heavenly places over the souls of human beings, and the fundamental elements of G-d's plan to provide salvation to mankind. These elements include the concept of sacrificial atonement and G-d's statement that a special individual would one day be born from the seed of Eve.

As the centuries moved on and prophets were appointed by G-d, additional details of His plan were revealed, and the life and ministry of the Messiah began to come into focus. We studied a number of messianic prophecies in Volume 2. Here is one from Isaiah Chapter 49:

> Listen to Me, O islands, and pay attention, you peoples from afar. The L-rd called Me from the womb; from the body of My mother He named Me. And He has made My mouth like a sharp sword; in the shadow of His hand He has concealed Me, and He has also made Me a select arrow; He has hidden Me in His quiver. And He said to Me, "You are My Servant, Israel, in Whom I will show My glory...."
>
> And now says the L-rd, who formed Me from the womb to be His Servant, to bring Jacob back to him, in order that Israel might be gathered to Him (for I am honored in the sight of the L-rd, and My G-d is My strength), He says, "It is too small a thing that You should be My Servant to raise up the tribes of Jacob, and to restore the preserved ones of Israel; I will also make You a light of the nations so that My salvation may reach to the end of the earth."[10]

This person is truly special. He would be called from His mother's womb to play an important role for G-d. Through Him, G-d's glory would be displayed on earth. He would reach out to both Jews and Gentiles with a message of salvation and lead them to G-d.

In closing, we should take note of how good G-d is. He is the opposite of the subtle lies that have been injected into society about Him. G-d's rescue plan proves how much He loves us.[11] Adam and Eve did not deserve a second chance. Yet, G-d went to great expense to provide a solution and offer a second chance to all of us. G-d would not compromise justice, but He paid the price for us so that we could go free. G-d knows and

---

[10] Isa. 49:1-3; 5-6.
[11] Rom. 5:8.

cares for each of us. He is offering us forgiveness free of cost. But He will not push Himself on anyone. We all have a free will choice to make—whether to accept or decline His offer to one day return to the wondrous existence that Adam and Eve once knew.

2

THE TOWER OF BABEL

Genesis Chapter 10 records the genealogies of Noah's three sons as the repopulation of the earth started to get underway following the flood. In the next chapter, beginning in verse 1, we read:

> Now the whole earth used the same language and the same words. It came about as they journeyed east, that they found a plain in the land of Shinar and settled there. They said to one another, "Come, let us make bricks and burn *them* thoroughly." And they used brick for stone, and they used tar for mortar. They said, "Come, let us build for ourselves a city, and a tower whose top *will reach* into heaven, and let us make for ourselves a name, otherwise we will be scattered abroad over the face of the whole earth." The L-rd came down to see the city and the tower which the sons of men had built. The L-rd said, "Behold, they are one people, and they all have the same

language. And this is what they began to do, and now nothing which they purpose to do will be impossible for them. Come, let Us go down and there confuse their language, so that they will not understand one another's speech." So the L-rd scattered them abroad from there over the face of the whole earth; and they stopped building the city. Therefore its name was called Babel, because there the L-rd confused the language of the whole earth; and from there the L-rd scattered them abroad over the face of the whole earth.[12]

That is quite a story. It almost sounds fanciful, but were these people really all that different from us today? Let's consider the context. This event took place a very long time ago. The height of technology at that time appears to have been the development of the kiln and the ability to bake bricks. That is not to put that technology down; rather, it is simply to say that this was a very long time ago. Abraham lived around 2000 BCE, and this story took place long before him. At that time, technology was in its infancy, as was societal development.

Life was harder then than it is today. Nonetheless, they had the same basic needs and wants that we have. They needed food, shelter, and love; they desired wealth and power.

It was so long ago that they knew of the great flood, G-d, and their ancestors who were irretrievably immoral. In fact, the earlier people of the earth were so pervasively evil that G-d removed them from history, except for one man of faith and his family.[13] For otherwise, their sin would have negatively impacted humanity from that time forward. Despite knowing all of this, the people in Genesis Chapter 11 started to go down the wrong path again.

---

[12] Gen. 11:1-9.
[13] Gen. 6:5-8.

These people had some building skills, and their leaders commissioned the master builders to design a great city and as big of a tower as they could imagine. Then the people got to work and started to build it.

Once the tower was finished, how big was it? Were they pleased with it, or was it a letdown? We do not know. But either way, the narrative makes it clear that it did not reach into heaven.[14] What we do know is the condition of their hearts. Their hearts were overflowing with rebellion. In verse 6, G-d said that they had reached a point where "nothing which they purpose to do will be impossible for them." He was not speaking about their ability to build cities and towers, but about their capacity to rebel. Once a society goes down a path of elevating themselves and their will over G-d and His will, first, sinful behavior becomes socially acceptable, and eventually, acts of heinous evil take place. We have seen this time and again in history, including multiple times in the Modern Age. Therefore, G-d split them up to save them from themselves.

How is this relevant to us today? We have impressive towers, but they are for conducting the affairs of business and government, not for shaking our fist at G-d. However, our society does have a metaphorical gate, and we have told G-d to wait outside. He is officially not welcome in our government or our schools. People declare, "separation of church and state" the second anyone tries to introduce Biblical morality into society. Of course, it is also taboo to bring up the subject of Jesus in polite conversation.

Though there are many people in America who love G-d, there appear to be more who do not. In fact, a plurality of people has formed in our nation today. They have essentially the same attitude towards G-d as the people from this story, and they have spoken loud and clear.

Shinar was Mesopotamia. Sociologists have long since known that civilization began there.[15] It is between the Tigris and Euphrates rivers in modern-day Iraq. The people of Shinar

---

[14] Gen. 11:5.

[15] Sociologists call this land the "Cradle of civilization."

were aware that G-d had told their forefathers, the three sons of Noah, to spread out and "fill the earth."[16] But they were satisfied with Shinar, and they wanted to stay together. They knew what happened to Noah's generation, so they came up with a plan. They would build a magnificent city and a tall tower, and they would show G-d how capable and independent they were. Then perhaps G-d would leave them be.

But G-d loved them. If they would not listen to Him and spread out and farm the land, as He had told them to do, then He would give them a little push. It was for their own good. So, He performed a miracle, and instead of speaking one language, they instantly began speaking a number of vastly different languages. Of course, there were no translators or dictionaries, so they could not communicate at all. Therefore, they moved apart with those who spoke their language.

To be clear, for the most part G-d leaves nations, as well as individuals, alone. If anyone seeks G-d, He is there for them.[17] But if people are not interested in Him, He leaves them be. In this story, we have one of the rare instances in history where He intervened. But after this event, G-d was very hands-off with these new peoples as they moved and began afresh in new lands. Perhaps unsurprisingly, they developed pagan religions with depraved rituals, including human sacrifice. Nonetheless, G-d caused the rain to fall on their fields as well as on those of "the righteous."[18] Though disgusted by the evil, G-d still loved every soul. Just as the father of the prodigal son waited for the return of his son, so too, G-d wanted them to return to Him so that He could bless them.[19] But He respected their free will, and He left it up to them to choose how they would respond to Him.[20] In the New Testament, the apostle Paul portrayed G-d as a patient, loving father. Here are his words as he was addressing a crowd in the pagan city of Lystra:

---

[16] Gen. 9:1.

[17] Mt. 7:7-8.

[18] Mt. 5:43-45.

[19] Lk. 15:11-32.

[20] Rom. 1:18-23.

> "Men, why are you doing these things? We are also men of the same nature as you, and preach the gospel to you that you should turn from these vain things to a living G-d, who made the heaven and the earth and the sea and all that is in them. In the generations gone by He permitted all the nations to go their own ways; and yet He did not leave Himself without witness, in that He did good and gave you rains from heaven and fruitful seasons, satisfying your hearts with food and gladness."[21]

The Bible is the story of G-d's creation of man, G-d's love for man, man's rebellion and downfall, and G-d's rescue plan for humanity. The story in Genesis 11 is a microcosm of all of these themes. We could delve into a number of theological points in this story, but they are beyond the scope of this book. For our purposes, we will just bring up one. Namely, this story is the beginning point of the division of humanity into the different people groups that would become the Gentile nations.

In the next chapter in Genesis, G-d moved forward with His rescue plan with one man, Abraham. Abraham grew up in Mesopotamia. His father, Terah, practiced paganism.[22] But Abraham was open to G-d, and in Chapter 12 of Genesis, we read about how he placed his faith in G-d. From that point forward, G-d would work exclusively for the next 2,000+ years with one people group, Abraham's descendants—the Jews. However, G-d was not done with the rest of humanity. In Chapter 12, He mentioned them to Abraham when He called them the "families of the earth."[23] Indeed, G-d's rescue plan would one day extend to the Gentiles as well.

---

[21] Acts 14:15-17. The term *gospel* refers to the message of salvation through the death of Jesus. It literally means "good news."
[22] Josh. 24:2.
[23] Gen. 12:3.

Then, after the 2,000+ years, Jesus came. Just before He died, He gave a famous prophetic speech, the Olivet Discourse. In it, He mentioned these people groups from Genesis 11. It was time for G-d's plan to shift and for G-d's people to go out from Judea and reach out to all of the different peoples of the earth.[24] We will discuss this subject in detail in Chapters 12 through 14 of this book.

---

[24] Mt. 24:14; Acts 1:7-8.

3

G-D'S PROMISES TO ABRAHAM

Multiple genealogies are recorded in the Tanakh. These genealogies are laid out formulaically in which the name of the father is featured as the central building block. Abraham's father was Terah. Terah had two other sons, Haran and Nahor. They lived in Ur, where Haran passed away. After Haran passed away, they moved northwest to, of all places, the city of Haran.[25]

Abraham lived approximately 4,100 years ago. Those were dark days spiritually. In fact, "both Ur and Haran were thriving centers of moon worship; thus it is probable that the theological milieu in which Abraham lived for a good bit of his life was one in which the cult focused its adoration on moon worship."[26]

---

[25] Gen. 11:26-32.

[26] Victor P. Hamilton, The Book of Genesis Chapters 1-17, The New International Commentary on the Old Testament, Gen. Ed. R. K. Harrison (Grand Rapids: William B. Eerdmans Publishing Company, 1990) 363.

What was Abraham's stance towards the pagan culture in which he grew up? We know that Terah worshipped the pagan gods of his homeland.[27] But what about Abraham? We do not know because the Tanakh is silent on his spiritual life prior to G-d approaching him at the beginning of Genesis Chapter 12.

There is a story about Abraham's early life that is presented in a series of passages in Rabbinic literature.[28] This story was not among those G-d gave Moses, as it is not part of the Oral Law (the Mishnah). It presents Abraham as a sort of spiritual superhero. Please read these passages if you are interested. But in this chapter, we will examine Abraham's life based only on what is written in the Tanakh.

An important interaction between G-d and Abraham takes place in Genesis Chapter 12:

> Now the L-rd said to Abram, "Go forth from your country, and from your relatives and from your father's house, to the land which I will show you; and I will make you a great nation, and I will bless you, and make your name great; and so you shall be a blessing; and I will bless those who bless you, and the one who curses you I will curse. And in you all the families of the earth shall be blessed." So Abram went forth as the L-rd had spoken to him; and Lot went with him. Now Abram was seventy-five years old when he departed from Haran.[29]

---

[27] Josh. 24:2.

[28] It can be found in Genesis Rabbah 38:13; Targum Pseudo-Jonathan, Gen. 11:28; Pirkey Rabbi Eliezer 26 (61a;) and Sefer ha-Yashar 7-13. It is also present in Jubilees 11-12 from the Pseudepigrapha. Part of the story is found in the Gemara in 'Erubin 53A; Pesahim 118A; Sanhedrin 93A; and 'Abodah Zarah 3A.

[29] Gen. 12:1-4. When we first meet Abraham in Genesis Chapter 12, his name is Abram. Later in his life, in Genesis 17:5, G-d changed his name from Abram to Abraham, which means "father of a multitude."

The lineage of Arpachshad, one of the sons of Noah's son Shem, is given in Genesis Chapter 11. In Chapter 12, G-d picked Abraham, a descendant of Arpachshad, to use in a key role in His plan to bless "all the families of the earth." G-d was the initiator in this conversation. Five times G-d said to Abraham, "I will," followed by a magnificent promise. In exchange, G-d commanded Abraham to do one thing, albeit, it was a big thing. G-d called on him to go to a new country and leave his family and the life he knew behind. Interestingly, G-d did not spell out exactly where it was that Abraham was to go. Unlike the people in Genesis Chapter 11, who did not want to leave their homeland when G-d called on them to do that, Abraham responded by trusting G-d and going.

All of these elements are important. Abraham needed to leave behind his pagan culture and begin life anew. In his new life, Abraham enjoyed a personal relationship with G-d and followed His will. Abraham chose wisely, for G-d is good. Not only did Abraham's choice change his life and his legacy for better, it changed history forevermore.

G-d's promises are so important that He repeated them to Abraham in Genesis Chapters 13, 15, 17, 18, and 22. In addition, G-d passed on these promises to Isaac in Chapter 26 and to Isaac's son Jacob in Chapters 28 and 35. G-d not only repeated them to Abraham, Isaac, and Jacob for their sakes, but He also had all nine of these instances recorded in the book of Genesis for our sakes. Surely, there is something very important in these passages that G-d wants us to learn.

These promises make up the Abrahamic Covenant.[30] Let us look at the details of this covenant from the passage in Genesis 15:

> Abram said, "O L-rd G-d, what wilt Thou give
> me, since I am childless, and the heir of my
> house is Eliezer of Damascus?" And Abram

---

[30] The Abrahamic Covenant is issued by G-d in Genesis 13:14-17; 15:1-21; 17:1-19; 18:9-19; 22:15-18; 26:1-5; 28:10-17; and 35:9-15.

said, "Since Thou hast given no offspring to me, one born in my house is my heir." Then behold, the word of the L-rd came to him, saying, "This man will not be your heir; but one who shall come forth from your own body, he shall be your heir." And He took him outside and said, "Now look toward the heavens, and count the stars, if you are able to count them." And He said to him, "So shall your descendants be." Then he believed in the L-rd; and He reckoned it to him as righteousness. And He said to him, "I am the L-rd who brought you out of Ur of the Chaldeans, to give you this land to possess it." And he said, "O L-rd G-d, how may I know that I shall possess it?" So He said to him, "Bring Me a three-year-old heifer, and a three-year-old female goat, and a three-year-old ram, and a turtledove, and a young pigeon." Then he brought all these to Him and cut them in two, and laid each half opposite the other; but he did not cut the birds. And the birds of prey came down upon the carcasses, and Abram drove them away.

Now when the sun was going down, a deep sleep fell upon Abram, and behold, terror and great darkness fell upon him. And G-d said to Abram, "Know for certain that your descendants will be strangers in a land that is not theirs, where they will be enslaved and oppressed four hundred years. But I will also judge the nation whom they will serve; and afterward they will come out with many possessions. And as for you, you shall go to your fathers in peace; you shall be buried at a good old age. Then in the fourth generation they shall return here, for the iniquity of the Amorite is not yet complete. And it came about when the sun had set, that it was very dark, and behold, there appeared a smoking oven and a flaming torch which passed between these pieces. On that day the L-rd made a covenant with Abram, saying "To your descendants I have given this land, from the river of Egypt as far as the great river, the river Euphrates; the Kenite and the Kenizzite and the Kadmonite and the Hittite and the Perizzite and the Rephaim and the Amorite and the Canaanite and the Girgashite and the Jebusite."[31]

Of note in this passage is the practice of killing these animals and cutting them in half to form two lines of severed carcasses. This was the way that two parties entered into a covenant in the ancient world. This practice signified that both parties were committing to fulfilling their obligations under the agreement—or paying the ultimate price if they failed. Should either of them fall short, then they would forfeit their lives just as these animals had before the ceremony. In this instance, only one party passed between the carcasses. Namely, the torch, signifying G-d, passed between the two lines, while Abraham slept restlessly through the ceremony. G-d was communicating that this was a unilateral covenant. It was conditional only for G-d. No matter how poorly Abraham, or his descendants, would follow G-d, He would honor His promises.

Another important part of this passage is where it says, "he [Abraham] believed in the L-rd; and He reckoned it to him as righteousness." In other words, this is what G-d is looking for from us: that we listen to Him and believe Him. That is not to say that living a moral life is not important, for surely it is. But moral living is not the way to gain right standing before G-d. It was on the basis of Abraham's trusting G-d that he was "reckoned" or deemed to be righteous. Certainly, G-d did not acknowledge Abraham as being righteous because he was

---

[31] Gen. 15:2-16.

sinless, for Abraham had sinned. For example, Abraham deceived a foreign ruler by concealing that he and Sarah were married. Abraham did this because Sarah was attractive, and he was afraid that the monarch would desire her and kill him to obtain her. Sure enough, Sarah was taken into the ruler's house as Abraham just stood there and allowed it to happen! Fortunately, G-d intervened and rescued her. Unbelievably, Abraham committed the same sin again, as the exact same scenario played out a second time in another foreign land.

This proposition of righteousness being accredited to a person who places their faith in G-d is developed further in the remainder of the Tanakh and in the New Testament.

There are three key promises in the Abrahamic Covenant as well as some other personal promises that pertained to Abraham. Not all of the three promises are repeated in every passage. The key promises are: 1) descendants of Abraham and Sarah who would one day become a great nation; 2) a particular plot of land for this people; and 3) blessing for every family on earth through Abraham. The first two promises are specific, and we know exactly what they mean. The third one is a general promise of blessing for all people. G-d did not reveal the specifics of this promise to Abraham. However, another event featuring Abraham in the book of Genesis may provide a clue to the meaning of the third key promise. This event takes place in Genesis 22, in which G-d called on Abraham to sacrifice Isaac. Here are the first few verses from this passage:

> Now it came about after these things, that G-d tested Abraham, and said to him, "Abraham!" And he said, "Here I am." And He said, "Take now your son, your only son, whom you love, Isaac, and go to the land of Moriah; and offer him there as a burnt offering on one of the mountains of which I will tell you." So Abraham rose early in the morning and saddled his donkey, and took two of his young men with him and Isaac his son; and he split

> wood for the burnt offering, and arose and
> went to the place of which G-d had told him.[32]

In this passage, we see similar elements to those in Genesis Chapter 12. G-d again called on Abraham to do something that was a big deal. In this case, it was scary and made no sense. But G-d had proven Himself to Abraham by this point, and even though this command did not make sense, Abraham knew he could trust G-d that it would all work out for good. So, he obeyed G-d, and like before, he packed up what was needed and went on a journey, not knowing the exact destination.

Of course, we know the outcome. G-d worked it all out. Father and son were just fine, as G-d provided an animal to sacrifice in place of Isaac. A few verses down, in verse 14, it says that Abraham was so moved by what just happened that he named the place "the L-rd will see." The verb in this sentence can also be translated as "will see to it" or "will provide." For this is what G-d did, He provided a substitute for Isaac. What is interesting is that Abraham used the future tense. You would think he would have used the past tense and named it "the L-rd provided," but he didn't. Abraham's usage of the future tense portended a future event that would be related to this event. Jesus claimed to be the future substitute.[33] Amazingly, Jesus' crucifixion took place in the location that Abraham named "the L-rd will provide."[34]

So, why did G-d call on Abraham to do this? Certainly, it was to refine Abraham's faith. But it was also a foreshadowing that would echo down through the ages. Namely, there would one day come a special individual who would offer up His life as a sacrifice for the sins of mankind.

In Volume 2, we studied the book of Isaiah, which includes four prophecies about a special servant. These passages are called "the servant songs." The most famous one is Isaiah Chapter 53. In that chapter, Isaiah unambiguously and

---

[32] Gen. 22:1-3.

[33] Mt. 20:28; Jn. 5:39; 1 Jn. 2:1-2.

[34] 2 Chron. 3:1.

repetitively foretells that this servant will die for his (Isaiah's) sins and those of his people, the Jews. Here are three verses from Isaiah 53:

> All of us like sheep have gone astray, each of us has turned to his own way; but the L-rd has caused the iniquity of us all to fall on Him. He was oppressed and He was afflicted, yet He did not open His mouth; like a lamb that is led to slaughter, and like a sheep that is silent before its shearers, so He did not open His mouth. By oppression and judgment He was taken away; and as for His generation, who considered that He was cut off out of the land of the living, for the transgression of my people to whom the stroke was due?[35]

But there is another element to the argument that is being presented in these verses. It comes from a few verses earlier in Chapter 52. The other element is that this special servant's sacrifice would also be for the sins of the Gentiles.[36] Yes, G-d is that big and that good. His plan all along was to provide salvation to everyone on earth. Herein lies the meaning of the third key promise G-d made to Abraham: "And in you all the families of the earth shall be blessed."[37]

* * * * *

G-d started His plan with one man and his descendants, the Jews. And although Isaac would not die as a sacrifice, another one of Abraham's descendants would come one day and bear this burden. Of course, it was not just Abraham, Isaac, Jacob, and the special servant who were to play roles in G-d's plan. Rather, every Jew had an important role to play in His plan. The

---

[35] Isa. 53:6-8.
[36] Isa. 52:15a. Cf. Isa. 49:5-6.
[37] Gen. 12:3b.

Jews were to be witnesses to the watching world of who the real G-d is. As Isaiah wrote:

> "You are My witnesses," declares the L-rd, "And My servant whom I have chosen, in order that you may know and believe Me, and understand that I am He. Before Me there was no G-d formed, and there will be none after Me."[38]

The Jews were not to know *of* G-d, but rather to know G-d. Then they would be able to show the world who He is. The Jewish G-d is the one who said "I will" multiple times to Abraham.[39] When G-d said "I" and spoke about Himself, it was different from when our leaders speak this way today. Usually, when our leaders speak about themselves, it reveals their arrogance. But G-d spoke this way to reveal all the good things He would do for the Jews and all the people of the world. Despite our unworthiness, G-d initiated a magnificent plan to provide salvation to us. He used this language pattern because it conveyed how His plan would be carried out based on His strength and ability, not ours. G-d's plan included thoroughly blessing the Jews so that the world could look upon their lives and see how good He is. G-d's care of the Jews included giving them an upright judicial system and set of laws so they could experience a civilized society. G-d also gave the Jews a set of religious practices that portrayed the correct way to worship Him. The Jewish rituals contrasted greatly with the depraved worship practices of their pagan neighbors. In addition to the rituals, G-d gave the Jews the Tanakh, which contains strong prophetic evidence and an explanation of spiritual truth that makes sense. As the Jews were faithful to follow G-d's commands, He prospered their crops and their health. He also

---

[38] Isa. 43:10; Rabbi Aryeh Kaplan, *The Handbook of Jewish Thought*, (Brooklyn, Maznaim Publishing Corporation, 1979) 56.
[39] Gen. 12:1-3.

gave them a day off every week. In fact, G-d commanded the Jews to observe the Sabbath, while He took care of their crops. Would-be enemy invaders could not defeat the Jews despite great numerical advantages. For example, Gideon defeated the Midianite army with a shockingly smaller number of soldiers.[40] All of these things spoke volumes to the people of the ancient world. Those who were wise turned to the G-d of the Jews. For example, Rahab, a Canaanite prostitute from Jericho, accepted G-d, and He accepted her.[41]

---

[40] Judges 7.
[41] Josh. 2:1-21; 6:15-25.

4

MOSES AND THE LAW

The Law is perfect and beautiful. However, I know that my appreciation of it is shallow. For I have only studied it in the Bible; I have never followed it, except for the Sabbath. Thus, I understand that, to some degree, I am unqualified to write to a Jewish audience about the Law. Hence, this chapter will be more about the underlying role of the Law in G-d's plan than it will be about following the Law.

We can view the Law in different ways. The Law is a picture of G-d's character. This is the way He acts. He is righteous, and the Law reflects His character: He never murders, He does not steal, He keeps His promises, and so on. The Law is also the set of conditions in the covenant which the Jewish people entered into with G-d at Mt. Sinai.[42] Each individual law is a condition the Jews were bound to observe. If they followed the Law, G-d was bound to bless them and protect them. If they broke the Law, they would receive His judgment, as this covenant was bilateral.[43] Therefore, by following the Law, the Jews would

---

[42] Ex. 24:1-8; 34:10-28.

[43] This covenant is the Mosaic Covenant. Deut. 27-28 (Deut. 27:1-28:68.)

show the world the right way to live, and they would be witnesses of G-d's love, for He would bless them and shower them with prosperity.

Of course, with the exception of some interludes in which the Jews turned toward G-d and obeyed Him from their hearts, throughout most of the millennium between Moses' receiving of the Law and the Tanakh's conclusion, the Jews failed to keep the Law. They chose to disobey G-d, and the results were tragic.

*   *   *   *   *

In G-d's first interaction with Abraham, recorded in Genesis 12, G-d commanded him to do a very strange thing in the ancient world: to leave his family and move far away.[44] The reason for this command was that Abraham lived in Mesopotamia, in a culture steeped in paganism. Abraham obeyed and set off with his wife, nephew, and some servants for a destination G-d would reveal to him once they headed out. He wound up in what is today the most hotly contested piece of real estate on earth— Israel. At the time, it was known as Canaan, and it was the home of the Canaanite peoples.[45]

The Canaanites were pagans too. But they were different from the Mesopotamians—they were worse! They were exceedingly evil. G-d knew that in a matter of centuries, their evil would reach a point at which He would have to judge them. Their culture became so sick, in fact, that He had to remove them from history for the sake of mankind. G-d knew in advance the exact moment these people would commit enough atrocities so as to forfeit their right to go on in history.[46] It would

---

[44] Gen. 12:1.

[45] Re: modern geopolitics, it should be noted that the Canaanites were defeated by the Jews and ceased to exist as a people approximately 3,500 years ago. Also, the Arabs moved into Israel over 2,000 years after this event. At that time, the land was no longer known as Israel but was called Palestine. It was renamed by the Romans as a final insult to the Jews, whom they had exiled in 70 CE. For the sake of clarity, there is no connection between the Canaanites and the Arabs.

[46] Gen. 15:13-16.

be hundreds of years after Abraham immigrated to their land. In fact, once the time came, Abraham's descendants had been in Egypt for over 400 years.[47] They moved to Egypt during the great famine that took place when Abraham's grandson, Jacob, was quite old.[48] Over time, they wound up becoming enslaved by the Egyptians, who severely oppressed them. Eventually, G-d sent Moses to set them free. From there, the Jews made their way back to Canaan where G-d used them to annihilate the wicked Canaanite peoples.

Finally, Abraham's descendants were living in a land that was mostly devoid of pagan influences. This setting was necessary for them to be able to follow His Law. For we are weak, and we cave easily to temptation.[49]

Even in the Promised Land, however, the neighboring peoples were still pagans, and that is why G-d commanded the Jews not to intermarry with them.[50] Hence, the Jews were a beacon of light amidst a sea of spiritual and moral darkness. This was G-d's plan—for the Jews to be witnesses of His glory to the watching world. The Jews did not need to fear their neighbors, for G-d would protect them. They had seen His might before when He defeated the Egyptian army and when He caused the walls of Jericho to crumble to the ground.[51] So G-d wanted the Jews to be separate from their pagan neighbors, lest they be seduced by the sins of their neighbors. But He also wanted them to be visible such that any G-d-fearing man, woman, or child from amongst their neighbors could look upon their way of life and find G-d. Tragically, all too often the Jewish people failed in their role as representatives of the one true G-d.

---

[47] Ex. 12:40.
[48] Gen. 47:1-12.
[49] Deut. 20:17-18.
[50] Deut. 7:1-6.
[51] Ex. 14:13-31; Josh. 6:1-25.

Indeed, in the days leading up to the Babylonian captivity, the Jews' hearts were far from G-d. In the words of G-d:

> "Hear the word of the L-rd, O house of Jacob, and all the families of the house of Israel. Thus says the L-rd, "What injustice did your fathers find in Me, that they went far from Me and walked after emptiness and became empty? They did not say, 'Where is the L-rd who brought us up out of the land of Egypt, who led us through the wilderness, through a land of deserts and of pits, through a land of drought and of deep darkness, through a land that no one crossed and where no man dwelt?' I brought you into the fruitful land to eat its fruit and its good things. But you came and defiled My land, and My inheritance you made an abomination. The priests did not say, 'Where is the L-rd?' and those who handle the law did not know Me; the rulers also transgressed against Me, and the prophets prophesied by Baal and walked after things that did not profit.
>
> Therefore I will yet contend with you," declares the L-rd, "and with your sons' sons I will contend. For cross to the coastlands of Kittim and see, and send to Kedar and observe closely and see if there has been such a thing as this! Has a nation changed gods when they were not gods? But My people have changed their glory for that which does not profit. Be appalled, O heavens, at this, and shudder, be very desolate," declares the L-rd. "For My people have committed two evils: they have forsaken Me, the fountain of living waters, to

hew for themselves cisterns, broken cisterns
that can hold no water...."[52]

These words hold great emotion. They almost sound like those of a man, don't they? But these are G-d's words. Actually, it is not G-d who displays our emotions, but rather we who display His emotions, for we are made in His image. In the case of ancient Israel, He was deeply saddened. He loved them and wanted to bless them, but they just would not exercise even a modicum of self-control in saying no to sin.

*   *   *   *   *

It was on their journey from Egypt to Canaan that the Jews were given G-d's Law. The first two of the ten commandments forbade them from turning aside from G-d and consorting with pagan deities.[53] G-d forbade this sin two times to make sure the warning was clear.[54] But it did not matter, because the Jews were not listening to Him.

This may be confusing to us today because we are not surrounded by nations where the people worship crude statues and commit child sacrifice in order to appease their gods. But this form of religion ruled the day in the ancient world. G-d knew, first and foremost, that the Jews needed to remain faithful to Him. For, once the sin of worshipping false gods is committed, all the other sins flow from it.

G-d's intention was for the Jews to follow His Law and live their best possible lives. Listen to G-d's words to Joshua as he took over the leadership of the nation following Moses' passing:

> "Be strong and courageous, for you shall give
> this people possession of the land which I
> swore to their fathers to give them. Only be
> strong and very courageous; be careful to do

---

[52] Jer. 2:4-13.
[53] Ex. 20:1-6.
[54] Ex. 20:3-6.

according to all the law which Moses My servant commanded you; do not turn from it to the right or to the left, so that you may have success wherever you go. This book of the law shall not depart from your mouth, but you shall meditate on it day and night, so that you may be careful to do according to all that is written in it; for then you will make your way prosperous, and then you will have success...."[55]

Joshua listened to G-d, and it worked out very well for him. Near the end of his life, Joshua encouraged the nation to do the same:

"Now, therefore, fear the L-rd and serve Him in sincerity and truth; and put away the gods which your fathers served beyond the River and in Egypt, and serve the L-rd. If it is disagreeable in your sight to serve the L-rd, choose for yourselves today whom you will serve: whether the gods which your fathers served which were beyond the River, or the gods of the Amorites in whose land you are living; but as for me and my house, we will serve the L-rd."[56]

Certainly, it was vitally important for the Jews to follow the Law. The first three verses of Psalm 1 put it this way:

How blessed is the man who does not walk in the counsel of the wicked, nor stand in the path of sinners, nor sit in the seat of scoffers! But his delight is in the law of the L-rd, and in His law he meditates day and night. He will be like a

---

[55] Josh. 1:6-8.
[56] Josh. 24:14-15.

tree firmly planted by streams of water, which
yields its fruit in its season and its leaf does not
wither; and in whatever he does, he prospers.

In fact, there were a number of reasons G-d gave the Jews
the Law. They include:

1. As stated in Psalm 1, one of the main purposes of the Law was
so that G-d could bless the Jews. This is who G-d is. He is a giver
of good things. G-d wanted to bless both the nation as a whole
and each individual Jew. If enough people chose to trust G-d
and obey Him, then the overall ethos of the nation would have
been godly, and G-d would have richly blessed them. As we
discussed in the last chapter, G-d wanted the surrounding
nations to see the Jews' prosperity so that they could find Him.[57]
Life was tenuous in the ancient world. G-d's provisions for the
Jews consisted of the very things their neighbors were seeking
from their gods. But they worshipped false gods who could not
answer their prayers and provide for them.

2. G-d gave the Jews the Law so they would have a just legal
system.[58] First and foremost, this was for their benefit. How
important it is to the health and wellbeing of any society for
there to be a just legal system as opposed to a corrupt one. But
also, this was part of the witness of the Jews to the watching
world. Indeed, it is a witness of G-d because He is just.

3. The Law reflected to the people what G-d is like, for the Law
is holy, and it defines His character. Again, G-d does not murder
or steal, or anything of that nature. But beyond these things, the
positive commandments reflect His kindness. For example, the
Jews became enslaved in Egypt, and they were severely
oppressed. It would have only been natural for them to fall into
the same sin once they became a powerful nation. But G-d

---

[57] Isa. 43:10.
[58] Ex. 21-23; Deut. 16:19-20.

commanded them not to do that. In Exodus 23:9, G-d said: "Do not oppress a foreigner; you yourselves know how it feels to be foreigners, because you were foreigners in Egypt." Who is G-d? He is not like us. He does not overpower people and take advantage of them; rather, He is concerned with the welfare of the vulnerable. Similarly, Lev. 23:22 says, "When you reap the harvest of your land, do not reap to the very edges of your field or gather the gleanings of your harvest. Leave them for the poor and for the foreigner residing among you. I am the L-rd your G-d." Hence, farmers were not to try to harvest every single plant. They were to intentionally leave some of their crops for the poor. Furthermore, they were to go through their fields once, but they were not go back a second time to harvest any of the plants they missed.[59] This was a provision for the widows and the orphans. This concern for the poor, embedded in the Law, is a reflection of G-d's character.[60]

4. The Law shows us the correct way to live. This is the way G-d designed us to live, and it is its own reward. We are to be givers, not takers. We are to be honest, humble, and kind. We are not to wound others with our words; we are to lift them up. Only by living this way can we have healthy souls. As it says in Psalm 19:

> The law of the L-rd is perfect, restoring the soul; the testimony of the L-rd is sure, making wise the simple. The precepts of the L-rd are right, rejoicing the heart; the commandment of the L-rd is pure, enlightening the eyes.[61]

Furthermore, it is possible to keep the Law—not perfectly, but to a degree such that godliness defines you. Like Joshua, the prophet Daniel is a good example of someone who lived this way. Ultimately, it comes down to a choice, or a series of

---

[59] Lev. 19:9-10; Deut. 24:20-22.

[60] Isa. 61:1-3.

[61] Ps. 19:7-8 (8-9.)

choices, and anyone can choose to live this way. In the words of King Solomon:

> My son, do not forget my teaching, but let your heart keep my commandments; for length of days and years of life and peace they will add to you. Do not let kindness and truth leave you; bind them around your neck, write them on the tablet of your heart. So you will find favor and good repute in the sight of G-d and man. Trust in the L-rd with all your heart and do not lean on your own understanding. In all your ways acknowledge Him, and He will make your paths straight. Do not be wise in your own eyes; fear the L-rd and turn away from evil. It will be healing to your body and refreshment to your bones.[62]

Solomon's wisdom is on full display in this passage. As important as obeying the Law was, your attitude was just as important. For example, you could follow the Law out of a sense of religious duty, but that was not what G-d wanted. G-d did not want the Jews to just fall in line and do what He told them. He wanted their hearts too—not for His sake, but for theirs. Thus, Solomon wrote that the Jews should be wise and fear G-d's righteous judgment. But more importantly, they should trust G-d and put their hearts into obeying Him because He is good.

Surely, trusting in G-d is a major theme in the Tanakh. Much of the Torah, Nevi'im, and Ketuvim is devoted to this subject. In the Torah, both Abraham and Moses trusted G-d and acted based on that trust, no matter what G-d called on them to do. Therefore, Abraham picked up a knife to slaughter Isaac, but G-d came through with a substitute at the last moment for

---

[62] Prov. 3:1-8.

him to sacrifice instead of Isaac.[63] That is how much Abraham trusted G-d.

G-d was so pleased with Moses that it says in Exodus: "Thus the L-rd used to speak to Moses as a man speaks to his friend."[64]

Having a close personal relationship was also important to David. In many psalms, David reveals his heart for G-d and speaks of G-d's goodness to him.

There is a pattern here. These men each had a personal relationship with G-d. What they discovered was that G-d actually loved them. One of the reasons there is so much written about these men in the Tanakh is so that we might learn from their example and seek a personal relationship with G-d. They obeyed G-d, and they did it out of a deep sense of trust. This is the correct way to follow the Law.

5.   Another important aspect of the Law was the subset of religious laws. This subset of laws prescribed the sacrificial system, the rituals that were to be performed during the festivals, and so on. These religious elements were symbolic, and they taught spiritual truths about G-d and man. Judaism contrasts greatly with paganism, which featured morally flawed gods and depraved worship practices. Indeed, child sacrifice was a central element of paganism.[65] This practice was detestable to G-d. Therefore, He gave the Jews a set of religious practices for all the world to see so that they could realize the error of their ways.[66]

6. In the New Testament, the apostle Paul teaches us that there was another purpose of the Law that the Jews were not told but were expected to notice. Namely, although G-d wanted them to do their best to follow the Law, He also wanted them to understand that they could not keep it perfectly. They were not

---

[63] Gen. 22:9-14.

[64] Ex. 33:11.

[65] Deut. 12:29-32 (12:29-13:1;) 18:9-14.

[66] Jer. 7:30-31.

righteous like G-d, and they needed atonement for their moral failures. In the words of Paul:

> Therefore the Law has become our tutor *to lead us* to Christ, so that we may be justified by faith.[67]

G-d knew they would not be perfect, and He wanted them to know that too. He did not want them to try to achieve perfection in order to gain salvation. That was not one of the reasons why G-d gave the Jews the Law. When the Jews sinned, G-d wanted them to approach Him through atonement, which is the exact opposite of approaching Him through your good works or your worthiness. There are ample passages in the Tanakh communicating this idea.[68] In fact, according to the Tanakh, ultimately it is G-d, not you yourself, who removes the stain of your sins.[69]

That following the Law would lead to G-d's blessing is stated in multiple places in the Torah,[70] but nowhere is it stated that following the Law would lead to justification before G-d. The issue of how to be justified before G-d is one of the fundamental theological differences between Christianity and Judaism. For example, Rabbi Tovia Singer writes:

> Bear in mind, there is good reason for the Church's uncompromising stand on this cherished doctrine. The founders of Christianity understood that if a man, through his devotion and obedience to God, can save himself from eternal damnation, the Church

---

[67] Gal. 3:24.

[68] e.g. Lev. 1:4; Lev. 17:11; et al.

[69] Ps. 32:1-5; 103:12-13; Isa. 1:18; 43:25.

[70] Ex. 23:20-33; Deut. 5:22-33 (19-30;) Deut. 28:1-14; Josh. 1:7-8; Ps. 1:1-3; Ps. 119:1-3; et al.

would have little to offer its parishioners. Moreover, if righteousness can be achieved through submission to the commandments outlined in the Torah, what possible benefit could Jesus' death provide for mankind?

... Moses declared that it is man alone who can and must merit his own salvation. Moreover, as he unhesitatingly speaks in the name of God, the lawgiver excoriates the notion that obedience to the Almighty is "too difficult or far off." According, he declared to the children of Israel that righteousness has been placed within their reach.

The thirtieth chapter of Deuteronomy discusses this matter extensively, and its verses read as though the Torah is bracing the Jewish people for the Christian doctrines that would confront them in the centuries to come.[71]

Here Singer is arguing against the Christian doctrine of "original sin."[72] He concludes that Christian beliefs are fundamentally wrong, and that "it is man alone who can and must merit his own salvation." Thus, Singer believes that people earn their salvation by obeying the commandments in the Torah. The doctrine of "original sin" is a Christian theological argument that explains why all humans sin. This argument may or may not be right, and I am not an advocate of it. But what I am arguing is that no one has ever been sinless. In fact, this is

---

[71] Rabbi Tovia Singer, *Let's Get Biblical*, New Expanded Edition (Forest Hills, NY: Outreach Judaism, 2014) 2:82-83.

[72] Please research this Christian doctrine on your own, if you are interested. I am not arguing for it in this chapter. I have brought up this quote from Rabbi Singer to deal with his associated argument that salvation is achievable through following the Law.

clearly stated as a proposition in both the Tanakh and the New Testament:

> Indeed, there is not a righteous man on earth who continually does good and who never sins.[73]

and,

> ...for all have sinned and fall short of the glory of G-d,[74]

These verses are crystal clear. Yet, the ramifications of our sin are so great that G-d had more to say on this subject:

> For all of us have become like one who is unclean, and all our righteous deeds are like a filthy garment; and all of us wither like a leaf, and our iniquities, like the wind, take us away.[75]

and,

> "The heart is more deceitful than all else and is desperately sick; who can understand it?"[76]

In Psalm 14, King David put it this way:

> The fool has said in his heart, "There is no G-d." They are corrupt, they have committed abominable deeds; there is no one who does good. The L-rd has looked down from heaven

---

[73] Eccl. 7:20; cf. 1 Kin. 8:46.
[74] Rom. 3:23.
[75] Isa. 64:6 (5.)
[76] Jer. 17:9.

upon the sons of men to see if there are any who understand, who seek after G-d. They have all turned aside; together they have become corrupt; there is no one who does good, not even one.[77]

This psalm has a universal element to it. According to this psalm, we are all morally corrupt, yet we do not fully comprehend it. For, we are surrounded by other corrupt people, and we are defensive by nature. Surely, it is very difficult for us to see our own shortcomings. That is why David wrote the following verses in Psalm 139:

Search me, O G-d, and know my heart; try me and know my anxious thoughts; and see if there be any hurtful way in me, and lead me in the everlasting way.[78]

The only way any of us can understand the depth of our sin is to turn to G-d and ask Him to show us. In addition to these propositional truths, 1,000 years' worth of examples of morally imperfect Jewish people are also recorded in the Tanakh. In fact, no one achieved a state of righteousness in ancient Israel by following the Law. Even Moses, the lawgiver, failed to do so.

Moses was so godly. He did an absolutely great job leading the people on behalf of G-d. When Miriam and Aaron spoke ill of Moses, G-d said to them:

"Hear now My words: If there is a prophet among you, I, the L-rd, shall make Myself known to him in a vision. I shall speak with him in a dream. Not so, with My servant Moses, he is faithful in all My household; with him I speak mouth to mouth, even openly, and not in dark

---

[77] Ps. 14:1-3.
[78] Ps. 139:23-24.

sayings, and he beholds the form of the L-rd. Why then were you not afraid to speak against My servant, against Moses?"[79]

Yet, the Tanakh also records Moses' sins. For example, Moses led the people all the way to the Jordan River, but, because he sinned, he was not allowed to cross the river and enter the Promised Land along with his countrymen.[80] Moses' sins may seem a bit trivial to us, but they were significant to G-d. This is because he represented G-d to the people, and that was a critically important assignment. One time, Moses had enough of all the complaining by the Jewish people, and he cracked and got angry with them.[81] That interaction misrepresented G-d, whose desire was to extend grace to the Jews in that moment and provide for their physical needs. For that, Moses was held accountable and was barred from entering the Promised Land.

The point is that although Moses was extraordinarily godly, he was not righteous. Even so, G-d loved Moses. Hence, G-d did not love Moses because he was righteous; He loved Moses because of His love. I am nothing compared to Moses, but G-d loves me too. And He loves you. G-d loves us because of His *hesed*, not because we deserve it.[82]

Rabbi Singer went on to quote Deuteronomy 30:10-14, which says:

> ...if you obey the L-rd your G-d to keep His commandments and His statutes which are written in this book of the law, if you turn to the L-rd your G-d with all your heart and soul.
>
> For this commandment which I command you today is not too difficult for you, nor is it

---

[79] Num. 12:6-8.

[80] Deut. 3:23-28.

[81] Num. 20:1-13.

[82] Cf. Volume 1, Chapter 12 for an explanation of this character quality.

> out of reach. It is not in heaven, that you should
> say, 'Who will go up to heaven for us to get it
> for us and make us hear it, that we may observe
> it?' Nor is it beyond the sea, that you should
> say, 'Who will cross the sea for us to get it for
> us and make us hear it, that we may observe it?'
> But the word is very near you, in your mouth
> and in your heart, that you may observe it.

Singer quotes this passage to show that obedience to the Law is possible, and in fact it is, but not perfectly. Certainly, no one in the Tanakh followed the Law perfectly in the 1,000 years of Jewish history that took place after G-d gave it to the Jews.[83]

Be that as it may, then why did Moses tell the Jewish people that obedience to the Law is possible? The answer is actually somewhat simple. As I explained in Volume 2, there are two levels of righteousness: godly living and moral perfection.[84] In the Mosaic Covenant, G-d was looking for the Jews to live godly lives. Then He would bless them greatly and use them to be His witnesses to the world. This means He expected them to follow His Law as the foundation of their lives, which many people accomplished in the Tanakh.[85] For instance, Moses lived this way, and G-d used Him mightily to accomplish His will.

The level of righteousness of moral perfection, on the other hand, can only be attained through faith according to the Tanakh. We saw this in the last chapter in which we read of

---

[83] However, it should be noted that Rabbi Singer offers a passage from the New Testament, Lk. 1:6, to prove his point. In this verse, it says that Zacharias and Elizabeth, who were to become the parents of John the Baptist, were righteous based on their performance of the Law. Yet, shortly thereafter, in Lk. 1:18-20, we see Zacharias being disciplined for his lack of faith in G-d's personal promise to him and his wife.

[84] Volume 2, Chapter 5.

[85] e.g. in 1 Kin. 19:9-18.

Abraham that "he believed in the L-rd; and He reckoned it to him as righteousness."[86] Habakkuk states this plainly as well:

> "Behold, as for the proud one, his soul is not
> right within him; but the righteous will live by
> his faith."[87]

Forgiveness comes through placing our faith in G-d's provision of the sacrifice of the special servant predicted by Isaiah.[88] Along with being forgiven, we are deemed to be righteous and we are able to enter G-d's presence.[89]

Also in response to Rabbi Singer's assertion, isn't it an oxymoron to say that man must merit his own salvation? For, the word *salvation* implies that you are in need of help from a savior. If you are able to earn your way into heaven, wouldn't you use words like "hard work" and "self-discipline" to describe the effort needed to make it to heaven? For example, if you are sick and tired of having massive credit card debt, and you tear up all your credit cards and slowly start to pay off your debts, you usually just say that. You describe the steps you are taking to get out of debt. On the other hand, if you were a soldier in a jungle in Vietnam, and you were under fire, and a helicopter pilot arrived and lifted you out of harm's way, then it would only be natural to say that the chopper pilot saved you. Therefore, if you are able to earn the right to enter G-d's presence by following the Law, there is no need to speak of being *saved* or of your *salvation*.

Of course, what really matters is not how we use the word *salvation* today but how they used it in ancient Israel when the Tanakh was written. Moses used the word four times. In each case, the Jews were in need of G-d's help, and He was their savior. In all, the word is used 111 times in the Tanakh. In almost

---

86 Gen. 15:6; Rom. 4:1-8; Gal. 3:1-11.
87 Hab. 2:4.
88 Isa. 53:5-6.
89 Gen. 15:6; Isa. 1:4-18; 6:1-7; 53:11; 61:10-11; Rom. 3:21-28; Gal. 3:20-21; 2 Tim. 4:7-8.

every case, *salvation* refers to receiving deliverance from G-d. Often, these passages are speaking of G-d's deliverance from human enemies.[90] Sometimes, these passages are referring to salvation from our sins, as in the case of David in Psalm 51.[91]

Actually, there are two Hebrew words that are translated into English as *salvation*. They are both derivatives of the same root word and are close to each other in spelling and meaning. They are yᵉshû'â and tᵉshû'â. Yᵉshû'â is usually translated as "salvation" but sometimes as "deliverance" or "help." Tᵉshû'â is translated as "salvation," "victory," or "deliverance." Yᵉshû'â is used in the Tanakh 78 times, and tᵉshû'â is used 33. Yᵉshû'â is Jesus' name in Hebrew. Of course, G-d picked this word to be His name on purpose.

Certainly, Jesus had much to say about righteousness and salvation. He taught that it is impossible for us to achieve eternity through following the Law.[92] For, although it is possible to set up a comprehensive set of rules based on the Law which can perhaps be performed perfectly,[93] no one has ever followed the Law from a completely pure and innocent heart. But this is the requirement to achieve justification before G-d. Jesus explained it this way in Matthew Chapter 5:

> "Do not think that I came to abolish the Law or the Prophets; I did not come to abolish but to fulfill. For truly I say to you, until heaven and earth pass away, not the smallest letter or stroke shall pass from the Law until all is accomplished. Whoever then annuls one of the least of these commandments, and teaches others to do the same, shall be called least in the kingdom of heaven; but whoever keeps and teaches them, he shall be called great in the

---

[90] e.g. Ps. 3:7-8 (8-9.)

[91] Ps. 51:11-14 (13-16.)

[92] Mt. 5:20-30.

[93] Phil. 3:6; A. Lukyn Williams, D.D., *Talmudic Judaism and Christianity* (London, England: Society for Promoting Christian Knowledge, 1933) 57.

> kingdom of heaven. For I say to you that unless your righteousness surpasses that of the scribes and Pharisees, you will not enter the kingdom of heaven.
>
> You have heard that the ancients were told, 'You shall not commit murder' and 'Whoever commits murder shall be liable to the court.' But I say to you that everyone who is angry with his brother shall be guilty before the court; and whoever says to his brother, 'You good-for-nothing' shall be guilty before the supreme court; and whoever says, 'You fool' shall be guilty *enough to go* into the fiery hell....
>
> You have heard that it was said, "You shall not commit adultery"; but I say to you that everyone who looks at a woman with lust for her has already committed adultery with her in his heart...."[94]

Notice that Jesus said your righteousness must surpass that of the Pharisees in order for you to spend eternity in heaven with G-d. He did not say that to provoke or insult the Pharisees. Rather, He said it to instruct His audience. For, although the Pharisees were dedicated to following the Law, their efforts were not good enough to gain salvation. Therefore, there must be another key to being reconciled with G-d.

In this sermon, Jesus taught the Jewish people that righteousness requires a pure heart as well as full compliance with all of G-d's laws. But how can Jesus say that calling someone a bad name is as bad as murder? Obviously, the damage is drastically worse for the murder victim. But, could it be that Jesus is right in terms of the person's attitude being the same in both cases? Think about the bitter person who detests

---

[94] Mt. 5:17-22, 27-28. In addition, per H. Polano, a similar statement can be found in the Talmud. Namely, it says, "To slander is to commit murder." (H. Polano, *The Talmud* (San Diego, California: The Book Tree, 2003) 303.)

someone else. They nurse their grudge, and they even fantasize about the other person experiencing failure, public humiliation, or worse. They may be able to hide their feelings and control themselves such that they do not break any of the 613 laws that deal with external behavior, but in their heart, they are not righteous. If you have ever heard a bitter person verbalize how they really feel about their enemy, it is sinful. Surely, Jesus is correct: a bitter person's attitude is actually not very different from that of a murderer.

Most people are not bitter, but no one's heart is pure. Everyone has wrestled with something, be it lust, greed, arrogance, impatience toward a child, or a judgmental attitude. Only G-d is different. His heart is pure and beautiful.

Jesus was not diminishing the Law in this sermon. On the contrary, He fully agreed with G-d's Law.[95] He was simply clarifying that none of us are good enough to enter G-d's presence in heaven. Rather, according to Jesus, the way to go to heaven is through faith in Him:

> "For G-d so loved the world, that He gave His
> only begotten Son, that whoever believes in Him
> should not perish but have eternal life."[96]

---

[95] Mt. 5:17-20.

[96] Jn. 3:16.

5

JEWISH HISTORY FROM MOSES TO THE BABYLONIAN EXILE

In this chapter we will discuss the success of the Jews in carrying out their mission once G-d gave them the Law through Moses. We will focus on the era in which they were governed by kings.

Moses was given the Law early on following the Jews' escape from Egypt. Then it took them 40 years until they crossed the Jordan River to enter into the Promised Land. Though the delay in entering the Promised Land was a judgment, it was not based on their failure to keep the Law. Rather, it was due to their lack of faith in G-d. There is a lengthy recounting of the events of these 40 years in the Tanakh, though little of lasting importance took place during this period. The reason for this section of the Tanakh is so that we may learn from their mistakes.

Their children learned, and when their moment came to trust G-d and enter the land, though that meant war, they obeyed. Under the leadership of Joshua, the next generation would conquer some of the land G-d had for them, and then go on to obey the Law.[97] Surprisingly, only one verse would be devoted to how well they obeyed the Law:

> Israel served the L-rd all the days of Joshua and all the days of the elders who survived Joshua, and had known all the deeds of the L-rd which He had done for Israel.[98]

Again, the Mosaic Covenant was a bilateral covenant. If the Jews followed the Law, G-d would bless them and they would show the world who He is. If they broke the Law, He would curse them and their witness would be regrettable. How did the Jews do going forward?

Sadly, the Jewish people did not remain faithful to G-d for very long at all. For, the second generation after Joshua's generation forgot about G-d and started to go down the wrong path.[99] In the book of Judges, Chapter 2, we read:

> All that generation also were gathered to their fathers; and there arose another generation after them who did not know the L-rd, nor yet the work which He had done for Israel.
>
> Then the sons of Israel did evil in the sight of the L-rd and served the Baals, and they forsook the L-rd, the G-d of their fathers, who had brought them out of the land of Egypt, and followed other gods from *among* the gods of the peoples who were around them, and bowed themselves down to them; thus they provoked the L-rd to anger. So they forsook the L-rd and served Baal and the Ashtaroth. The anger of the L-rd burned against Israel, and He gave them

---

[97] Josh. 11:23; 13:1 ff.
[98] Josh. 24:31.
[99] Judg. 2:6-10.

into the hands of plunderers who plundered them; and He sold them into the hands of their enemies around *them,* so that they could no longer stand before their enemies.[100]

As the narrative continues, eventually the Jews experienced such extreme negative circumstances that they cried out to G-d, and He heard them and raised up a godly judge who led them to victory over their enemies.[101] But then, as the years passed and the judge died, the Jews fell back into idolatry again.[102] Several such cycles are recorded in the book of Judges. The period of the judges lasted roughly 300 years. These centuries could loosely be compared to the Wild West period in American history. It was at times lawless.[103] It was filled with colorful characters, such as Gideon and Samson, and it can be summed up in the final verse of the book:

> In those days there was no king in Israel; everyone did what was right in his own eyes.[104]

Now we come to the period of the kings. The first king was the physically impressive Saul.[105] Unfortunately, spiritually, Saul was only ordinary. But since he was the king of G-d's people, that was not good enough. He made two critical mistakes, and G-d rejected him.[106] In the first mistake, Saul assumed a priestly role and offered sacrifices he had no right to offer. In the second mistake, he disobeyed a direct order from G-d. As per G-d's patience, He allowed Saul's life to play out naturally over the course of many years. But once Saul perished,

---

[100] Judg. 2:10-14.
[101] Judg. 2:15-18.
[102] Judg. 2:19.
[103] Judg. 20-21.
[104] Judg. 21:25.
[105] 1 Kin. 9:1-2; 10:23-24.
[106] 1 Sam. 13:1-14; 15:1-35.

that was it. No king would ever come forth from his descendants.[107]

Then came King David. David's most striking feature was his heart. He had a heart for G-d, which stands out because it is so very rare.[108] David wrote over 70 of the Psalms in the Tanakh. Each one was a personal letter to G-d in which David welcomed G-d into His life, no matter what his circumstances were. For example, in Psalm 19, we read:

> The law of the L-rd is perfect, restoring the soul; the testimony of the L-rd is sure, making wise the simple. The precepts of the L-rd are right, rejoicing the heart; the commandment of the L-rd is pure, enlightening the eyes. The fear of the L-rd is clean, enduring forever; the judgments of the L-rd are true; they are righteous altogether.... Let the words of my mouth and the meditation of my heart be acceptable in Your sight, O L-rd, my rock and my Redeemer.[109]

David did not follow the Law out of a sense of duty. Rather, he embraced it. He even wanted his words and the concealed thoughts of his heart to be pure and pleasing to G-d. But of course, he was human, and he made mistakes. When he did, he turned to G-d then as well:

> Be gracious to me, O G-d, according to Your lovingkindness; according to the greatness of Your compassion blot out my transgressions. Wash me thoroughly from my iniquity and cleanse me from my sin. For I know my transgressions, and my sin is ever before me. Against You, You only, I have sinned and done

---

[107] 1 Sam. 13:13-14.
[108] 1 Sam. 13:14; 16:7.
[109] Ps. 19:7-9, 14 (8-10, 15.)

what is evil in Your sight, so that You are justified when You speak and blameless when You judge.[110]

It crushed David to think that he had damaged his relationship with G-d, and he threw himself on G-d's mercy and asked for forgiveness. David was not perfect, but he genuinely sought to do G-d's will. He was the right man to be the king of G-d's people. Unfortunately, he was the king in a time of war. But G-d blessed him and gave him victory over the Philistines.

David was succeeded by his son Solomon. Solomon was a unique king, to say the least. Clearly, he had observed his father's love for G-d, and he started out strong.

In Gibeon the L-rd appeared to Solomon in a dream at night; and G-d said, "Ask what *you wish* Me to give you."

Then Solomon said, "You have shown great lovingkindness to Your servant David my father, according as he walked before You in truth and righteousness and uprightness of heart toward You; and You have reserved for him this great lovingkindness, that You have given him a son to sit on his throne, as *it is* this day. Now, O L-rd my G-d, You have made Your servant king in place of my father David, yet I am but a little child; I do not know how to go out or come in. Your servant is in the midst of Your people which You have chosen, a great people who are too many to be numbered or counted. So give Your servant an understanding heart to judge Your people to discern between good and evil. For who is able to judge this great people of Yours?"

---

[110] Ps. 51:1-4 (3-6.)

It was pleasing in the sight of the L-rd that Solomon had asked this thing. G-d said to him, "Because you have asked this thing and have not asked for yourself long life, nor have asked riches for yourself, nor have you asked for the life of your enemies, but have asked for yourself discernment to understand justice, behold, I have done according to your words. Behold, I have given you a wise and discerning heart, so that there has been no one like you before you, nor shall one like you arise after you. I have also given you what you have not asked, both riches and honor, so that there will not be any among the kings like you all your days.[111]

Hence, Solomon was specially gifted with wisdom to rule G-d's people. After receiving this gift, Solomon built a temple for G-d.[112] It took seven years to build, and it was magnificent.[113] Thus, Solomon honored G-d, and he led the people to follow G-d. But alas, he was just a human, and he would eventually be led astray and sin against G-d:

Now King Solomon loved many foreign women along with the daughter of Pharaoh: Moabite, Ammonite, Edomite, Sidonian, and Hittite women, from the nations concerning which the L-rd had said to the sons of Israel, "You shall not associate with them, nor shall they associate with you, *for* they will surely turn your heart away after their gods." Solomon held fast to these in love. He had seven hundred wives, princesses, and three hundred concubines, and his wives turned his heart

---

[111] 1 Kin. 3:5-13.

[112] 1 Kin. 6:1, 7, 9.

[113] 1 Kin. 6:37-38.

away. For when Solomon was old, his wives turned his heart away after other gods; and his heart was not wholly devoted to the L-rd his G-d, as the heart of David his father *had been*. For Solomon went after Ashtoreth the goddess of the Sidonians and after Milcom the detestable idol of the Ammonites. Solomon did what was evil in the sight of the L-rd, and did not follow the L-rd fully, as David his father *had done*. Then Solomon built a high place for Chemosh the detestable idol of Moab, on the mountain which is east of Jerusalem, and for Molech the detestable idol of the sons of Ammon. Thus also he did for all his foreign wives, who burned incense and sacrificed to their gods.[114]

Solomon's personal collapse is hard to fathom. First he violated G-d's command not to marry wives from any of the Canaanite peoples.[115] Then he broke the first two commandments and led the nation into rebellion against G-d. As you might guess, things only got worse from there.

Solomon's son was named Rehoboam. He did not get off to a good start when his turn came to be king. In fact, he was so bad that the nation split into two kingdoms.

And Solomon slept with his fathers and was buried in the city of his father David, and his son Rehoboam reigned in his place.

Then Rehoboam went to Shechem, for all Israel had come to Shechem to make him king. Now when Jeroboam the son of Nebat heard *of it*, he was living in Egypt (for he was yet in Egypt, where he had fled from the presence of

---

[114] 1 Kin. 11:1-8.
[115] Deut. 7:1-4.

King Solomon). Then they sent and called him, and Jeroboam and all the assembly of Israel came and spoke to Rehoboam, saying, "Your father made our yoke hard; now therefore lighten the hard service of your father and his heavy yoke which he put on us, and we will serve you." Then he said to them, "Depart for three days, then return to me." So the people departed.

King Rehoboam consulted with the elders who had served his father Solomon while he was still alive, saying, "How do you counsel *me* to answer this people?" Then they spoke to him, saying, "If you will be a servant to this people today, and will serve them and grant them their petition, and speak good words to them, then they will be your servants forever." But he forsook the counsel of the elders which they had given him, and consulted with the young men who grew up with him and served him. So he said to them, "What counsel do you give that we may answer this people who have spoken to me, saying, 'Lighten the yoke which your father put on us'?" The young men who grew up with him spoke to him, saying, "Thus you shall say to this people who spoke to you, saying, 'Your father made our yoke heavy, now you make it lighter for us!' But you shall speak to them, 'My little finger is thicker than my father's loins! Whereas my father loaded you with a heavy yoke, I will add to your yoke; my father disciplined you with whips, but I will discipline you with scorpions.'"

Then Jeroboam and all the people came to Rehoboam on the third day as the king had directed, saying, "Return to me on the third day." The king answered the people harshly, for he forsook the advice of the elders which they had given him, and he spoke to them according to the advice of the young men,...

When all Israel *saw* that the king did not listen to them, the people answered the king, saying, "What portion do we have in David? *We have* no inheritance in the son of Jesse; to your tents, O Israel! Now look after your own house, David!" So Israel departed to their tents. But as for the sons of Israel who lived in the cities of Judah, Rehoboam reigned over them. Then King Rehoboam sent Adoram, who was over the forced labor, and all Israel stoned him to death. And King Rehoboam made haste to mount his chariot to flee to Jerusalem.... And it came about when all Israel heard that Jeroboam had returned, that they sent and called him to the assembly and made him king over all Israel.[116]

Rehoboam's arrogance was breathtaking. He sounded like Moses' adversary, Pharaoh. Ten tribes seceded. Only Judah and Benjamin remained for him to rule. They formed the Southern Kingdom, or Judah, and the other tribes formed the Northern Kingdom, or Israel. At least there was no bloodshed in this separation.[117]

After 20 generations of kings in each kingdom, the kings were so ungodly, and the idolatry was so rampant, that G-d was forced to send the Jews into exile. First, the Northern Kingdom was vanquished, and sometime later, the Southern Kingdom was defeated.

Jeroboam was the first king in the Northern Kingdom. Jerusalem was in the Southern Kingdom, and that made him insecure. He was afraid that as His people returned to

---

[116] 1 Kin. 11:43; 12:1-14a, 16-18, 20a.
[117] 1 Kin. 12:21-24.

Jerusalem to visit the Temple and worship G-d, they might reunify under Rehoboam, and he would lose his kingship. Therefore, he decided to alter the Jewish religion so that the Jews of the Northern Kingdom would no longer need to return to the Temple in Jerusalem. We read about this in 1 Kings Chapter 12:

> Then Jeroboam built Shechem in the hill country of Ephraim, and lived there. And he went out from there and built Penuel. Jeroboam said in his heart, "Now the kingdom will return to the house of David. If this people go up to offer sacrifices in the house of the L-rd at Jerusalem, then the heart of this people will return to their lord, *even* to Rehoboam king of Judah; and they will kill me and return to Rehoboam king of Judah." So the king consulted, and made two golden calves, and he said to them, "It is too much for you to go up to Jerusalem; behold your gods, O Israel, that brought you up from the land of Egypt." He set one in Bethel, and the other he put in Dan. Now this thing became a sin, for the people went *to worship* before the one as far as Dan. And he made houses on high places, and made priests from among all the people who were not of the sons of Levi. Jeroboam instituted a feast in the eighth month on the fifteenth day of the month, like the feast which is in Judah, and he went up to the altar; thus he did in Bethel, sacrificing to the calves which he had made.[118]

Jeroboam did not care about G-d's will. In the Law, G-d instituted three pilgrimage festivals: Passover, Pentecost, and Sukkot. On those occasions, the Jews were to go to the Temple

____

[118] 1 Kin. 12:25-32a.

and worship G-d by offering grain and animal sacrifices.[119] Jeroboam was like Saul, and what he cared about was his power and fame. So he had craftsmen fabricate two golden calves, and he proclaimed them to be the gods of Israel. Then he placed them in Bethel and Dan so that his people did not need to travel to Jerusalem to worship. As if that were not enough, he revoked G-d's prescription for the Levites to be the sole priests.[120] Hence, Jeroboam violated the first two commandments, and he altered the religious portion of the Law. His actions were so grievous that they are titled "the sins of Jeroboam" in the Tanakh.[121] As has often been the case in history, his conduct was not repudiated but rather repeated by his successors.

In their synopsis of 1 Kings and 2 Kings, The Bible Project established a rating system for the Jewish kings consisting of three criteria.[122] One, did they worship G-d alone or also pagan deities? Two, did they build idols and pagan worship facilities or tear them down? And three, did they follow the Law and stand against corruption and injustice?[123] Under this rating system, all 20 of the kings of the Northern Kingdom failed.

Eventually, the rebellion of these kings, and of the people who followed them, reached a point where G-d had to judge them. For at that point, they were not just representing G-d poorly to the Gentile world, but rather, they had become a pagan nation. The period from Jeroboam to Hoshea, the final king of the Northern Kingdom, lasted a little over 200 years. Then, in 722 BCE, the Assyrians conquered the Northern Kingdom, and it was all over.

But long before the end came, G-d sent prophets who called the people to turn back to G-d and warned them of the

---

[119] Ex. 23:14-19.

[120] Ex. 29:1-9; Num. 1:47-54; 3:1-10.

[121] E.g. 2 Kin. 13:2.

[122] The Bible Project is a nonprofit organization that creates educational resources to help people understand the Bible.

[123] The Bible Project, "Books of 1-2 Kings Summary: A Complete Animated Overview," 8:51, https://bibleproject.com/videos/kings (accessed June 3, 2025.)

consequences they would face if they continued to rebel. For example, during the reign of King Ahab, G-d sent the prophet Elijah. Ahab was a particularly bad king:

> Now Ahab the son of Omri became king over Israel in the thirty-eighth year of Asa king of Judah, and Ahab the son of Omri reigned over Israel in Samaria twenty-two years. Ahab the son of Omri did evil in the sight of the L-rd more than all who were before him. It came about, as though it had been a trivial thing for him to walk in the sins of Jeroboam the son of Nebat, that he married Jezebel the daughter of Ethbaal king of the Sidonians, and went to serve Baal and worshiped him. So he erected an altar for Baal in the house of Baal which he built in Samaria. Ahab also made the Asherah. Thus Ahab did more to provoke the L-rd G-d of Israel than all the kings of Israel who were before him.[124]

Alas, Baal and his consort, Asherah, were abominations. Ahab was a fool. He had been given an important role to be the king of the Jews and represent G-d to the world. What did he do? He bowed down to Baal and trampled on his position of honor. For her part, Jezebel started executing Jewish prophets as she attempted to do away with the worship of G-d.[125] Thus, G-d sent the prophet Elijah to deal with the damage caused by Ahab and his wife:

> Now Elijah the Tishbite, who was of the settlers of Gilead, said to Ahab, "As the L-rd, the G-d of Israel lives, before whom I stand, surely there

---

[124] 1 Kin. 16:29-33.
[125] 1 Kin. 18:3-4.

shall be neither dew nor rain these years, except by my word."[126]

Baal was the Canaanite G-d of rain/fertility. Hence, G-d applied some pressure in order to get the Jews' attention and make it clear who the real G-d is.

> Now it happened *after* many days that the word of the L-rd came to Elijah in the third year, saying, "Go, show yourself to Ahab, and I will send rain on the face of the earth." So Elijah went to show himself to Ahab. Now the famine *was* severe in Samaria.
>
> ...When Ahab saw Elijah, Ahab said to him, "Is this you, you troubler of Israel?" He said, "I have not troubled Israel, but you and your father's house *have*, because you have forsaken the commandments of the L-rd and you have followed the Baals. Now then send *and* gather to me all Israel at Mount Carmel, *together* with 450 prophets of Baal and 400 prophets of the Asherah, who eat at Jezebel's table."
>
> So Ahab sent *a message* among all the sons of Israel and brought the prophets together at Mount Carmel. Elijah came near to all the people and said, "How long *will* you hesitate between two opinions? If the L-rd is G-d, follow Him; but if Baal, follow him." But the people did not answer him a word. Then Elijah said to the people, "I alone am left a prophet of the L-rd, but Baal's prophets are 450 men. Now let them give us two oxen; and let them choose one ox for themselves and cut it up, and place it on the wood, but put no fire *under it*; and I will prepare the other ox and lay it on the wood,

---

[126] 1 Kin. 17:1.

and I will not put a fire *under it*. Then you call on the name of your god, and I will call on the name of the L-rd, and the G-d who answers by fire, He is G-d." And all the people said, "That is a good idea."

So Elijah said to the prophets of Baal, "Choose one ox for yourselves and prepare it first for you are many, and call on the name of your god, but put no fire *under it*." Then they took the ox which was given them and they prepared it and called on the name of Baal from morning until noon saying, "O Baal, answer us." But there was no voice and no one answered. And they leaped about the altar which they made. It came about at noon, that Elijah mocked them and said, "Call out with a loud voice, for he is a god; either he is occupied or gone aside, or is on a journey, or perhaps he is asleep and needs to be awakened." So they cried with a loud voice and cut themselves according to their custom with swords and lances until the blood gushed out on them. When midday was past, they raved until the time of the offering of the *evening* sacrifice; but there was no voice, no one answered, and no one paid attention.

Then Elijah said to all the people, "Come near to me." So all the people came near to him.... Then he arranged the wood and cut the ox in pieces and laid *it* on the wood. And he said, "Fill four pitchers with water and pour *it* on the burnt offering and on the wood." And he said, "Do it a second time," and they did it a second time. And he said, "Do it a third time," and they did it a third time. The water flowed around the altar and he also filled the trench with water.

At the time of the offering of the *evening* sacrifice, Elijah the prophet came near and said, "O L-rd, the G-d of Abraham, Isaac and Israel, today let it be known that You are G-d in Israel and that I am Your servant and I have done all these things at Your word. Answer me, O L-rd, answer me, that this people may know that You, O L-rd, are G-d, and *that* You have turned their heart back again." Then the fire of the L-rd fell and consumed the burnt offering and the wood and the stones and the dust, and licked up the water that was in the trench. When all the people saw it, they fell on their faces; and they said, "The L-rd, He is G-d; the L-rd, He is G-d." Then Elijah said to them, "Seize the prophets of Baal; do not let one of them escape." So they seized them; and Elijah brought them down to the brook Kishon, and slew them there.[127]

What an odd response, Ahab called Elijah the "troubler of Israel." This means that Ahab knew that G-d is the real, all-powerful G-d. Yet, instead of bowing to Him and beseeching Him for forgiveness, Ahab was angry with His prophet. Ahab's heart was in the things of this world—like being the king and being rich. He did not care about the will of G-d.

Following this event, Jezebel sought to kill Elijah, and he ran away. Elijah escaped, but it took a toll on him, and he became depressed.[128] Not only was he overwhelmed by everything that had just happened, but he was also disheartened by the spiritual state of the people. He could not understand how they could have fallen away so easily and begun to worship the false gods of the Canaanites. Yet, as G-d told him, there was a remnant of 7,000 people who had not fallen away

---

[127] 1 Kin. 18:1-2, 17-30a, 33-40.
[128] 1 Kin. 19:1-5.

but had remained faithful to G-d.[129] Therein lies the hope for the Jewish people. There has always been a remnant of godly Jews in every era.

As time went on, the rebellion of the Jewish kings and the people continued. G-d would send more prophets, but He would not override their free will. In the end, it was a losing battle.[130] They broke the Mosaic Covenant so badly for so long that He removed His protection from over them, and they were conquered by the Assyrians.[131] Their defeat was a disaster. Not only did the Jews suffer a crushing military defeat to a savage enemy, but then Assyria deported most of them and scattered them throughout their empire.[132] The Jews who stayed in the land were inundated with settlers from other places in the Assyrian Empire.[133] The result was that the Jews remaining in the Northern Kingdom intermarried to the point that they were no longer a Jewish people. Rather, they became the Samaritans, a half-breed people who were confused about Judaism.[134]

This tragic story is revealing in terms of who G-d is and who we are. G-d is extremely patient as He allowed this rebellion to last for over two centuries. G-d is not controlling. It was never His will for the Jews to choose this path, and He tried to counsel them not to go down it, but they were stubborn and would not listen. They even performed human sacrifices to please their pagan deities.

> The sons of Israel did things secretly which were not right against the L-rd their G-d. Moreover, they built for themselves high places in all their towns, from watchtower to fortified city. They set for themselves *sacred* pillars and Asherim on every high hill and under every

---

[129] 1 Kin. 19:18.

[130] 2 Kin. 17:7-23.

[131] Deut. 26:16-19; Josh. 24:14-28.

[132] 2 Kin. 17:1-23.

[133] 2 Kin. 17:24-41.

[134] Jn. 4:19-24.

green tree, and there they burned incense on all the high places as the nations *did* which the L-rd had carried away to exile before them; and they did evil things provoking the L-rd. They served idols, concerning which the L-rd had said to them, "You shall not do this thing." Yet the L-rd warned Israel and Judah through all His prophets *and* every seer, saying, "Turn from your evil ways and keep My commandments, My statutes according to all the law which I commanded your fathers, and which I sent to you through My servants the prophets." However, they did not listen, but stiffened their neck like their fathers, who did not believe in the L-rd their G-d..... They forsook all the commandments of the L-rd their G-d and made for themselves molten images, *even* two calves, and made an Asherah and worshiped all the host of heaven and served Baal. Then they made their sons and their daughters pass through the fire, and practiced divination and enchantments, and sold themselves to do evil in the sight of the L-rd, provoking Him. So the L-rd was very angry with Israel and removed them from His sight; none was left except the tribe of Judah.[135]

Thanks be to G-d, there is one positive in this story. Namely, G-d was not caught off guard by their epic failure, and He vowed to redeem the Jews of the Northern Kingdom at the end of time. For G-d had made promises to Abraham regarding the Jewish people,[136] and though our word often means very little, He remains faithful to His word. So, not only did the prophets warn the Jews that they would face judgment if they

---

[135] 2 Kin. 17:9-14, 16-18.
[136] Gen. 12:1-3; 15:1-5.

did not repent from their idolatry, but they also prophesied that one day G-d would restore the Jews of the Northern Kingdom.[137]

The Southern Kingdom fared somewhat better than the tribes in the north. For, the Southern Kingdom would go on to have eight godly kings out of 20 total.[138] Since the reigns of their kings were longer, the Southern Kingdom would last 136 years longer than the Northern Kingdom before they would fail and incur G-d's judgment.

An example of a bad king from the Southern Kingdom is King Ahaz. He reigned from 732 to 715 BCE, during the time of the fall of the Northern Kingdom.

> In the seventeenth year of Pekah the son of Remaliah, Ahaz the son of Jotham, king of Judah, became king. Ahaz *was* twenty years old when he became king, and he reigned sixteen years in Jerusalem; and he did not do what was right in the sight of the L-rd his G-d, as his father David *had done*. But he walked in the way of the kings of Israel, and even made his son pass through the fire, according to the abominations of the nations whom the L-rd had driven out from before the sons of Israel. He sacrificed and burned incense on the high places and on the hills and under every green tree....
>
> So Ahaz sent messengers to Tiglath-pileser king of Assyria, saying, "I am your servant and your son; come up and deliver me from the hand of the king of Aram and from the hand of the king of Israel, who are rising up against

---

[137] Isa. 11:11-12; Jer. 31:31-33 (30-32;) Ezek. 47:13-21; Hos. 14 (14:2-10;) Rev. 7:1-8.

[138] The Bible Project, "Books of 1-2 Kings Summary: A Complete Animated Overview," 8:51, https://bibleproject.com/videos/kings (accessed June 3, 2025.)

me." Ahaz took the silver and gold that was found in the house of the L-rd and in the treasuries of the king's house, and sent a present to the king of Assyria.[139]

He was as bad as any king from the Northern Kingdom. He even sacrificed his own child to a pagan deity.

An example of a good king is King Josiah. He reigned for 31 years, from 640 to 609 BCE.

> Josiah was eight years old when he became king, and he reigned thirty-one years in Jerusalem; and his mother's name *was* Jedidah the daughter of Adaiah of Bozkath. He did right in the sight of the L-rd and walked in all the way of his father David, nor did he turn aside to the right or to the left....
> Moreover, Shaphan the scribe told the king saying, "Hilkiah the priest has given me a book." And Shaphan read it in the presence of the king.
> When the king heard the words of the book of the law, he tore his clothes. Then the king commanded Hilkiah the priest, Ahikam the son of Shaphan, Achbor the son of Micaiah, Shaphan the scribe, and Asaiah the king's servant saying, "Go, inquire of the L-rd for me and the people and all Judah concerning the words of this book that has been found, for great is the wrath of the L-rd that burns against us, because our fathers have not listened to the words of this book, to do according to all that is written concerning us."
> So Hilkiah the priest, Ahikam, Achbor, Shaphan, and Asaiah went to Huldah the

---

[139] 2 Kin. 16:1-4, 7-8.

prophetess,... She said to them, "Thus says the L-rd G-d of Israel, 'Tell the man who sent you to me, thus says the L-rd, "Behold, I bring evil on this place and on its inhabitants, *even* all the words of the book which the king of Judah has read. Because they have forsaken Me and have burned incense to other gods that they might provoke Me to anger with all the work of their hands, therefore My wrath burns against this place, and it shall not be quenched."' But to the king of Judah who sent you to inquire of the L-rd thus shall you say to him, 'Thus says the L-rd G-d of Israel, "*Regarding* the words which you have heard, because your heart was tender and you humbled yourself before the L-rd when you heard what I spoke against this place and against its inhabitants that they should become a desolation and a curse, and you have torn your clothes and wept before Me, I truly have heard you," declares the L-rd. "Therefore, behold, I will gather you to your fathers, and you will be gathered to your grave in peace, and your eyes will not see all the evil which I will bring on this place."'"[140]

What a great man Josiah was. Can you imagine that in the midst of repairing the Temple, they found a copy of the Law?[141] The Law had been disregarded for so long that it became forgotten, and the king did not know about it! Fortunately, Josiah "walked in all the way of his father David," and his "heart was tender" toward the Law. He was godly, and he was wise. He immediately perceived that Judah was in trouble, for he knew that idolatry and paganism had been rampant throughout the land for a long time. His first response was to inquire of the L-rd

---

[140] 2 Kin. 22:1-2, 10-14a, 15b-20a.
[141] 2 Kin. 22:8.

about their standing before Him. Josiah was not concerned only for himself, but rather for "all Judah." His response was to follow the Law himself and to lead the nation to follow the Law.[142] Then he went on a campaign to tear down all the pagan shrines, burn all the paraphernalia used in performing pagan rites, tear down the houses of the male cult prostitutes, and end the practice of child sacrifice. His mission extended throughout both the Southern Kingdom and the Northern Kingdom.[143] Then he reinstituted the observance of Passover.[144]

Nonetheless, eventually, enough bad kings rose to power and enough evil was perpetrated that G-d was forced to judge the Southern Kingdom. Again, the kings were amply warned by prophets. Notably, Isaiah and Jeremiah prophesied for a very long time in the Southern Kingdom. But in the end, the Jews gave themselves over to sin to an almost inconceivable degree. When they finally broke their covenantal agreement with G-d one too many times, His patience ran out, and their fall was hard.[145]

> Zedekiah was twenty-one years old when he became king, and he reigned eleven years in Jerusalem; and his mother's name was Hamutal the daughter of Jeremiah of Libnah. He did evil in the sight of the L-rd like all that Jehoiakim had done.... Now it came about in the ninth year of his reign, on the tenth day of the tenth month, that Nebuchadnezzar king of Babylon came, he and all his army, against Jerusalem, camped against it and built a siege wall all around it. So the city was under siege until the eleventh year of King Zedekiah. On the ninth day of the fourth month the famine was so severe in the city that there was no food

---

142 2 Kin. 23:1-3.
143 2 Kin. 23:4-20.
144 2 Kin. 23:21-23.
145 Isa. 5:24-30.

for the people of the land. Then the city was broken into, and all the men of war fled and went forth from the city at night by way of the gate between the two walls which was by the king's garden, though the Chaldeans were all around the city. And they went by way of the Arabah. But the army of the Chaldeans pursued the king and overtook Zedekiah in the plains of Jericho, and all his army was scattered from him. Then they captured the king and brought him up to the king of Babylon at Riblah in the land of Hamath, and he passed sentence on him. The king of Babylon slaughtered the sons of Zedekiah before his eyes, and he also slaughtered all the princes of Judah in Riblah. Then he blinded the eyes of Zedekiah; and the king of Babylon bound him with bronze fetters and brought him to Babylon and put him in prison until the day of his death.

Now on the tenth day of the fifth month, which was the nineteenth year of King Nebuchadnezzar, king of Babylon, Nebuzaradan the captain of the bodyguard, who was in the service of the king of Babylon, came to Jerusalem. He burned the house of the L-rd, the king's house and all the houses of Jerusalem; even every large house he burned with fire. So all the army of the Chaldeans who were with the captain of the guard broke down all the walls around Jerusalem.[146]

Even after their defeat, the Jews could not stop debasing themselves and disrespecting G-d. Although most of the Jews

---

[146] Jer. 52:1-14.

were exiled to Babylon, some of them wound up in Egypt. Here is what happened to them:

> The word that came to Jeremiah for all the Jews living in the land of Egypt, those who were living in Migdol, Tahpanhes, Memphis, and the land of Pathros, saying, "Thus says the L-rd of hosts, the G-d of Israel, 'You yourselves have seen all the calamity that I have brought on Jerusalem and all the cities of Judah; and behold, this day they are in ruins and no one lives in them, because of their wickedness which they committed so as to provoke Me to anger by continuing to burn sacrifices *and* to serve other gods whom they had not known, *neither* they, you, nor your fathers. Yet I sent you all My servants the prophets, again and again, saying, "Oh, do not do this abominable thing which I hate." But they did not listen or incline their ears to turn from their wickedness, so as not to burn sacrifices to other gods. Therefore My wrath and My anger were poured out and burned in the cities of Judah and in the streets of Jerusalem, so they have become a ruin and a desolation as it is this day. Now then thus says the L-rd G-d of hosts, the G-d of Israel, "Why are you doing great harm to yourselves, so as to cut off from you man and woman, child and infant, from among Judah, leaving yourselves without remnant, provoking Me to anger with the works of your hands, burning sacrifices to other gods in the land of Egypt, where you are entering to reside, so that you might be cut off and become a curse and a reproach among all the nations of the earth?
>
> …

Then all the men who were aware that their wives were burning sacrifices to other gods, along with all the women who were standing by, *as* a large assembly, including all the people who were living in Pathros in the land of Egypt, responded to Jeremiah, saying, "As for the message that you have spoken to us in the name of the L-rd, we are not going to listen to you! But rather we will certainly carry out every word that has proceeded from our mouths, by burning sacrifices to the queen of heaven and pouring out drink offerings to her, just as we ourselves, our forefathers, our kings and our princes did in the cities of Judah and in the streets of Jerusalem; for *then* we had plenty of food and were well off and saw no misfortune. But since we stopped burning sacrifices to the queen of heaven and pouring out drink offerings to her, we have lacked everything and have met our end by the sword and by famine."[147]

Unbelievable! The Jews who went to Egypt would do anything rather than turn to G-d.

The good news for the Jews from the Southern Kingdom was that G-d would rescue them one day too, but not at the end of history. Of all things, G-d had given Jeremiah a prophecy that

---

[147] Jer. 44:1-8, 15-18. Note: there were actually four events in which Jewish people were exiled. They occurred in 605, 597, 586, and 581 BCE. In the first event, Babylonia exerted its power and took control of Judah. In the second one, the Babylonians returned to reassert their dominance. In the third one, the Babylonians responded to another rebellion, and this time they obliterated Jerusalem. The fourth one consisted of Jeremiah and many of the other Jews who had been allowed to remain in Judah, fleeing to Egypt.

He would rescue them from their captivity in Babylon after 70 years![148] And so He did.

*   *   *   *   *

From the time G-d used Moses to set the Jews free, their overall record of following the Law and representing Him to the Gentile world was a failure. This period lasted for approximately 850 years. It started when the Jews received the Law at Mt. Sinai, and it ended when the Southern Kingdom went into exile. Early on, Moses prophesied that the Jews would fail G-d and break their covenantal vow to follow the Law.[149] And so they did. This was not the outcome G-d wanted, but it is what they chose.

Their role was to follow G-d's Law. They were to work hard, be honest in business, and establish a just society. They were to leave some of the crops in their fields for the poor. They were also to treat foreign visitors well, even though they had been oppressed and held hostage when they were strangers in a foreign land.[150] Of course, trying your best to live this way is its own reward. But on top of that, G-d would bless them richly. He would bless the work of their hands, their crops, and their flocks. He would bless them with children and long lives.[151] He also gave them a day off.[152] That was unheard of in the ancient world.

G-d prescribed physical boundaries for their nation, and they were not to go beyond them.[153] To their credit, they never did. Should any empire attempt to invade them, G-d would protect His people, as He did spectacularly on numerous occasions.[154] All G-d asked was for them to give Him thanks and be faithful to Him.

---

148 Jer. 25:11-12; 29:10-14 (9-13.)
149 Deut. 4:25-31; 31:16-22.
150 Lev. 19:33-34.
151 Deut. 28:1-14.
152 Ex. 20:8-11.
153 Gen. 15:18; Num. 34:1-15.
154 Deut. 28:7.

G-d gave them scripture. It still holds up today. And G-d's presence was with them in the Holy of Holies! Their religion included none of the sick, depraved worship practices required by the other gods of the ancient world. But it did include the concept of sacrificial atonement coupled with the promise of a savior.

If the Jews had tried their best to follow G-d's path, then all of their neighbors would have seen the contrast between their lives and the Jews' lives, and between their society and the Jews' society.[155] Any Gentile whose heart was open to G-d could have looked upon them and found G-d. This was the role G-d gave to the Jewish people. They could have done their best to follow G-d's path for them, and for brief moments, they did.[156]

But in the end, the Jews went too far, and they forfeited their roles as G-d's representatives on earth. He told them not to intermarry with their pagan neighbors, but they did not listen. He gave them a law code with 613 laws—the most well-known of these were the Ten Commandments. The first two commandments were the starting point: to worship only G-d and not to make an idol.[157] It is hard to conceive of the Jews violating the first two commandments any worse than they did. Then they broke all of the other laws. In the end, all G-d could do was salvage His reputation by disciplining the Jews to show that He would not stand for that level of rebellion from His people.[158]

*　　*　　*　　*　　*

Yet, there were signs of hope. When Elijah lost all hope, G-d told him there was a remnant of 7,000 faithful Jews. It was not the case that all of the Jewish people had given themselves over to evil. So too, there has always been a faithful remnant.

---

[155] Deut. 30:11-20.

[156] E.g., they succeeded in honoring their covenant with G-d in the days of Joshua.

[157] Ex. 20:1-4.

[158] Deut. 29:22-28 (21-27.)

Daniel's associates, Shadrach, Meshach, and Abed-nego, were resolute in their faith, even in the face of death. They were captives in Babylon, where they had been taken as young men in the first deportation.[159] They had been hand-picked to be in a special program. They ate dinner with the Babylonian king, King Nebuchadnezzar, and they were being raised up to be officials in his government.[160]

On one occasion, King Nebuchadnezzar built a large, gold statue in his own honor. Then he held a dedication in which Shadrach, Meshach, and Abed-nego were present. A herald ordered everyone to bow down to the statue when they heard the sound of instruments, but Shadrach, Meshach, and Abed-nego refused. For they were Jews, and they worshipped G-d alone. Nebuchadnezzar was caught off guard by their response. So, he gave them a direct order to bow down, lest they be cast into a "furnace of blazing fire."[161] Then they said,

> "O Nebuchadnezzar, we do not need to give you an answer concerning this matter. If it be *so*, our G-d whom we serve is able to deliver us from the furnace of blazing fire; and He will deliver us out of your hand, O king. But *even* if *He does* not, let it be known to you, O king, that we are not going to serve your gods or worship the golden image that you have set up."[162]

The king was incensed, and he had them thrown in the furnace. Alas, G-d was with them, and, like the burning bush,

---

[159] There were three invasions of Judah by Babylonia. The third was the catastrophic defeat in 586 BCE. Daniel and his associates were taken captive in the first invasion, in 605 BCE. Gleason L. Archer, Jr., Daniel, The Expositor's Bible Commentary, Volume 7, Gen. Ed. Frank E. Gaebelein (Grand Rapids: Zondervan Publishing House, 1985) 31.

[160] Dan. 1:1-7.

[161] Dan. 3:15.

[162] Dan. 3:16a-18.

they were unharmed by the flames.[163] The king was astounded. He had them brought out of the furnace, and he gave honor to their G-d. This is quite a story. It involves an extraordinary miracle. But for our purposes, in this story we see three Jewish men who had faith in G-d and obeyed Him. The end result was that all the Gentiles in attendance that day learned who the real G-d is.

Just before the 70 years of Babylonian exile were up, after apologizing profusely for the sins of the Jews, including his own sins, Daniel prayed:

> "O L-rd, in accordance with all Your righteous acts, let now Your anger and Your wrath turn away from Your city Jerusalem, Your holy mountain; for because of our sins and the iniquities of our fathers, Jerusalem and Your people *have become* a reproach to all those around us. So now, our G-d, listen to the prayer of Your servant and to his supplications, and for Your sake, O L-rd, let Your face shine on Your desolate sanctuary. O my G-d, incline Your ear and hear! Open Your eyes and see our desolations and the city which is called by Your name; for we are not presenting our supplications before You on account of any merits of our own, but on account of Your great compassion. O L-rd, hear! O L-rd, forgive! O L-rd, listen and take action! For Your own sake, O my G-d, do not delay, because Your city and Your people are called by Your name."[164]

Surely, G-d did bring the exiles home and place them in their land, and He blessed the work of their hands. G-d is

---

163 Ex. 3:2; Dan. 3:25-27.
164 Dan. 9:16-19.

faithful, and ultimately, He will fulfill every promise He ever made to the Jews, and to the Gentiles too.

6

MALACHI

In the canon of the Tanakh, there are a number of famous books. For example, Genesis, Exodus, Psalms, and Isaiah, to name a few, are very well known. But what about the book of Malachi? Malachi was a postexilic prophet. He wrote this book in approximately 450 BCE to the Jews who returned from the Babylonian exile.

Perhaps the Jews living in the intertestamental period should have paid more attention to its message. The book of Malachi is the twelfth book among the minor prophets, and it contains the last words G-d spoke to the Jews. What was He trying to tell them?

We know that the Jews returning from the Babylonian exile had learned the message of Isaiah and let go of worshipping pagan idols. That was very good.

But stopping a wrong behavior is not the same as replacing it with the right behavior. Ceasing to worship false deities does not mean that you have started worshipping the one true G-d. Herein lies the message of the prophet Malachi.

Malachi was trying to warn them. Listen to this quote from G-d as He directly addressed the priests in that day:

> "Behold, I am going to rebuke your offspring, and I will spread refuse on your faces, the refuse of your feasts; and you will be taken away with it."[165]

These words are scandalous. G-d was trying to use shock appeal to wake them up. It turns out that the priests were at the forefront of the commission of a new strain of sin. The priests were the spiritual leaders of the nation at that time, but they were leading the people in the wrong direction. Here G-d had saved His people and given them another fresh start, but they were heading down another path that would lead to exile! So G-d called out to them to try to get them to think, turn back, and take the right path.

What the priests were doing was running the sacrificial system shoddily. In Malachi Chapter 1, verses 6 and 8, G-d says:

> "A son honors his father, and a servant his master. Then if I am a father, where is My honor? And if I am a master, where is My respect?" says the L-rd of hosts to you, O priests who despise My name. But you say, "How have we despised Thy name?" ... "But when you present the blind for sacrifice, is it not evil? And when you present the lame and sick, is it not evil? Why not offer it to your governor? Would he be pleased with you? Or would he receive you kindly?" says the L-rd of hosts.

The priests were not offering unblemished animals as sacrifices, but rather the blind and lame of the flocks. The

---

[165] Mal. 2:3. Note: the word *refuse* literally means *fecal matter* in Hebrew.

problem for G-d was not the animals, per se. The problem was the hearts of both the priests and the people. There is a G-d, and the Jews are His people, but that meant very little to them. Even the priests did not respect Him.

The setting of the book of Malachi consists of the returnees struggling to rebuild their nation, as well as their personal lives, following the exile. They had not regained their sovereignty, as they were under the rule of the Persian Empire. They also had local enemies who were annoyingly putting obstacles in their way. Their lives were difficult, and they viewed having to carry out the Mosaic sacrificial system as burdensome.

The Jews forgot that G-d was sovereign over the Persian Empire. They failed to appreciate that it was their honor to be the people of G-d and to follow His will, including performing all the prescribed sacrifices. Their thinking was askew. If they would have simply turned to G-d for help, He would have seen to their well-being. He could have taken better care of them than they could have ever done for themselves.

So G-d sent Malachi to wake His people up, but they did not listen well. In fact, for 480 years after Malachi gave them G-d's message, they never really heard it. They went down a path of emphasizing the Mosaic Law in order to merit G-d's favor and avoid His judgment.[166] It was during this period that the Sages and Pharisees came into being. They led the way by breaking each of the 613 laws down into a massive number of sub-laws.

Even though it would take the Sages, and later the Rabbis, all the way to the beginning of the sixth century CE to complete the Talmud, when Jesus came along at the beginning of the millennium, Pharisaic Judaism was already well underway, in which following the Law was the emphasis. Indeed, the Pharisees devoted themselves to following the Law, including all of the sub-laws they had developed by that time. They clashed with Jesus over their sub-laws, for example the sub-

---

[166]Rom. 10:3; F. F. Bruce, *Israel and the Nations* (Grand Rapids: William B. Eerdmans Publishing Company, 1969, 1985) 109, 111, 117; Paul Johnson, *A History of the Jews* (New York, N.Y.: HarperPerennial, 1987) 103, 105-106.

laws they created to define what constitutes work on the Sabbath. (We will examine this subject in the next chapter.)

The Pharisees' approach to G-d was different from Moses' or David's in that it minimized turning to Him in their hearts and welcoming Him into their lives as their loving Father. In addition, even though the priests no longer offered blind and lame animals as sacrifices, and even though the Pharisees followed the Law meticulously, their love for their fellow man had grown cold. Yet, isn't caring for your fellow man as important as offering religious sacrifices? Jesus put it this way to the Pharisees:

> Woe to you, teachers of the law and Pharisees, you hypocrites! You give a tenth of your spices— mint, dill and cumin. But you have neglected the more important matters of the law—justice, mercy and faithfulness. You should have practiced the latter, without neglecting the former. You blind guides! You strain out a gnat but swallow a camel.
>
> Woe to you, teachers of the law and Pharisees, you hypocrites! You clean the outside of the cup and dish, but inside they are full of greed and self-indulgence. Blind Pharisee! First clean the inside of the cup and dish, and then the outside also will be clean.[167]

Again, G-d was not concerned with the actual sacrificial animals in the book of Malachi. He was concerned with the hearts of the people, which led them to offer up deficient animals. Unfortunately, the Jews in the intertestamental period understood Malachi's message superficially. Therefore, they focused on offering the right animals so they would not get in trouble, but their hearts were still far away from G-d. In Jesus' day, the condition of the Pharisees' hearts could be seen by their

---

[167] Mt. 23:23-26.

judgmental treatment of those who were considered the sinners of society. The Pharisees were also callous to the suffering of those who had diseases and deformities for which there was no medical treatment in that day. We will see an example of their hardheartedness towards those who suffer in the next chapter.

*   *   *   *   *

It is interesting that in the New Testament, Jesus' most shocking actions were in response to how the Temple was being run. When Jesus saw what was going on in the Temple grounds, He reacted strongly. As He came to Jerusalem for the final time, He entered the Temple grounds and saw a flea market taking place in the outermost court. The business that was being conducted there consisted of exchanging currency and merchandising sacrificial animals that were certified to be unblemished. As Jesus gazed upon this scene, He raised His voice and began overturning the money changers' tables and the dove sellers' benches. Then He threw them out.[168]

In our modern culture, we are used to greed and commercialism, so His reaction may seem excessive. But the Temple of G-d was not the right place for merchants to push the bounds of ethical business practice. All of Jewish society visited the Temple, including people who travelled great distances and the poor, who could not afford to be extorted. Gentiles as well were welcome to come to the Temple, where a court was provided just for them. People came to the Temple to pray and beseech G-d for help with their deepest needs. They came to make thank offerings to G-d and to seek atonement for their sins. The priests oversaw the Temple and the sacrificial system, but they were misrepresenting G-d, for He is generous and does not take advantage of anyone. Rightly did Jesus take a stand against this corrupt system.

So, between the priests misrepresenting G-d in the Temple and the Pharisees misrepresenting G-d in the streets, the

---

[168] Mt. 21:12, 13.

spiritual leadership in Jerusalem was lacking, to say the least. G-d was not pleased.

Thank G-d that He is not like us. As Paul wrote to his disciple Timothy in 2 Tim. 2:13:

> ...if we are faithless, He remains faithful; for He cannot deny Himself.

So too, in the book of Malachi, G-d said in Chapter 3:

> "For I the L-rd, do not change; therefore you, O sons of Jacob, are not consumed."[169]

Other nations, such as the Edomites, committed sins that were also unacceptable.[170] Upon reaching a level of rebellion in which these nations were only contributing negatively to mankind, G-d mercifully revoked their right to continue as sovereign nations. But He would never terminate the national identity of the Jews. Yes, He would discipline them, and He would even allow the Romans to send them into exile, but He would preserve them. He did not preserve them because they deserved it but because He had made promises to Abraham regarding them.

*　　*　　*　　*　　*

In G-d's plan, it was at the turn of the millennium when He would send the world a savior.[171] Sure enough, Malachi prophesied this as well:

> "Behold, I am going to send my messenger, and he will clear the way before Me. And the L-rd, whom you seek, will suddenly come to His temple; and the messenger of the covenant, in

---

[169] Mal. 3:6.
[170] Mal. 1:2 ff.
[171] Dan. 9:24-27.

whom you delight, behold He is coming," says
the L-rd of hosts.[172]

Quite a bit is revealed in this concise statement. First of all, there would be a forerunner who would appear before the Messiah. This seemingly insignificant detail was actually important. In fact, there are a total of three prophecies predicting that a forerunner would precede the coming of the Messiah: Isa. 40:3, Mal. 3:1, and Mal. 4:5-6 (3:23-24.)[173]

John the Baptist was Jesus' second cousin, and his ministry preceded Jesus'. Both John and Jesus acknowledged that John was the forerunner prophesied by Isaiah and Malachi.[174] One day, as John was performing his ministry of preaching and baptizing people in the Jordan River, Jesus came to him. John humbly baptized Him, and in that moment, the Spirit of G-d descended upon Jesus. Then G-d spoke from heaven and said: "This is my beloved Son, in whom I am well pleased," and everything changed.[175]

John was devoted to the mission G-d had given him. His food and clothing were unusual compared to other Jews, but people were drawn to him.[176] John had a twofold job: to spiritually prepare the Jewish people for the coming of the Messiah and to announce Jesus to the world. In the New Testament book of Mark, we read of his first role:

> John the Baptist appeared in the wilderness preaching a baptism of repentance for the forgiveness of sins.[177]

---

[172] Mal. 3:1.

[173] Mal. 4:5-6 (3:23-24) may be a double reference prophecy referring both to the coming of John the Baptist and a future return of Elijah. This makes sense in that there are similarities between the two men and their ministries (2 Kings 1:8; Mt. 3:4; 1 Kings 19:1-2; Mk. 6:17-29.)

[174] Mt. 11:10; Jn. 1:23.

[175] Mt. 3:17.

[176] Mk. 1:6.

[177] Mk. 1:4.

Again, in Jesus' day, the people's love for G-d was faint. They were living out their faith perfunctorily or mechanically. John was saying, Wake up! You are the people of G-d, but you do not understand Him. He is not concerned with how meticulously you follow all of the sub-laws. Your problem is that you sin, and you are not fit to be in G-d's presence. He wants to help you, but you have to change your perspective and receive His forgiveness.

John caught the attention of the nation. A large number of people went out to the Jordan River to see what was happening. Many of them wound up confessing their sins and getting baptized in the river.[178]

But the paramount detail revealed in Mal. 3:1 is that the Messiah would be none other than G-d Himself! Thus, we read: "...he will clear the way before Me...says the L-rd of hosts," and, "...the L-rd whom you seek, will suddenly come to His temple...."

How could that be, for the Messiah had been promised for centuries to be a descendant of King David? How could the Messiah be both G-d and a man? Malachi does not tell us how; he just tells us that it is so.

The Jewish people of Jesus' day were eagerly awaiting the Messiah. They were bristling under the iron fist of Rome, and they longed for G-d to send a descendant of David to rise up and set them free.[179] But they were not ready for Jesus. John tried to prepare them, but the people as a whole did not understand, as they were waiting for a military/political deliverer. Of course, Rome was a big problem for the Jewish people. But from G-d's perspective, Rome was a secondary problem. Their real problem was themselves. G-d could set them free from other nations, even Rome. But they would still have hearts that were captured by the shiny objects of life, mouths that spoke words that were not true, and lives that were largely devoid of acts of lovingkindness towards others. From G-d's perspective, this was their fundamental problem. That is why Jesus came the

---

[178] Mk. 1:5.
[179] 2 Sam. 7:12-16; Jer. 23:5, 6; Dan. 2:44-45.

first time—to provide for their forgiveness so that they could go to heaven and experience relief from their sinful hearts in this life. But the Jews did not comprehend G-d's plan.

Interestingly, in the book of Malachi, where it predicts the coming of the Messiah, the context is not the oppression of the Jews by a hostile foreign power. But rather, the context is the struggle the Jews were experiencing as a result of their lack of faith. The implication is that Malachi's messianic prophecy pertains to the first coming of the Messiah, not the second one, in which the Messiah will deliver the Jews from the Gentile nations at the end of history.

*　*　*　*　*

No further Jewish history was recorded in the Tanakh; Malachi was the last book written. Approximately 500 years later, the writing of the New Testament began. The New Testament covers Jesus' three- to three-and-a-half-year ministry period as well as events involving His disciples that took place over the next few decades. The question is, why did G-d not record approximately 480 years of Jewish history?[180]

We know about this period from other historical sources, including the apocryphal books, Josephus' books, and other historical sources. The Jews started out the period having returned from exile in Babylonia. Unfortunately, they were ruled by the Persians after they returned to their land. When the Persians fell to the Greeks, Israel still remained an occupied territory, as the Greeks took over at that point.

About three centuries later, a Greek king crossed a line he should not have. To be specific, he was a Seleucid King.[181] His

---

[180] Malachi was written in approximately 450 BCE, and Jesus was crucified in the early 30s CE. Furthermore, the New Testament was started approximately 20 years after Jesus' crucifixion. Stephen M. Miller, *How to Get into the Bible* (Nashville, Tennessee: Thomas Nelson Publishers, 1998) 275, 379, 421.

[181] After Alexander the Great, the Greek Empire divided into four sub-empires, and the Seleucid Empire was one of them. It encompassed western Asia and also included Syria and Judea.

name was Antiochus IV Epiphanes, and he assaulted the Jews' faith. He abolished the Law, and he placed a statue of Zeus on the altar in the Temple courtyard.[182] In addition, on Zeus' birthday, December 25, 168 BCE, he desecrated the Temple by offering a pig on the altar.[183] He also ordered the Jews to erect pagan altars and offer swine upon them throughout the land.[184] Indeed, he demanded the observance of his religion and prohibited the practice of the Jewish faith. The sentence was death for anyone who violated these commands. Many pious Jews refused to go along with him and paid the ultimate price.[185]

Eventually, the Jews could take no more, and a revolt broke out. A family of six men, one father and five sons, started and led the revolt.[186] The father's name was Mattathias. Within the first year, he passed away from an illness, and his son, Judas Maccabaeus, took over. Judas was a brilliant military leader, and within three years, the Jews defeated the Greeks.[187]

On December 25, 165 BCE, three years after the day the Temple was desecrated, the Jews cleansed the Temple and rededicated the altar.[188] Hanukkah is an eight-day feast that celebrates this event. In fact, the word *Hanukkah* means "dedication."[189] There is a reference to this holiday in the New Testament in which we see Jesus observing Hanukkah.[190]

This was truly a historic event, as the Jews took a righteous stand against evil and prevailed. Indeed, the Jews would go on to regain their sovereignty in 142 BCE, 463 years after they lost

---

[182] Kevin Howard and Marvin Rosenthal, *The Feasts of the Lord* (Nashville, Tennessee: Thomas Nelson, Inc., 1997) 163.

[183] Ibid., 163.

[184] Flavius Josephus, *Antiquities*, 12.5.4 (253) from: *The Works of Josephus, Complete and Unabridged*, New Updated Edition, trans. William Whiston, A.M. (Peabody, MA: Hendrickson Publishers, Inc., 2009) 324.

[185] Howard and Rosenthal 163-164.

[186] Ibid., 164-165.

[187] Ibid., 165.

[188] Ibid., 165-166.

[189] Ibid., 157.

[190] Jn. 10:22-23; Howard and Rosenthal 171.

it to the Babylonians. They would retain their sovereignty for the next 69 years until they lost it again to the Roman Empire.

The question is, why did G-d not record this important event? The answer is because this 480-year period was a waiting period as far as G-d's long-term rescue plan was concerned. Very little progress was made toward His plan during these centuries. For whatever reason, G-d chose the early 30s CE to be the time for the Messiah to come and pay for the sins of the world.[191] During the preceding centuries, G-d was patiently waiting on history to run its course. We do not need to know about the events that took place in those centuries to be able to understand G-d's plan of salvation. That is not to say that the righteous stand leading to independence was not important. It certainly was. It is just that G-d's plan was not altered by this victory. Likewise, in no way does the absence of these Jewish people's lives from scripture indicate that they were less important than people from other ages. G-d loves all of His children, and the Jews who lived during this 480-year period were priceless to Him.

There are a number of parallels between this period and the 400+ years in which the Jews were enslaved in Egypt. In both periods the Jews were in a decent place at the start. In Egypt, the pharaoh at that time loved Joseph and welcomed his family as guests.[192] Similarly, at the time of the return from exile, the Persian kings were good and decent men, such as Cyrus and Artaxerxes. Cyrus granted the Jews the right to return, and Artaxerxes shockingly provided the materials for the rebuilding of the city wall of Jerusalem.[193] Such permission was never granted by an emperor in the ancient world, lest the subject people rebel.

In Egypt, the Jews became enslaved at some point. By the end, they were horribly oppressed by Pharaoh.[194] In the case of the intertestamental Jews, they were not enslaved, but they

---

[191] Dan. 9:24-27.
[192] Gen. 47:1-12.
[193] 2 Chron. 36:22-23; Ezra 1:7; 6:3-5; Neh. 2:7-8.
[194] Ex. 1:8-22; 2:23-25; 5:4-19.

remained an occupied people. As we detailed above, the time came when they were horribly oppressed by the Greek tyrant Antiochus IV Epiphanes. They did gain their independence temporarily, but eventually their situation became untenable again under the Roman prefect, or governor, Pontius Pilate. He was a sinful despot who, like Antiochus Epiphanes, attacked the Jews' faith.[195]

As with the intertestamental period, G-d did not have the history of the Egyptian period recorded either. The reason appears to be the same. However, again, it was not the case that these people's lives and struggles were unimportant. But rather, the Bible is only so big, and it would not be necessary for people in the future to know their stories. Similar to the intertestamental period, the Egyptian captivity was a long period in which G-d patiently allowed man to do his thing until it was time for Him to step in.[196]

---

[195] Flavius Josephus, *Antiquities*, 18.3.1-3 (55-64); *Wars*, 2.9.2-4 (169-177) from: *The Works of Josephus, Complete and Unabridged*, New Updated Edition, trans. William Whiston, A.M. (Peabody, MA: Hendrickson Publishers, Inc., 2009) 479-480; 608-609. Pilate was the governor in the 30s CE. In the 60s, the Jews would be subjected to Roman cruelty under Governor Florus (*Antiquities*, 20.11.1 (252-258).) These offenses, coupled with the earlier assaults on their religion by Emperor Caligula, caused the Jews to revolt (*Antiquities*, 18.8.1-8 (257-309).) Tragically, this revolt was unsuccessful, and the Jews were either killed or sent into exile in 70 CE.

[196] Gen. 15:12-16.

7

THE SABBATH

There is the letter of the law, and then there is the spirit of the law. The letter of the law is the wording of a statute. The spirit of the law is the intention behind it.

The fourth commandment states:

> "Remember the Sabbath day, to keep it holy. Six days you shall labor and do all your work, but the seventh day is a Sabbath of the L-rd your G-d; *in it* you shall not do any work, you or your son or your daughter, your male or your female servant or your cattle or your sojourner who stays with you. For in six days the L-rd made the heavens and the earth, the sea and all that is in them, and rested on the seventh day; therefore the L-rd blessed the Sabbath day and made it holy."[197]

---

[197] Ex. 20:8-11.

What was G-d's intention when He wrote this law? What is the spirit of this law? To answer this, we must go back to just before G-d sent the first plague on Egypt. When Moses first approached Pharaoh in Exodus Chapter 5, he asked Pharaoh to let the Jews go and celebrate a feast to G-d in the wilderness, but Pharaoh spurned Moses' request. Indeed, not only did Pharaoh refuse to let the people take a break from their labors to offer sacrifices to G-d, but he also increased their workload. Specifically, he stopped providing straw for their bricks and ordered them to go out and gather it for themselves. Yet, he still required them to produce the same amount of bricks per day. Of course, just like other historic slaveowners, Pharaoh had some of them beaten to ensure his demands would be met.[198] It was unbearable.

Fast forward to three months after the tenth plague and the Jews' escape from Egypt, when G-d gave Moses the Ten Commandments on Mount Sinai.[199] The Jews were no longer subject to the wicked pharaoh. Now G-d was leading them. Pharaoh had viewed the Jews as mere instruments to do his bidding. He had no concern for their well-being as his fellow humans. But G-d is different. He cared about their needs. So instead of demanding more and more work, G-d told them to work less. In the fourth commandment, He gave them a day off every week so they could catch their breath and recharge.[200] G-d even called for all the animals to be given a day off. He cared about them too.

What is the spirit of the fourth commandment? The purpose was to make life bearable, for G-d is good. Just as Moses had requested that the Jews be allowed to go and "celebrate a feast to G-d,"[201] the Sabbath was to be a joyous, celebratory occasion. Sure enough, this is the manner in which Jewish people observe the Sabbath today. Today, Jews enthusiastically greet each other with "Shabbat Shalom," and

---

[198] Ex. 5:1-14.
[199] Ex. 20.
[200] Deut. 5:15.
[201] Ex. 5:1.

they celebrate G-d's provision of food and the people in their lives. In addition, they remember the Law and His selection of them as His people.

Indeed, appropriate responses to G-d's gift of the Sabbath are thankfulness and joy. The other appropriate response to G-d is trust. This goes back to Adam and Eve in Genesis Chapter 3. When they chose to rebel, G-d remained true to His word, and He carried out their sentence. The consequences were severe. Humanity left a relationship with their loving Father in paradise and entered a broken world in which they were alienated from Him. In addition, work became difficult. Whereas there were no weeds in the garden of Eden, we all know what a pain weeds are today. Of course, not only were gardeners and farmers cursed, but this curse carried over to every profession. There are numerous frustrations each day for everyone who works. We each have our own "weeds" that tax our spirit and diminish our productivity. But perhaps it was even worse in the ancient world, where they were subject to the elements to a far greater degree. For example, farmers were subject to droughts, blights, insects, and pests. They did not have fertilizers, pesticides, combines, and irrigation systems. They worked from sunup to sundown every day, performing backbreaking labor. Despite their efforts, some years their harvests were slim, and they did not have enough to eat. In the words of G-d,

> Cursed is the ground because of you; in toil you will eat of it all the days of your life. Both thorns and thistles it shall grow for you; and you will eat the plants of the field; by the sweat of your face you will eat bread, till you return to the ground, because from it you were taken; for you are dust, and to dust you shall return.[202]

---

[202] Gen. 3:17b-20.

Again, still today work is hard. It stresses us out, and it takes a toll on our health. In third-world countries it is even worse. In some places, it is no more advanced than it was in the days after Adam and Eve were removed from Eden.

But then G-d gave Moses the Law, which included the Sabbath. The Sabbath is actually the removal of one seventh of the curse G-d placed on work. This is an enormous gift G-d gave to the Jews. Did He want anything in return from them for this gift? The answer is no. It was a pure gift. He just wanted them to take a day off, relax their aching muscles, forget about their work, and connect with Him and others. In order to succeed at this, they needed to trust G-d to take care of their crops while they were off.[203] If the Sabbath day was right in the middle of planting season, they needed to trust Him that taking a day off would not hinder their harvest that year. Likewise, if the Sabbath was in the middle of the prime time to harvest, they needed to trust G-d that their crops would be ripe and on the vines on the day after the Sabbath just the same as they were on the morning of the Sabbath. This was hard to do because they needed their crops in order to live. But G-d's message to them was "I have your farms covered. Take a day off and don't worry—so that your spirit may be refreshed. Then, when you come back to work on the first day of the week, you will be able to do a better job, and you will have a bigger harvest."

Of course, G-d is faithful to His promises, and to the extent they trusted G-d, their lives improved. Those who let go of worrying about their crops were able to rest and enjoy their families. In addition, they grew closer to G-d. They appreciated Him more, and they understood Him better. Indeed, G-d wanted them to grow in their faith, not for His sake, but for theirs.

*　*　*　*　*

An incorrect response to G-d's gift of the Sabbath is to approach it as a statute to be followed legalistically. The Pharisees of

---

[203] Lev. 26:1-5.

Jesus' day approached the Sabbath this way, and it grieved and even angered Jesus.

The Pharisees were following the letter of the law, but they were not acting in accordance with the spirit of the law. The result was that they turned G-d's beautiful gift into an exercise of walking on eggshells. In short, they took the gift of a well-needed day off and turned it into a cumbersome event.

Jesus violated the Pharisees' sub-laws on multiple occasions when they ran counter to G-d's intention for the Sabbath. This led to a series of heated exchanges between Jesus and the Pharisees.[204] Jesus used these exchanges to teach the onlookers about His mission and the true nature of the Sabbath.

About 475 years after Jesus' death, the rabbis, who came after the Sages, completed the Talmud. There are 63 tractates, or books, in the Talmud. Tractate Shabbat deals with activities that are prohibited on the Sabbath. Thus, Jewish scholars worked tirelessly for centuries, examining every activity that could be considered work. They broke each of the activities down into a series of actions as they attempted to identify the exact point at which work was being performed. The tractate they produced is nearly 400,000 words long.

Here is an example from Tractate Shabbat showing how narrowly they defined work:

Talmud – Mas. Shabbath 96a

CHAPTER XI

MISHNAH:

If one throws [an object] from private [ground]
into public ground [or] from public [ground]
into private ground, he is culpable. [If one
throws an object] from one private domain to
another, and public ground lies between, R.

---

[204] E.g., Jn. 9.

Akiva holds him liable, but the sages declare him exempt. How so? If there are two balconies facing each other across the street, [or public ground,] he who reaches over or throws [an object] from one to the other is not culpable. If both [balconies] are on the same story [and the same side of the street,] he who reaches over is culpable, while he who throws [an object] is not. For, so was the labor of the Levites: two wagons [stood] behind each other in public ground, [and] they reached the boards over from one to another, but [they] did not throw [them.]²⁰⁵

Talmud – Mas. Shabbath 96b

GEMARA:

Throwing is a derivative of carrying out.²⁰⁶ Where is carrying out itself written [in the Torah?] — Said R. Johanan, Scripture saith, "And Moses gave a command, and they caused a proclamation to pass throughout the camp."²⁰⁷ Now, where was Moses stationed? He was in the camp of the Levites, which was public ground, and he said to the Israelites, "Do not carry out from your private dwellings into public ground."... We have thus found [a prohibition against] carrying out; how do we know [that] carrying in [is forbidden?] — That

---

²⁰⁵ This labor was performed in connection with the Tabernacle in the Wilderness.

²⁰⁶ Throwing is a derivative act of labor since it is not enumerated in the list of principal acts of labor in 73a. Furthermore, it is a derivative of carrying out, for it is not similar to any of the other principal acts of labor.

²⁰⁷ Ex. 36:6.

is common sense. Consider: it is [transference of an object] from one domain to another, what does it matter whether one carries out or carries in? Nevertheless, carrying out is a principal [act of labor, whereas] carrying in is a derivative [act of labor.]

Yet let us consider: [if] one is culpable for both, why is one designated a principal [act of labor] and the other a derivative [act of labor?] — The practical difference is that if one performs [either] two principal or two derivative [acts of labor,] he is liable for two [sin offerings,] whereas if he performs a principal [act of labor] along with its derivative, he is only liable for one.[208]

This is the beginning of Chapter 11 of Tractate Shabbat. Chapter 11 is part of a section in this tractate dealing with the prohibited act of transporting objects from one domain to another.[209] An example of transporting objects would be movers carrying a dryer from the laundry room of a house and loading it onto a moving van. Clearly, this is work. But the sages and rabbis did not name moving as a forbidden activity. Rather, they broke the act of transporting an object down into multiple scenarios. Then they analyzed each scenario and explained when work would be taking place and when it would not.

Chapter 11 deals specifically with throwing objects, which the Sages and rabbis saw as a form of transporting an object. After all, the end result is the same, albeit there are some

---

[208] *The Complete Babylonian Talmud, in one volume*, (The Soncino Babylonian Talmud, Tractate Shabbat, Chapter 11, Folios 96a-96b,) Rab. Dr. H. Freedman, trans., Rab. Dr. I. Epstein, ed., 1938, https://halakhah.com/Complete-Babylonian-Talmud-English.pdf (accessed April 15, 2026.)

[209] It should be noted that transporting objects is one of 39 categories of work, or acts of labor, that are prohibited on the Sabbath. Approximately a third of Tractate Shabbat deals with this category.

differences between throwing and carrying. Hence, they wrote Chapter 11 in order to ascertain when throwing an object reaches the level of work.

The above excerpt is long enough to give you an idea of what Tractate Shabbat is like and what it has to say about throwing objects on the Sabbath. But this excerpt is only just the beginning of Chapter 11. Chapter 11 is actually over 13,000 words long. In the above text, we can see that the Talmud is composed of legal jargon, and it is complicated. This passage discusses throwing an object from one balcony to another. It states that it is permissible to throw an object from your balcony onto a balcony across the street. It is also permissible to lean a long object over to another balcony on the other side of the street. But leaning a long object off your balcony onto another balcony that is on the same side of the street is not permitted. Though, you can throw an object onto such a balcony, provided it is on the same story as your balcony.

Of course, throwing can certainly be work. For example, throwing hay bales up onto the bed of a truck is hard work. But what about a father spending some time throwing a baseball with his child? Is that work? Common sense tells us that it is not work but play. Would that be forbidden per this tractate because it involves the physical act of throwing an object? There is some debate today over the answer to this question. Lengthy papers about this debate are available online for those who are interested.[210] Here is a simple, conclusory statement from an article written for laypeople[211]:

---

[210] E.g. Rabbi Daniel Neustadt, "Games On Shabbos Ball Playing On Shabbos," 2007, https://torah.org/torah-portion/weekly-halacha-5767-kisavo/ (accessed October 11, 2024); Saul J. Berman, "Playing Ball on *Shabbat* and *Yom Tov*," The Edah Journal 1:1 (2000,) https://library.yctorah.org/files/2016/09/Playing-Ball-On-Shabbat-And-Yom-Tov.pdf (accessed October 11, 2024.)

[211] Nechoma Greisman and Chana Ne'eman, "Baby and Toddler Care on Shabbat," https://www.chabad.org/library/article_cdo/aid/77897/jewish/Baby-and-Toddler-Care-on-Shabbat.htm (accessed October 11, 2024.)

Below three years children have little conception of what Shabbat is and can exercise no responsibility in keeping it. Halacha reflects this fact. Thus, most authorities allow babies to play with their rattles and other noise-producing toys on Shabbat, though adults may not shake or even touch them. Similarly, small children may play with soap bubbles on Shabbat, whereas adults may not make them at all.

As they grow older, children play with an ever larger variety of toys, and a good many of them are permitted on Shabbat as well. For example, balls (but not inflated ones) may be played with indoors and, if there is an eruv, also outdoors. Wind-up toys, if they do not make musical sounds and do not run on batteries, are permitted. Blocks are allowed, if they do not attach permanently together. Permitted, too, are beads and strings, as long as no knot is made in them; out-door games not involving carrying; running and jumping games; swings (unless attached to a tree); and tricycles if the custom is to ride them in your community, if there is an eruv, and if the bell is removed. Trikes may be ridden indoors, in any case. Playing in a sandbox is controversial. Wagschal states flatly that playing with sand is forbidden on Shabbat. Matzner-Beckerman, on the other hand, says that playing with sand in a sandbox (not on the beach) is permitted, as long as children are not allowed to mix it with water, which constitutes kneading, one of the 39 forbidden categories of melacha. Consult your rabbi on this issue.

Hence, their conclusion is that fathers may not play catch with their children on the Sabbath. Children, on the other hand, can throw a baseball indoors, or in an eruv outside.[212]

This is the kind of reasoning, and imposition on the general public, that angered Jesus. Here is a passage from the New Testament in which Jesus clashed with the Pharisees over how to observe the Sabbath:

> As He passed by, he saw Levi the *son* of Alphaeus sitting at the tax booth, and He said to him, "Follow Me!" And he got up and followed Him.
>
> And it happened that He was reclining at the table in his house, and many tax collectors and sinners were dining with Jesus and His disciples; for there were many of them, and they were following Him. When the scribes of the Pharisees saw that He was eating with the sinners and tax collectors, they said to His disciples, "Why is He eating and drinking with tax collectors and sinners?" And hearing this, Jesus said to them, "It is not those who are healthy who need a physician, but those who are sick; I did not come to call the righteous, but sinners."
>
> John's disciples and the Pharisees were fasting; and they came and said to Him, "Why do John's disciples and the disciples of the

---

[212] An eruv is a technical enclosure which surrounds both private and hitherto public domains and thus creates a large private domain in which carrying is permitted on Shabbat. . . . The eruv is usually large enough to include entire neighborhoods with homes, apartments and synagogues, making it possible to carry on Sabbat, since one is never leaving one's domain." (This explanation is from: Lome Rozovsky, "What Is an Eruv?," https://www.chabad.org/library/article_cdo/aid/700456/jewish/What-Is-an-Eruv.htm (accessed December 9, 2024.))

Pharisees fast, but Your disciples do not fast?" And Jesus said to them, "While the bridegroom is with them, the attendants of the bridegroom cannot fast, can they? So long as they have the bridegroom with them, they cannot fast. But the days will come when the bridegroom is taken away from them, and then they will fast in that day.

"No one sews a patch of unshrunk cloth on an old garment; otherwise the patch pulls away from it, the new from the old, and a worse tear results. No one puts new wine into old wineskins; otherwise the wine will burst the skins, and the wine is lost and the skins as well; but one puts new wine into fresh wineskins."

And it happened that He was passing through the grainfields on the Sabbath, and His disciples began to make their way along while picking the heads of grain. The Pharisees were saying to Him, "Look, why are they doing what is not lawful on the Sabbath?" And He said to them, "Have you never read what David did when he was in need and he and his companions became hungry; how he entered the house of G-d in the time of Abiathar the high priest, and ate the consecrated bread, which is not lawful for anyone to eat except the priests, and he also gave it to those who were with him?" Jesus said to them, "The Sabbath was made for man, and not man for the Sabbath. So the Son of Man is L-rd even of the Sabbath."

He entered again into a synagogue; and a man was there whose hand was withered. They were watching Him to see if He would heal him on the Sabbath, so that they might accuse Him. He said to the man with the withered hand,

"Get up and come forward!" And He said to them, "Is it lawful to do good or to do harm on the Sabbath, to save a life or to kill?" But they kept silent. After looking around at them with anger, grieved at their hardness of heart, He said to the man, "Stretch out your hand." And he stretched it out, and his hand was restored. The Pharisees went out and immediately began conspiring with the Herodians against Him, as to how they might destroy Him.[213]

This passage is about two fundamentally different perspectives on the Law. The Pharisees' approach to the Law was religious, which implies that G-d is religious. Jesus' approach was based on the view that G-d loves people and seeks their welfare. At the beginning of this passage, we see Jesus sharing a meal with a group of "tax collectors and sinners." These people were rejected by the religious leaders, and society as a whole, for living sinfully. Jesus saw them as human beings who were in need of rescue. Jesus' view is the same as the view of parents who have a drug-addicted child. They will do anything to help their child become sober and turn their life around. But the Pharisees and scribes in this passage were disgusted by these people, and they did not want to have anything to do with them. They believed that G-d rejects people such as these. Hence, they were confused by Jesus, for they heard that He was a man of G-d.[214]

They were not sure what to make of John the Baptist either. But at least his disciples fasted. Jesus' disciples were not fasting. The Pharisees questioned Jesus about this, and He responded with a parable. In the parable, He said that His disciples were not fasting because they were enjoying a wedding, referring to the brief moment they had to spend with Him prior to His crucifixion.

---

[213] Mk. 2:14-3:6.
[214] Lk. 7:11-17, 36-50.

Then He told the Pharisees a parable that was somewhat cryptic. It was not meant as an insult, but if they got His point, they probably would not have liked it. Whether it is a new piece of cloth patching a hole in an old piece of clothing, or new wine being poured into an old wineskin, the result will be the same. Either the old, threadbare piece of clothing will be ripped apart by the new piece of cloth as it shrinks, or the old wineskin will burst as the new wine ferments and expands. For, the old wineskin will no longer be able to stretch to accommodate the new wine as it expands. Jesus' point was that the Jewish religion started out in accord with G-d's instructions, but it had changed over the centuries. He came with a new message, and it conflicted with those changes. His parable implied that if you tried to combine the two messages, it would not work. His message emphasizing the forgiveness of sins would destroy the Pharisees' message of earning salvation through strict observance of the Law. This was difficult for the Pharisees to hear, for they were human, and it hurts to hear someone say that what you have devoted your life to is wrong. In their defense, it should be noted that their motives were good.

The Jews had rebelled badly for centuries. G-d sent prophet after prophet to them to give them a warning. But the Jews ignored the prophets, or worse. For example, in the book of Jeremiah, we see where Jeremiah was in danger multiple times for speaking the words of G-d. In Isaiah's case, tradition tells us that the Jews sawed him in half![215] Eventually, G-d had to deal with the Jews for the sake of justice. Furthermore, He did not want to be associated with them because of the way they were living. Thus, He allowed the Babylonians to conquer them and send them into exile. It was horrific. Hence, it is understandable why the Jewish religious leaders were perfectionists when it

---

[215] F. F. Bruce, *The Epistle to the Hebrews*, Revised, The New International Commentary on the New Testament, Gen. Ed. Gordon D. Fee (Grand Rapids, William B. Eerdmans Publishing Company, 1990) 328. In this commentary, the apocryphon titled the *Ascension of Isaiah* is cited as the source.

came to following the Law. Their goal was to prevent anything like the Babylonian exile from ever happening again.

In addition to the Pharisees' desire to protect the nation, they were also leaders in Israel, and they viewed Jesus' parable as a threat to their positions of power. Yet, if Jesus was right, ultimately they needed to humble themselves and obey G-d's will. But they were unwilling to consider that Jesus might be right. Therefore, a schism arose. Some Jews followed Jesus and began the Christian movement. But most of the Jews followed the Pharisees. Their religious system is still around today, as the Pharisees' beliefs and practices are the foundation of Rabbinic Judaism.

Jesus' parable sets the context for the remainder of Mark Chapters 2 and 3, which cover His conflict with the Pharisees over the Sabbath. There are two parts to His conflict with them in this passage. In the first part, Jesus' disciples broke some of the Pharisees' sub-laws regarding the Sabbath. When the Pharisees challenged Jesus about their behavior, He responded strongly, and then He made a shocking claim. He told them that "the Son of Man is L-rd even of the Sabbath." This was a claim to deity! Jesus was angry with them. Why? The answer is that, from Jesus' perspective, they hijacked G-d's gift of the Sabbath and put themselves in charge of it. They turned it into an exercise of following rules. G-d had given the Sabbath to the Jews as a day off. Would G-d give a father a day off work and then say that he could not play catch with his son? But rather, that he had to be careful and walk on eggshells lest he be found guilty of doing anything that could be considered work? So, instead of the Jews experiencing G-d's goodness, they were subjected to the Pharisees' complicated set of sub-laws. The net result was that the Sabbath did not communicate G-d's kindness and draw the Jews to Him, but rather, it taught them to approach Him in a religious fashion. This is why Jesus was upset.

The logic of Jesus' argument is that His disciples were not farming on the Sabbath but were simply picking some grain along their way and eating it because they were hungry and poor, and that was all they had to eat that day. Furthermore, they were not violating the Law by picking the heads of the grain as they walked through the grainfields.[216] Then Jesus referenced the story of David famously eating the priests' food and thereby violating the Law.[217] But David was not in trouble, because he was on the run and hungry. Therefore, it is acceptable to violate a ceremonial law in order to come to the aid of someone who is in desperate need. David's breach was not a Sabbath violation, but it worked as an illustration of the principle Jesus was teaching. Namely, it is better to take care of people in need than to be a perfectionist in observing the Sabbath. To be clear, Jesus was not opposed to the Sabbath; He was opposed to the Pharisees' version of it.[218] In fact, He was fully in favor of following the Law.[219]

The second part of the conflict starts in Chapter 3, verse 1. In this event, Jesus performed a beautiful miracle—He healed a man with a withered hand. That would have really been a sight to see. However, Jesus healed him on the Sabbath. In the eyes of the Pharisees, Jesus broke the Sabbath because He healed a man, which is tantamount to performing the work of a doctor.[220]

Have you ever seen someone with a withered hand? There may be webbing between the fingers, or there may be missing fingers or fingers that never grew to full size. Their hand does not work well, and it definitely looks different. The damage to their self-worth is not small. Jesus crossed paths with this man and felt compassion for him. So He performed a miracle and healed him. Was Jesus working? No, He merely spoke, and the man's hand was formed. Jesus wanted the man to know that G-d knew how hard his life was and that He cared. Then Jesus

---

[216] Deut. 23:25 (26.)

[217] 1 Sam. 21:1-6 (2-7.)

[218] Mt. 22:34-40.

[219] Mt. 5:17-19.

[220] The Pharisees had a category for giving medical attention to someone in mortal danger but not to someone who could wait until the following day to receive treatment.

reiterated to the Pharisees that lovingly helping someone in need is more important than using a microscope to make sure that no work is performed.

When Jesus healed the man's hand, it validated His claim to be G-d. For, He did not just heal someone's aching back, which no one can see. No, Jesus healed a man whose withered hand was visible to everyone. Every onlooker knew whether or not Jesus performed this miracle. For example, we know that the Pharisees saw the miracle because they were upset with Jesus. Had nothing happened, they would not have cared. It upset them because He was challenging their beliefs and undermining their authority. The story ends with the Pharisees seeking the counsel of the Herodians in order to come up with a plan to destroy Jesus.[221]

Jesus' bold claim is still important and worthy of consideration today. Is He who He said He was? For, the answer to that question may hold the key to each of our eternal destinies. Of course, this question is the subject of this four-volume series.

*　　*　　*　　*　　*

For some reason, human beings gravitate towards approaching G-d in a religious fashion. But is that what He wants? Does G-d have a religious heart? He did not act that way in the Garden of Eden with Adam and Eve. There were no rituals. Adam and Eve approached G-d as their loving father. Their relationships with Him consisted of spending time together, talking, and expressing love to one another.

Jesus' relationships with His disciples were similar. He spent night and day with them. He camped with them, cooked and ate with them, taught them, and had them assist Him with His ministry. The disciples were open and honest with Jesus. That makes sense because Jesus accepted them, and they knew it.

---

[221] The Herodians were the supporters of Herod Antipas, the man who executed John the Baptist.

On the night before Jesus' execution, Peter denied that he knew Jesus three times to save his skin. He felt deeply ashamed, and he left the courtyard of the High Priest in tears.[222] Following Jesus' crucifixion and resurrection, one evening the disciples decided to go fishing, which was their old profession. They caught nothing all night. At dawn, they were close to shore, and a solitary figure on the beach shouted out to them to cast their net on the right side of the boat. They did that, and immediately their net was bursting with fish. At that point, it dawned on them that it was Jesus who was standing on the shore. Without hesitation, Peter jumped in the water with his clothes on and ran to the beach to be with Jesus. He could not wait to see Him.[223]

Peter found Jesus cooking fish and baking bread for their breakfast. After breakfast, Jesus addressed Peter's abandonment of Him in His hour of need. Jesus was not going to brush it under the table. But He brought it up lovingly to resolve the matter for Peter's sake. In the end, He reaffirmed Peter. Jesus told Peter that He still wanted him to play the role he was given earlier.[224] The point is that Jesus dealt with His disciples as if they were His actual brothers, and they knew they were fully loved by Him.

This is who G-d is, and this is the relationship He wants to have with the Jews on the Sabbath. He does not want them to be focused on an encyclopedic set of sub-laws. That is not who He is. He wants them to draw close to Him and speak to Him in a real way, like David did. In the Psalms, David opened up about everything with G-d. He sought G-d's help with his enemies, he asked for forgiveness when he sinned, and he thanked and praised G-d when things were going well. These are the kinds of prayers we should offer on the Sabbath.[225] This is also the way

---

[222] Mt. 26:75.

[223] Jn. 21:1-14.

[224] Mt. 16:17-19; Jn. 21:15-17.

[225] Jesus agreed with David. He, too, was opposed to formulaic prayer and instead taught people to pray to G-d in a personal manner (Mt. 6:6-8.)

we should be relating with our loved ones on the Sabbath. In addition, we should have fun with each other and bond with each other.

Unfortunately, the Pharisees turned the Sabbath into something different. No longer was it the sweet gift G-d gave them. Rather, it became complicated and burdensome. Furthermore, onlookers who observed the Jews practicing the pharisaic version of the Sabbath were not drawn to G-d. G-d's role for the Jews was to bear witness of Him. They were to show the world who He is and how good He is, so that Gentiles could find Him too. But that was not happening, and that is also why Jesus was angry with the Pharisees.

This was the state of Judaism in Judea 2,000 years ago when Jesus arrived on the scene. In the next chapter, we will discuss what Jesus did outside of debating theology with the Jewish religious leaders.

8

THE INCARNATION

What is more beautiful than the love between a mother and her child? It is not surprising that G-d gave the gift of motherhood to women in the opening chapters of the book of Genesis. It also tells us in Gen. 1:26 that G-d created us in His image! What an absolute honor and great fortune it is to be a human being. How are we like G-d? The answer is that we are like Him in many ways, such as our creativity and intelligence. But perhaps the most important way in which we are similar to G-d is in our capacity to love others. For example, the love a mother has for her children is from G-d and is a reflection of who He is. At the heart of who each of us is, is the capacity to give and receive love. In fact, we should each be experiencing a relationship with G-d in which we are receiving His life-giving love and expressing love back to Him.

That was G-d's plan. That was the existence He created for us, and that is who He made us to be. But we believed a lie—that G-d is not good—and we rebelled.[226] Now we are all confused, and we live in a state of alienation from G-d.

---

[226] Gen. 3.

The good news is that G-d has a plan to rescue us. G-d's plan consists of sending a savior to correct our misconceptions about Him and to die for our sins. Jesus claimed to be that savior.[227] He also claimed to be G-d.[228] This makes sense, for both Isaiah and Jeremiah predicted that the Messiah would be G-d in the form of a man.

> For a child will be born to us, a son will be given to us; and the government will rest on His shoulders; and His name will be called Wonderful Counselor, Mighty G-d, Eternal Father, Prince of Peace. There will be no end to the increase of *His* government or of peace, on the throne of David and over his kingdom, to establish it and to uphold it with justice and righteousness from then on and forevermore. The zeal of the L-rd of hosts will accomplish this.[229]

and,

> "Behold, *the* days are coming," declares the L-rd, "when I will raise up for David a righteous Branch; and He will reign as king and act wisely and do justice and righteousness in the land. In His days Judah will be saved, and Israel will dwell securely; and this is His name by which He will be called, 'the L-rd our righteousness.'...."[230]

Wouldn't it make sense that if G-d was going to take the form of a man and appear to us, He would do it by being born? G-d had been foreshadowing Jesus' birth throughout history in

---

227 Mt. 16:13-17; Mk. 14:60-63; Jn. 4:25-26.
228 Jn. 8:53-59; 10:22-30; 17:1-5.
229 Isa. 9:6-7 (5-6.)
230 Jer. 23:5-6.

the form of a string of miraculous births by mothers such as Sarah, Rebekah, and Rachel, all of whom are ancestors of Jesus.

How can G-d be born of a woman? Well, He can do anything. He can appear as a pillar of fire in the desert, as a cloud in the Holy of Holies, and, yes, as a human being.[231] In fact, He had already appeared this way to Abraham.[232] Of course, Jesus was not conceived the usual way. The Holy Spirit touched Mary's body such that an embryo formed in her womb,[233] yet Mary remained a virgin.[234] So, Jesus was G-d, and yet He became a human. He was born and grew up with His mother, Mary, His adoptive father, Joseph, and His brothers and sisters. At about the age of thirty, Jesus began His public ministry.[235]

Jesus' ministry period lasted only three to three and a half years. Yet, He changed the world. He came to accomplish five main tasks:

First, He came to clear up the lies that have been told about G-d by showing us His character. Jesus' disciple John put it this way:

> In the beginning was the Word, and the Word was with G-d, and the Word was G-d. He was in the beginning with G-d. All things came into being through Him, and apart from Him nothing came into being that has come into being. In Him was life, and the life was the Light of men. The Light shines in the darkness, and the darkness did not comprehend it.
>
> There came a man sent from G-d, whose name was John. He came as a witness, to testify about the Light, so that all might believe

---

231 Ex. 13:21-22; 1 Kin. 8:10-11.
232 Gen. 18.
233 Lk. 1:35.
234 Mt. 1:24-25.
235 Lk. 3:23.

through him. He was not the Light, but *he came* to testify about the Light.

There was the true Light which, coming into the world, enlightens every man. He was in the world, and the world was made through Him, and the world did not know Him. He came to His own, and those who were His own did not receive Him. But as many as received Him, to them He gave the right to become children of G-d, *even* to those who believe in His name, who were born, not of blood nor of the will of the flesh nor of the will of man, but of G-d.

And the Word became flesh, and dwelt among us, and we saw His glory, glory as of the only begotten from the Father, full of grace and truth. John testified about Him and cried out, saying, "This was He of whom I said, 'He who comes after me has a higher rank than I, for He existed before me.'" For of His fullness we have all received, and grace upon grace. For the Law was given through Moses; grace and truth were realized through Jesus Christ. No one has seen G-d at any time; the only begotten G-d who is in the bosom of the Father, He has explained *Him*.[236]

Here we see that He is G-d the Son, who created the universe with G-d the Father.[237] He came to bring light into the darkness, or in other words, to bring the truth about Himself

---

[236] Jn. 1:1-18. For the sake of clarity, it should be noted that this passage mentions John the Baptist, though it was written by a different John—Jesus' disciple.

[237] The concept of the Trinity is one of the main reasons Jewish people reject Christian theology. Based on the Shema in Deut. 6:4-9, they do not believe in the Trinity, including the deity of Jesus. Much is written on this subject, including a brief explanation in Volume 2, Chapter 10.

into a world filled with lies. He came to His people, the Jews. What did they see in Jesus? They saw a man who was honest and gracious. Yet, most of them were not interested in what He had to say and did not receive Him as their savior.

Who is G-d, really? The Jews saw in Jesus that He is kind, gentle, patient, and brave. It should be noted that John, Jesus' disciple, lived with Him day and night for the entire three-plus years. John knew of what he wrote.

Second, Jesus spent a large percentage of His time raising up His disciples to carry on after His death and resurrection. We will cover this subject in detail in Chapter 12. Along with the apostle Paul, these men fearlessly took the message of Jesus across the Roman Empire and started a worldwide movement. With the exception of John, who died at a ripe old age as a prisoner on an island, all the other disciples went to their deaths as martyrs rather than recant their testimonies of Jesus' resurrection.

Third, Jesus provided evidence that He was G-d by healing people with visible handicaps and diseases, fulfilling messianic prophecy from the Tanakh, and rising from the dead after His crucifixion. In fact, He appeared to as many as 500 people at one time after He was resurrected.[238] We covered the subject of messianic prophecy in Volume 2. For example, Isaiah 53 is a gratuitously obvious prophecy. People who hear it for the first time may even say, "That is about Jesus." They are right, but what they may not know is that this passage was written 650 years before Jesus' death on the cross.

Regarding Jesus' resurrection, as stated above, His disciples went to their deaths rather than take back their testimony that He rose from the dead. There is no explanation in the world for why they would do that, other than it really happened. Also, it is undeniable that despite His tomb being guarded by Roman soldiers, Jesus' body went missing and was never found. In the words of English theologian N. T. Wright,

---

[238] 1 Cor. 15:6.

> If nothing happened to the body of Jesus, I cannot see why any of his explicit or implicit claims should be regarded as true. What is more, I cannot as a historian, see why anyone would have continued to belong to his movement and to regard him as the Messiah.[239]

But something did happen to Jesus' body. He rose from the dead.

Fourth, Jesus came to teach us spiritual truth. Not only did He teach about who G-d is, but He also explained who we are, how dire our predicament is, and what G-d's solution is to rescue us. He taught publicly to large crowds and one on one to people He came across. His words were profound yet down to earth. They were also true and seasoned with grace. His teachings are often quoted still to this day. Some of His notable teachings include the Parable of the Good Samaritan, the Parable of the Prodigal Son, and the Sermon on the Mount.

Unfortunately, Jesus had enemies. His enemies were, of all people, the Jewish religious leaders. He debated them publicly on a number of occasions, as we saw in the last two chapters. He utilized these occasions to teach spiritual truth as well.

Fifth, Jesus came to die as a sacrifice to atone for the sins of the world. Of course, this task surpassed all the others by far in terms of importance. In several different conversations, Jesus made it clear that He came to provide forgiveness for sinners. For example,

> Getting into a boat, Jesus crossed over *the sea* and came to His own city. And they brought to Him a paralytic lying on a bed. Seeing their faith, Jesus said to the paralytic, "Take courage, son; your sins are forgiven." And some of the scribes said to themselves, "This

---

[239] Eric Chabot, *The Resurrection of the Jewish Messiah* (Made in Columbia, SC, 2019) 67.

fellow blasphemes." And Jesus knowing their thoughts said, "Why are you thinking evil in your hearts? Which is easier, to say, 'Your sins are forgiven,' or to say, 'Get up, and walk'? But so that you may know that the Son of Man has authority on earth to forgive sins"—then He said to the paralytic, "Get up, pick up your bed and go home." And he got up and went home. But when the crowds saw *this*, they were awestruck, and glorified G-d, who had given such authority to men.[240]

This could not be clearer. We all need forgiveness.[241] But forgiveness requires a perfect sacrifice to pay for the sins of humanity. Hence, Jesus allowed Himself to be arrested, beaten, and crucified.[242] Jesus' great act of sacrificial love is the centerpiece of G-d's plan to rescue humanity. In the words of Jesus' disciple, Peter,

> For you have been called for this purpose, since Christ also suffered for you, leaving you an example for you to follow in His steps, who committed no sin, nor was any deceit found in his mouth; and while being reviled, He did not revile in return; while suffering, He uttered no threats, but kept entrusting *Himself* to Him who judges righteously; and He Himself bore our sins in His body on the cross, so that we might die to sin and live to righteousness; for by His wounds you were healed. For you were continually straying like sheep, but now you have returned to the Shepherd and Guardian of your souls.[243]

---

[240] Mt. 9:1-8.
[241] Ps. 14:1-3; Rom. 3:23.
[242] Isa. 53:5-10; Mt. 5:17-20; Heb. 4:14-16; 1 Pet. 2:21-25.
[243] 1 Pet. 2:21-25. Cf. Isa. 53:5-10.

This is why He came: to offer Himself up for the sake of others. He was a human, yet He committed no sins. Therefore, He was able to step in and take the punishment of the guilty on His shoulders.[244] Of course, being in the form of a man, he went through this hellish trial fully. There was no heavenly anesthetic to relieve His pain. In fact, it was worse for Him than it was for others who were crucified. For, while He was on the cross, He was rejected by G-d, and He absorbed G-d's punishment for all of the sins of mankind.[245] I cannot comprehend how that worked, but I am certain it was awful.

He was in great anguish the night before His death, as He knew what He was facing. Here are the words He spoke to the disciples, and the ones He spoke to G-d:

> They came to a place named Gethsemane; and He said to His disciples, "Sit here until I have prayed." And He took with Him Peter and James and John, and began to be very distressed and troubled. And He said to them, "My soul is deeply grieved to the point of death; remain here and keep watch." And He went a little beyond *them*, and fell to the ground and *began* to pray that if it were possible, the hour might pass Him by. And He was saying, "Abba! Father! All things are possible for You; remove this cup from Me; yet not what I will, but what You will."[246]

Jesus came to the brink of the cross, and it hit Him. He prayed for G-d to take it away, but G-d said no. The price of justice had to be paid in order for men to be forgiven. Jesus had a choice to make. He could have quit, but He chose to go through with it.

Thank you Jesus!

---

[244] Mt. 5:17; Heb. 4:14-16.
[245] Mt. 27:46.
[246] Mk. 14:32-36.

*　　*　　*　　*　　*

The question is, how do you receive this gift of forgiveness? First of all, it is a gift. In fact, it is made clear in both the Tanakh and the New Testament that salvation is a free gift.[247] You cannot work for it or earn it.[248] Jesus' offer of salvation is like a wedding ceremony. All the bride and groom need to do is say, "I do." If they want to be married, then they simply verbalize it. Ultimately, it comes down to a choice the bride and groom both have to make. So too, G-d is offering each person a second chance to enter into a Father-son or Father-daughter relationship.[249] If you want to do that, you just pray and say yes to G-d's offer of reconciliation through Jesus. If you are not interested, you either say no, or you simply ignore Him. But if you say yes, that is all it takes. In the words of Paul,

> ...that if you confess with your mouth Jesus *as* L-rd, and believe in your heart that G-d raised Him from the dead, you will be saved; for with the heart a person believes, resulting in righteousness, and with the mouth he confesses, resulting in salvation.[250]

It would be foolish to simply ignore Jesus. In the words of Hebrews 2:3, which was written to Jews,

> ...how will we escape if we neglect so great a salvation? After it was at the first spoken through the L-rd, it was confirmed to us by those who heard....

---

[247] Isa. 55; Rom. 6:23.

[248] Isa. 55:1-3; Eph. 2:8-9.

[249] Rom. 8:15-16.

[250] Rom. 9:9-10.

How could anyone say no to this offer? Jesus said the reason is that we are too proud. In Matthew 18, it says:

> At that time the disciples came to Jesus and said, "Who then is greatest in the kingdom of heaven?" And He called a child to Himself and set him before them, and said, "Truly I say to you, unless you are converted and become like children, you will not enter the kingdom of heaven. Whoever then humbles himself as this child, he is the greatest in the kingdom of heaven. And whoever receives one such child in My name receives Me; but whoever causes one of these little ones who believe in Me to stumble, it would be better for him to have a heavy millstone hung around his neck, and to be drowned in the depth of the sea.[251]

Jesus was right. Little children have an unpolluted innocence and an understanding of what is truly important in life, namely love and relationships. They are not proud, and they have an undeveloped facade. Therefore, they are able to give and receive forgiveness easily.

---

[251] Mt. 18:1-6.

9

70 CE

Four short decades after Jesus burst on the scene came another awful year for the Jews. The catastrophic events of 70 CE were eerily similar to those of 586 BCE. In both years, protracted sieges came to an end as the soldiers finally breached the walls and rushed into the city. Both sieges led to starvation and cannibalism, and both events culminated in the destruction of Jerusalem and the exile of the Jewish survivors.[252] However, there was one difference. Prior to the first event, the Jews had been warned for hundreds of years by the prophets to turn from their sinful ways and thereby prevent their defeat to the Babylonians. But, similar warnings were not given to the Jews prior to 70 CE. Indeed, G-d sent no prophets at all to the Jews for five hundred years. That is, except for Jesus, who did predict the events of 70 CE.

The Jews of Jeremiah's day had no one to blame but themselves for the fall of Jerusalem. But what about the Jews of the first century? They were no longer worshipping idols. In fact, they were striving to follow the Law. In addition, tension

---

[252] Lam. 4:1-13.

had been brewing between the Jews and the Romans for decades. Rightly did the Jews resist every Roman affront to their faith. Therefore, one may ask, were the Jews properly warned, and what did they do to deserve the catastrophic defeat in 70 CE?

Yet, there were some warnings of a destruction that would be coming upon Israel that were issued by both the exilic and post-exilic prophets. But these warnings tended to be subtle and not explicit.[253]

Both Jesus and Daniel predicted the fall of Jerusalem to the Romans. Their predictions stemmed from G-d's knowing that in the future the Jews would make a fateful choice that would lead to their downfall. The siege of 70 CE and the resultant exile were never G-d's will; rather, they were the fruit of the free will choice the Jews made. Here are the prophecies of Jesus and Daniel:

> And when He approached, He saw the city and wept over it, saying, "If you had known in this day, even you, the things which make for peace! But now they have been hidden from your eyes. For the days shall come upon you when your enemies will throw up a bank before you, and surround you, and hem you in on every side, and will level you to the ground and your children within you, and they will not leave in you one stone upon another, because you did not recognize the time of your visitation."[254]

> "O Jerusalem, Jerusalem, who kills the prophets and stones those who are sent to her! How often I wanted to gather your children together, the way a hen gathers her chicks under her wings, and you were unwilling. Behold, your house is

---

253 Zech. 11:4-14.
254 Lk. 19:41-44.

> being left to you desolate! For I say to you, from now on you shall not see Me until you say, 'Blessed is he who comes in the name of the L-rd!'"[255]

And from Daniel:

> "So you are to know and discern *that* from the issuing of a decree to restore and rebuild Jerusalem until Messiah the Prince *there will be* seven weeks and sixty-two weeks; it will be built again, with plaza and moat, even in times of distress. Then after the sixty-two weeks the Messiah will be cut off and have nothing, and the people of the prince who is to come will destroy the city and the sanctuary. And its end *will come* with a flood; even to the end there will be war; desolations are determined."[256]

Both Jesus and Daniel predicted a crushing defeat by the Romans, and Jesus explained why. In the words of Jesus, the Jews were "unwilling" to receive Him and His message of approaching G-d through the forgiveness of their sins. They wanted to earn G-d's acceptance through strict adherence to the Mosaic Law, including the sub-laws prescribed by the Sages. These two paths are opposed to one another, and the Jews chose the latter.

The problem is that although Jesus claimed to be G-d in the form of a man, and He provided evidence, the Jews chose to reject Him. That would explain why G-d allowed the Romans to conquer the Jews and exile them in 70 CE. Jesus never wanted this fate for the Jews.[257] Luke recorded that as Jesus approached the city and gazed into the future, He saw the

---

[255] Mt. 23:37-39.
[256] Dan. 9:25-26.
[257] Mt. 23:37.

suffering that would come upon the people, and He wept. But the Jews made their choice, and He accepted it.

In the Garden of Eden, G-d gave Adam and Eve a simple choice. It consisted of eating versus not eating the fruit from one particular tree in the midst of a substantial orchard of fruit trees.[258] The prohibition on eating the fruit from this tree was just a mechanism by which they could register their choice. The real choice was whether they wanted to stay in the garden with G-d, or jettison Him and venture out on their own. They did not get hundreds of years of warnings. It was a straightforward choice. They experienced love from G-d over a period of time, and that was enough for them to know Him and be responsible for their choice. A malevolent being approached them and lied about G-d, and they believed his lies. Then they chose to rebel, and they and all their descendants, including us, have suffered the consequences of that choice ever since.[259]

When Jesus left home and stepped onto the public stage, He captured the attention of the nation. He did not make a small ripple; He made a big splash. However, His goal was not to draw attention to Himself, but rather to G-d. He wanted to bring G-d's plan to undo the damage caused by Adam and Eve to the forefront of the conversation in Israel. Jesus demonstrated the love of G-d through His interactions with people. In addition, He performed miracles of healing as well as other miracles. Some of them were personal, like giving a fishing crew an enormous haul of fish after they had fished all night and caught nothing.[260] He also performed some very large-scale, public miracles, such as feeding thousands of people despite starting with only a small amount of bread and fish.[261] He had a strong grasp of the Tanakh,[262] and He taught the people about G-d's love. He also told the nation that they had gotten off course in the way they were trying to approach

---

[258] Gen. 2:14-16.
[259] Gen. 3.
[260] Lk. 5:1-11.
[261] Mk. 6:33-44.
[262] Mk. 1:21-22; Jn. 7:14-17.

G-d.[263] Some people saw that Jesus was from G-d, and they followed Him. Most of the people viewed Jesus' ministry as a spectacle, but they were not really interested in what He was saying. The religious leaders felt threatened by Jesus' stance that their legalistic approach to following the Law was wrong. Not surprisingly, they opposed Him.[264] In the midst of His popularity, Jesus discussed with His disciples how the Jewish people viewed Him:

> Now when Jesus came into the district of Caesarea Philippi, He *began* asking His disciples, saying, "Who do people say that the Son of Man is?" And they said, "Some *say* John the Baptist; and others, Elijah; but still others, Jeremiah, or one of the prophets." He said to them, "But who do you say that I am?" And Simon Peter answered and said, "Thou art the Christ, the Son of the living G-d." And Jesus answered and said to him, "Blessed are you, Simon Barjona, because flesh and blood did not reveal *this* to you, but My Father who is in heaven."[265]

The people believed that Jesus was one of the prophets of old who had come back to life to speak to them on behalf of G-d. In one sense, the people were on the right track, for Jesus was sent by G-d.[266] But they did not fully consider His message, and for that, they were held responsible. After all, the people who thought Jesus might be Elijah would have been duty-bound to listen to Jesus and follow what He was saying. For, when Elijah was alive, he was not given much due by the people. Yet, the Jewish people living at the time of Elijah's ministry should have been listening very intently to what he was saying since he was

---

[263] Mk. 2:23-28; 7:1-23; Mt. 23:23-24.
[264] Mt. 12:9-14.
[265] Mt. 16:13-17.
[266] Jn. 3:17; 5:37-38; 6:38; 12:49.

speaking the words of G-d to them. But only a remnant had any interest in the things of G-d. The rest were willing to cast G-d aside to worship the repugnant pagan god, Baal, essentially at the drop of a hat.[267]

Interestingly, King Ahab and his wife, Jezebel, loathed Elijah and wanted to see him dead.[268] Still today, these two are recognized as two of the greatest villains in all of history, while Elijah is held in very high regard. Hence, when the religious leaders grew to loathe Jesus and sought his life, why did the public go along with it?[269] Again, some of them thought He might be Elijah. They should have known better than to go along with their leaders.

However, there was a remnant of the nation who followed Jesus from their hearts. Over the course of the next few decades, this set of Jewish people would go on to start Christianity.

There is a spiritual component that is necessary to be able to understand who Jesus is, as was the case for Peter. That was true then, and it still is today, as it was for me when I asked G-d to show me the way to heaven. You can hear the Christian message and not know what to think about it. But if your heart is open to whatever it is that is true, and you ask G-d to show you, He will.[270] On the other hand, if you do not really care, then G-d may leave you be. For, He does not force His will on us. That is not to say that G-d does not care about you, for He definitely does. He pursues all of us like a loving shepherd searching for a lost sheep.[271] However, if you say no to Him, He will accept it.[272] Of course, there are consequences to saying no to G-d. Namely, you will remain separated from Him. This is true on an individual basis for all human beings, and it was true for the Jews on a national basis 2,000 years ago.

---

[267] 1 Kings 19:18.

[268] 1 Kings 19:1-8.

[269] Mt. 21:14-15, 45-46; 22:15-22; 27:20-26.

[270] Jn. 7:17.

[271] Lk. 15:3-7.

[272] Rev. 3:20.

Because the Jews said no to Jesus, 70 CE came crashing down upon them. In the words of His disciple John, "He came to His own, and those who were His own did not receive Him."[273] I believe that if the Jews had received Jesus, there would not have been a Diaspora. Yes, Jesus came to die for the sins of the world, but Satan could have just as easily triggered a conflict between Jesus and the Romans, and they would have been perfectly capable of executing Jesus all on their own.

In fact, even though the Jews did not get hundreds of years of warnings like their ancestors, they were still abundantly guilty before G-d. Simply put, they were like most humans—wrapped up in their lives and not really interested in the things of G-d. That is not to say they were not religious, because they were. But to some degree, they were just going through the motions.

Jesus' life lined up with many Messianic prophecies. For all who wanted to know who He was, the evidence was right before their eyes.[274] For one thing, He was a descendant of King David. In addition, if they were paying attention, like Daniel was when the 70-year Babylonian exile was drawing to a close, then they should have been waiting expectantly for their Messiah's arrival as the 483-year period that started with King Artaxerxes' decree was drawing to a close.[275] Also per prophecy, Jesus performed many public miracles.[276] He did not just heal a couple of people. He healed hundreds and perhaps thousands of people. There were days when large crowds brought their loved ones who were blind, lame, disfigured, and suffering from other physical maladies, and Jesus healed them from sunup to sundown.[277] These healings were miraculous, and the people who were healed, as well as those who were close to them, had absolutely no doubt that G-d healed them. Furthermore, not only were these poor, suffering people healed, but they were also touched

---

[273] Jn. 1:11.
[274] Lk. 19:44; 24:24-27.
[275] Dan. 9:24-26.
[276] Isa. 35:5-6; 61:1-2.
[277] Mk. 3:7-10; 6:53-56; Lk. 4:40.

by Jesus' personal love in the moments they got to spend with Him. Based on these healings alone, people should have come to Jesus with listening ears. They should have looked to G-d and been willing to do whatever it was He was calling them to do. Jesus put it this way:

> "When you see a cloud rising in the west, immediately you say, 'A shower is coming,' and so it turns out. And when *you see* a south wind blowing, you say, 'It will be a hot day,' and it turns out *that way*. You hypocrites! You know how to analyze the appearance of the earth and the sky, but why do you not analyze this present time?"[278]

Here, Jesus called them out on their disregard for the evidence He provided them that He was the Messiah. But G-d is so good. Jesus gave them another chance. He told them there would be one more miraculous sign, and this time they better pay attention. Luke wrote:

> And as the crowds were increasing, He began to say, "This generation is a wicked generation; it seeks for a sign, and yet no sign shall be given to it but the sign of Jonah. For just as Jonah became a sign to the Ninevites, so shall the Son of Man be to this generation. The Queen of the South shall rise up with the men of this generation at the judgment and condemn them, because she came from the ends of the earth to hear the wisdom of Solomon; and behold, something greater than Solomon is here. The men of Nineveh shall stand up with this generation at the judgment and condemn it, because they repented at the preaching of

---

[278] Lk. 12:54-56.

Jonah; and behold, something greater than Jonah is here."[279]

Surely, just as Jonah emerged alive from the belly of the great fish after three days, so too, Jesus emerged from the grave three days after He was laid to rest. Many people saw Jesus resurrected, or heard of it from eyewitnesses, and turned to Him for salvation.[280] Again, these people started Christianity. But most of the Jews continued to follow their religious leaders, who opposed the Jewish Christians.[281] Due to their decision, G-d stopped working with the Jews and began working with the Christian Church to accomplish His plan. In addition, the Jews forfeited G-d's protection and were vulnerable. Sure enough, a few decades later, they fell to Rome, and so began their very long and very difficult exile.

So much persecution has been inflicted upon the Jews over the centuries that it would take a multivolume set of books to cover this subject. Here is a small sampling of events to give you an idea of the nature of the hatred the Gentile world expressed towards the Jews:

> The bishop of Speyer, Rüdiger, in order to protect the Jews against the mob, conceived the idea in c. 1084 of confining them to a special quarter of the town. Gradually, what was at first a measure of protection became a place of involuntary confinement enforced by law.[282]

Thus began the ghettos. They were started with good intentions, but of course, the Gentiles found a way to use this provision to punish the Jews.

---

[279] Lk. 11:29-32.

[280] Acts 2:14-42; 1 Cor. 15:6.

[281] Acts 8:1-2.

[282] Jakob Jocz, *The Jewish People and Jesus Christ* (London, England: SPCK, 1949) 81-82.

Paul IV (1554–1557) excelled his predecessors in harshness and intolerance towards the Jews. He ordered synagogues to be destroyed, the practice of Judaism to be severely restricted, the enforcement of a distinctive headgear for Jewish men and women, and every form of intercourse with Christians to be avoided. Jews were precluded from belonging to guilds, forbidden to own property; even the number of annual marriages was strictly limited by law.[283]

What a poor job this pope did of leading the Catholic flock to love their fellow man. Of course, we know what happens when prejudice is not just permitted, but mandated: violence is never far behind. Here is an account of an event that took place in Germany during the Crusades, when forced conversion was being imposed upon the Jewish people:

"...They said to one another, 'Let us be strong, in order to endure what the holy faith imposes upon us.... Soon enemies will kill us...our souls will survive for the eternal bright paradise. Blessed is the one who perishes in behalf of the One and Eternal.... Whoever has a knife... let him cut our throats in the Name of the Eternal One—and let him cut his own throat, or stick it into his belly.' ...(the) women summoned courage, and killed their sons and daughters, and then themselves. Men killed their wives and children.... A father sacrificed his son, a brother his sister, a mother her daughter, a neighbor another, a bridegroom his bride...."[284]

---

[283] Ibid., 77-78.
[284] Arthur Blech, *The Causes of Anti-Semitism*, A Critique of the Bible, rev. ed. (Amherst, NY: Prometheus Books, 2006) 247.

The Crusaders were either forcibly baptizing or killing the Jews in the communities along the Rhine River. The above horrifying account took place in 1096 CE in the German city of Mainz. The Jews chose this course of action as they felt it was their best option! Astonishingly, events of violent persecution were not isolated, but rather, they took place throughout the Diaspora.

What on earth possessed the Catholics to use coercion, including violence, to force Jews to convert to Christianity? Did they not read the Bible? Here is how Jesus told His followers to tell people about Him:

> And He (Jesus) summoned the twelve and began to send them out in pairs; and He was giving them authority over the unclean spirits; and He instructed them that they should take nothing for *their* journey, except a mere staff; no bread, no bag, no money in their belt; but *to* wear sandals; and *He added*, "Do not put on two tunics." And He said to them, "Wherever you enter a house, stay there until you leave town. And any place that does not receive you or listen to you, as you go out from there, shake off the dust from the soles of your feet for a testimony against them." And they went out and preached that *men* should repent. And they were casting out many demons and were anointing with oil many sick people and healing them.[285]

These instructions seem foreign to us in America today. Jesus' followers were to set out without provisions or money, trusting G-d for their needs. Then they were to tell people the news of Jesus, which makes more sense. If the town rejected Jesus, His followers were to simply leave. But as they left, they

---

[285] Mk. 6:7-13.

were to shake the dust off their feet. By performing this cultural custom, Jesus' followers were communicating to the townspeople that they had heard the message of Jesus' offer of forgiveness and turned it down, and for that, they were responsible.[286] But nowhere did Jesus call on His followers to use coercion.

The Protestant Reformation was begun by people who read the Bible for themselves and saw that the Catholic hierarchy had violated the plain meaning of the text. Yet, the Protestants held onto the unbiblical view of anti-Semitism. Following is a quote from Martin Luther. This was his advice to the governing authorities regarding the Jews:

> First, their synagogues should be set on fire, and whatever does not burn up should be covered or spread over with dirt so that no one may ever be able to see a cinder or stone of it. And this ought to be done for the honor of God and of Christianity in order that God may see that we are Christians, and that we have not wittingly tolerated or approved of such public lying, cursing, and blaspheming of His Son and His Christians.
>
> Secondly, their homes should likewise be broken down and destroyed. For they perpetrate the same things there that they do in their synagogues. For this reason they ought to be put under one roof or in a stable, like gypsies, in order that they may realize that they are not masters in our land, as they boast, but miserable captives, as they complain of incessantly before God with bitter wailing.
>
> Thirdly, they should be deprived of their prayer-books and Talmuds in which such

---

[286] William L. Lane, *The Gospel of Mark*, The New International Commentary on the New Testament (Grand Rapids: William B. Eerdmans Publishing Company, 1974) 208-209.

idolatry, lies, cursing, and blasphemy are taught.

Fourthly, their rabbis must be forbidden under threat of death to teach any more....

Fifthly, passport and traveling privileges should be absolutely forbidden to the Jews. For they have no business in the rural districts since they are not nobles, nor officials, nor merchants, nor the like. Let them stay at home....[287]

How well thought out these recommendations were by Luther. He really covered every area of life so that the Jews would be oppressed and treated like subhumans. Earlier in his career, he was more favorable to the Jews. But when they did not convert to Christianity, he turned on them.[288] Sadly, he never repented from his sinful position, and he and others set the tone for the continued oppression of the Jews over the next five centuries. These men acted like tyrants and misrepresented Jesus.

Thank G-d, the suffering of the Jews is drawing to a close. Yes, on one hand, the restoration in which everything will be made right, and G-d will dwell among the Jews,[289] still lies in the future. But, on the other hand, we see the end approaching. The Jews have returned to their land! In addition, many of the signs that Jesus said would precede the end of time are happening right now.[290]

Thus far in this chapter, we have discussed the reason G-d stopped working with the Jews, and the persecution they have been subjected to in the Diaspora. The apostle Paul wrote the book of Romans a number of years before 70 CE. But already, it appeared to Paul that G-d had stopped working with Israel and had begun working with the Christian Church. Paul wondered

---

[287] Rabbi Singer 1:4.

[288] James M. Kittelson, *Luther the Reformer* (Minneapolis: Augsburg Publishing House, 1986) 273-275.

[289] Isa. 35; Ezek. 36:33-36; 37:25-28; Zech. 11:16-17; 14:9-11.

[290] Mt. 24.

what was going to happen to his beloved countrymen. He wrote about this subject in Romans Chapters 9 through 11. One of the points that catches your attention in this passage is how much Paul cared for his Jewish brethren:

> I am telling the truth in Christ, I am not lying, my conscience bearing me witness in the Holy Spirit, that I have great sorrow and unceasing grief in my heart. For I could wish that I myself were accursed, *separated* from Christ for the sake of my brethren, my kinsmen according to the flesh, who are Israelites, to whom belongs the adoption as sons and the glory and the covenants and the giving of the Law and the *temple* service and the promises, whose are the fathers, and from whom is the Christ according to the flesh, who is over all, G-d blessed forever. Amen.[291]

Paul was a very serious man, and though some may disagree with him on certain issues, no one doubts his sincerity. He opens this passage with these words, and it is reminiscent of the way Moses felt about the Jews of his day, whom he feared were in deep trouble with G-d. Moses pleaded with G-d for their lives. He even asked to die with them if G-d was going to take their lives.[292] But just as G-d did not hold Moses accountable for the sins of the nation in his day, neither would He hold Paul accountable for the Jews' rejection of Jesus.

Then Paul considered the state of the Jews in his day by looking at G-d's dealings with the Jews in the past. Paul mentioned Jacob and Esau and said that, in their case, G-d chose to work with only one of them.[293] That is interesting because in the next generation, G-d chose to work with all twelve of Jacob's sons. But not so with Jacob and Esau. They

---

[291] Rom. 9:1-5.
[292] Ex. 32:31-35.
[293] Rom. 9:10-13.

each had the same choice every Jew has had. Namely, were they interested in G-d's will and His choosing of Abraham's descendants to be His people, or were they not? As it turned out, they both followed their hearts; Jacob was interested in the things of G-d, but Esau was not. On that basis, G-d chose Jacob and his children to be His people whom He would use to accomplish His will. That only makes sense. For example, in marriage, you marry someone who gives you their heart. You marry someone who accepts you and will be loyal to you. You are not looking for someone who is perfect, for no such person exists. But you do hold out for someone who loves you, and you do not marry anyone who is halfhearted in their love and devotion to you. So too with G-d, He is looking for people who appreciate Him and desire to receive His love in their lives.

The point Paul is making is that it was G-d's choice which brother to use. For, G-d is sovereign. We tend to gravitate to G-d's attribute of love, and sometimes to His attribute of justice, when we gaze upon moral evil. But we are not typically drawn to His attribute of sovereignty. His sovereignty means that even though He gives us wide latitude to act, ultimately He can and does make decisions that affect humanity as a whole and each of us as individuals. Truth be told, this offends us as Americans, because we are all, to some degree, controlling. We do not like the idea of G-d ultimately being in control of our lives. Be that as it may, this is Paul's main point in Romans Chapter 9. Sometimes, G-d picks people to play certain roles in His mission. We do not get to pick our roles, He does. G-d picked Isaac and not Ishmael to be the father of the people He would use to be His witnesses to the world.[294] Then He chose the younger of Isaac's twin sons, Jacob, rather than the older, Esau, to carry on as the progenitor of His people. This choice broke with the custom of that time in which the eldest was the principal heir.[295] But G-d is sovereign over history, and especially over the plan that He has been executing down

---

[294] Rom. 9:6-9.
[295] Hamilton 185.

through the ages. Paul's point is that even though G-d had made promises to Abraham, Isaac, and Jacob about their children, He was taking a break from working with the Jewish people. Yes, G-d is faithful, and one day He will return to work with them again, as Paul mentions in Romans 11.[296] But He put the Jews on hiatus in the first century CE, for He has the right to do so.

---

[296] Rom. 11:25-30.

10

G-D LOVES GENTILES TOO

The Jewish people recognize that some Gentiles are noble, honorable, and courageous. On the grounds of Jerusalem's Yad Vashem are commemorative sites to honor the Gentiles who risked their lives to protect Jews from the Holocaust. Lamentably, only a precious few Gentiles went against the grain to protect the Jews during the war. Indeed, the German people were responsible en masse for this shocking event of evil perpetrated against their fellow human beings. Yes, there were degrees of culpability. At the top of the list was the cabal of leaders who became drunk with racial hatred and had the audacity to plot the genocide of the entire Jewish population in Europe. Following closely behind them was the large group of henchmen in the SS who strutted around in their fancy uniforms and sneered as they rounded up innocent Jewish citizens. At the death camps, SS monsters performed the mass murders. Behind these evil men were all the people who participated in the support roles of this operation, be they secretaries, delivery people, accountants, and others. There were also companies that made a profit by producing the

Zyklon B poison gas and by manufacturing the specialty pieces of equipment that were used in these factories of death.

Then there were the masses. They turned a blind eye to save their skin. It could not have happened without their tacit approval.

But there was a remnant. There were those precious few brave souls who refused to go along with the evil. They acted like human beings and did what they could to shelter Jewish people, and they saved many lives. Today, these people have been singled out in Yad Vashem as the Righteous Among the Nations. Yad Vashem is an amazing place. The artistry of the museum, and the dignity and classiness of this institution are par excellence. The museum does not respond to the blind hatred of the Nazis with reciprocal hatred. Rather, they have a healthy perspective. They work tirelessly to uncover the identity of every single Jewish Holocaust victim in order to restore their dignity. They also present actual physical evidence of the crimes to lay to rest any absurd claims against the historicity of the Holocaust. Another one of their goals is to keep the story alive in order to prevent any nation from attempting to commit a similar crime against humanity ever again.

There is another element of the museum, and it is somewhat surprising. It consists of the healing that began the day the Nazis were defeated. The museum is laid out chronologically. Near the end is a room that is devoted to how the surviving European Jews started to put their lives back together. Surely, the wisdom and maturity of the Jewish people are on display in this exhibit.

Then, at the very end of the long, tunnel-like museum is a glass wall exiting to a veranda. The glass wall provides daylight, and as you make your way through this museum of darkness and death, it is symbolic of the fact that there was light at the end of the tunnel. Outside on the veranda is a beautiful view of Jerusalem, the capital once more of the Jewish people.

So the Jews praise the Righteous Among the Nations, and they have a healthy attitude towards the German people. They are not bitter. Rather, the Jews have moved on with their lives.

But, for the sake of the victims, and for the sake of humanity, they remember.

G-d's character and His ability to simultaneously execute justice and extend mercy are beyond our ability to fully grasp. Surely, there must be justice for this great sin, and we trust G-d that there will be. But could G-d extend mercy to those who to one degree or another were responsible for this unimaginable act of evil?

Of course, much evil has been perpetrated against the Jewish people over the last 2,000 years across the Gentile world. It is a fair question to ask: How can G-d love Gentiles?

*　　*　　*　　*　　*

In the book of Jonah, we have a loosely analogous situation. Jonah was a Jewish prophet who was ordered by G-d to warn the heathen Ninevites to repent or face certain doom. The Ninevites were enemies of the Jews. Two of Jonah's contemporaries, Hosea and Amos, were both given prophesies that one day a foreign nation would be used as an instrument by G-d to conquer the ten faithless Jewish tribes living in the Northern Kingdom. In the book of Hosea, G-d revealed that it would be the Assyrians who would rule over them.[297] And indeed, one day the Assyrians did go on to conquer Israel. We do not know if Jonah knew about those prophecies at the time G-d called him to go to Nineveh. But even if he didn't know about them, he would have been well aware of the Assyrians, as they were notorious in the ancient world for their barbaric treatment of the people they conquered. To stand out in the ancient world in this regard was no easy task. Time has moved on, and their deeds have largely been forgotten, but these people were monsters. Among other things, they were known for doing undignified things with the skin of their victims. If you lived at that time in a neighboring land and saw the Assyrian army appear on the horizon in battle formation, you knew you were facing horror followed by death. Hence, it is

---

[297] Hos. 9:1-11:7.

understandable why Jonah was not just reluctant to speak G-d's warning to the Ninevites—he was repulsed by this task. Indeed, he booked passage on a boat that was headed for Spain, which was as far away from Nineveh as you could get in that day.[298]

But G-d was serious about delivering the Ninevites from judgment, if only they would repent. Therefore, the L-rd caused a great storm to arise and then exposed Jonah to the sailors on the ship as the cause of that storm. Upon Jonah's being thrown overboard, G-d abrogated the laws of nature and caused Jonah to be swallowed whole by a great fish and remain alive in its belly for three days.[299] At this point, G-d had Jonah's attention, and Jonah repented and prayed for his own deliverance. Then the fish vomited Jonah onto the shore.[300]

So Jonah went to Nineveh and, despite his lack of enthusiasm, delivered G-d's message. The Ninevites, from the greatest to the least, believed the message. They fasted, they dressed in sackcloth, and, individually, they repented before G-d of their wickedness and their violent ways. G-d saw their repentance, and He spared them.[301]

In the fourth and final chapter of his book, we learn that Jonah was displeased by this result, and he became angry and depressed. Jonah wanted judgment, not mercy, for this wicked people. Jonah was very dramatic. (Three times in this short story, he either wished to die or attempted suicide.[302]) Thus, instead of going back to Israel, Jonah encamped himself east of the city, where he watched to see what would happen.[303]

Enter G-d. Not to deal with Nineveh, but to deal with Jonah. G-d must have really loved this man. He took the time to perform another miracle and use it as an object lesson to teach Jonah about Himself and about compassion. In this second miracle, G-d caused a plant to grow up overnight and provide

---

[298] Jon. 1:3.

[299] Jon. 1:17.

[300] Jon. 2.

[301] Jon. 3:3-10.

[302] Jon. 1:12; 4:3, 8.

[303] Jon. 4:5.

shade for Jonah. But then the next day it withered and died. Then G-d used the weather again to get Jonah's attention. This time a scorching hot sun rose in the sky, and a strong wind came and blew the oven-like air on Jonah. He became weary, and he begged G-d to let him die. Again G-d had his attention, and then He spoke the following words to Jonah in the final three verses of the book:

> Then G-d said to Jonah, "Do you have good reason to be angry about the plant?" And he said, "I have good reason to be angry, even to death." Then the L-rd said, "You had compassion on the plant for which you did not work, and *which* you did not cause to grow, which came up overnight and perished overnight. And should I not have compassion on Nineveh, the great city in which there are more than 120,000 persons who do not know *the difference* between their right and left hand, as well as many animals?"[304]

The lesson is that G-d loves all of us, both Jews and Gentiles. Yes, the Jews are His people, and they have been selected by Him to play a special role in His plan. But that plan always included one day reaching the Gentiles—for G-d loves all of us, despite our many sins. He loves us because His ability to love is infinitely great. He is so very different from us that it is hard for us to understand His love.

Jesus told the following parable to try to illustrate G-d's love in a way we could understand:

> And He said, "A certain man had two sons; and the younger of them said to his father, 'Father, give me the share of the estate that falls to me.' And he divided his wealth between them. And not many days later, the younger son gathered everything together and went on a journey into

---

[304] Jon. 4:9-11.

a distant country, and there he squandered his estate with loose living. Now when he had spent everything, a severe famine occurred in that country, and he began to be in need. And he went and attached himself to one of the citizens of that country, and he sent him into the fields to feed the swine. And he was longing to fill his stomach with the pods that the swine were eating, and no one was giving *anything* to him. But when he came to his senses, he said, 'How many of my father's hired men have more than enough bread, but I am dying here with hunger! I will get up and go to my father, and will say to him, "Father, I have sinned against heaven, and in your sight; I am no longer worthy to be called your son; make me as one of your hired men."' And he got up and came to his father. But while he was still a long way off, his father saw him, and felt compassion *for him*, and ran and embraced him, and kissed him. And the son said to him, 'Father, I have sinned against heaven and in your sight; I am no longer worthy to be called your son.' But the father said to his slaves, 'Quickly bring out the best robe and put it on him, and put a ring on his hand and sandals on his feet; and bring the fattened calf, kill it, and let us eat and be merry; for this son of mine was dead, and has come to life again; he was lost, and has been found.' And they began to be merry. Now his older son was in the field, and when he came and approached the house, he heard music and dancing. And he summoned one of the servants and *began* inquiring what these things might be. And he said to him, 'Your brother has come, and your father has killed the fattened calf, because he has received him back safe and sound.' But he became angry, and was not willing to go in; and his father came out and *began* entreating him. But he answered and said to his father, 'Look! For so many years I have been serving you, and I have never neglected a command of yours; and yet you have never given me a kid, that I might be merry with my friends; but when this son of yours came, who has devoured your wealth with harlots, you killed the fattened calf for him.' And he said to him, '*My* child, you have always been with me, and all that is mine is yours. But we had to be merry and rejoice, for this brother of yours was dead and *has begun* to live, and *was* lost and has been found.' "[305]

In this story, the father's love overcomes his son's capacity to sin. The only thing that matters to the father is that his child has seen the error of his ways and come home. Indeed, his son was wholly unworthy to come before him. But the father cared more about being reunited with his own flesh and blood than about the loss of money or the shameful nature of the things his son had done. There were no recriminations from the father. There was just forgiveness and joy. He was so happy that he ran to his son and embraced and kissed him. He even threw a celebration! The ring that was put on the young man's finger signified that he was fully restored to his position as the rich man's son.

Of course, the father represents G-d, and the simple message of this parable is that G-d loves each of us with a shocking amount of love. He is just that good, and He has provided a way by which each of us may be fully restored to our position as His child.

However, our love is not like G-d's; it is like the older brother's. It is imperfect. We keep score. We struggle to feel joy

---

[305] Lk. 15:11-32.

for the good fortune of another. Could it be that Jesus was implying that the Jews are the older brother? For they had worked so hard to follow all of G-d's commands. Jesus understood that, like Jonah, Jewish people would be disgusted by the thought of G-d simply forgiving Gentiles who have sinned so awfully for so long.[306]

G-d's love is otherworldly. But He is also just. In fact, true love requires justice. Herein lies a great dilemma. Only G-d in His infinite wisdom could resolve this dilemma. Only G-d in His infinite love could bring about the solution.

Humans came up with the Final Solution, consisting of unspeakable hatred, brutality, and death. It was directed against G-d's chosen people and, ultimately, against G-d Himself.

G-d responded to the problem of human sin with a different solution. His solution consisted of taking our judgment upon Himself so that we could receive forgiveness, kindness, and rebirth. There had to be two comings of the Messiah. There was no other way. So, Jesus came the first time, and He went through with it—He died as a sacrifice.

In the critical moment, the self-serving Jewish religious leaders engineered His execution. The uncaring Jewish masses fell in line and cried out for Him to be killed. The self-serving Roman governor stepped aside and allowed the crime to take place. The heartless Roman soldiers stripped Him of His robe and gambled for it. Then they drove spikes through his flesh into a wooden cross, and they hoisted it upright.

In that moment, Jesus responded to all the sin, evil, and rebellion against G-d by stepping forward. The hero took it on His shoulders. His bravery and love are incomprehensible.

As if that was not enough, He then rose from the grave to authenticate what He accomplished on the cross.

Quite a plan, isn't it? G-d was incarnated as Jesus, underwent a horrific execution, and then was resurrected. We did not see that coming. That is how dire our situation is. That

---

[306] Rom. 9:30-33.

is the cost that had to be paid in order for sinners to gain entrance into eternity.

Here is a passage from Isaiah about the Messiah's role being to bring salvation to the Gentiles as well as to the Jews:

> Listen to Me, O islands, and pay attention, you peoples from afar. The L-rd called Me from the womb; from the body of My mother He named Me. And He has made My mouth like a sharp sword; in the shadow of His hand He has concealed Me, and He has also made Me a select arrow; He has hidden Me in His quiver. And He said to Me, "You are My Servant, Israel, in Whom I will show My glory." But I said, "I have toiled in vain, I have spent My strength for nothing and vanity; yet surely the justice *due* to Me is with the L-rd, and My reward with My G-d."
>
> And now says the L-rd, who formed Me from the womb to be his Servant, to bring Jacob back to Him, in order that Israel might be gathered to Him (for I am honored in the sight of the L-rd, and My G-d is My strength), He says, "It is too small a thing that You should be My Servant to raise up the tribes of Jacob, and to restore the preserved ones of Israel; I will also make You a light of the nations so that My salvation may reach to the end of the earth." Thus says the L-rd, the Redeemer of Israel, *and* its Holy One, to the despised One, to the One abhorred by the nation, to the Servant of rulers, "Kings shall see and arise, princes shall also bow down; because of the L-rd who is faithful, the Holy One of Israel who has chosen You."[307]

---

[307] Isa. 49:1-7.

This is an obvious prophecy of Jesus' first coming. Although, there are a few intellectual "fig leaves" to provide cover for those who are desperately opposed to Jesus. For example, the L-rd calls this person "My Servant, Israel." In the Tanakh, *Israel* typically refers to Jacob, the Jewish people, or the land. So why would this usage be referring to Jesus? Furthermore, no one ever called Jesus by this name in the New Testament. Also, G-d refers to the Jewish people as His servant in Isa. 41:8. Therefore, Jewish scholars state that the above passage from Isaiah Chapter 49 is talking about the Jews, not the Messiah or Jesus.[308]

Yet, this prediction is of a special Servant of G-d whose role it would be to bring Jacob back to G-d. In addition, this Servant would be a light to the nations such that G-d's salvation would reach to the end of the earth. But something would go wrong. This Servant, who was a "select arrow" hidden in G-d's "quiver," would become defeated and utter the words "I have toiled in vain." In fact, Jesus failed in reaching the Jewish people as He was "abhorred by the nation." Thus, these details line up with Jesus' life and death and the movement that began following His resurrection.

In response to the arguments of Jewish theologians who disagree with this interpretation, just because G-d calls this person Israel, it does not mean He is speaking to the nation. After all, it was this person's role to "bring Jacob back to Him, in order that Israel might be gathered to Him." In other words, it was the role of Israel, the select arrow, to gather Israel, the nation, back to G-d. It would be illogical to interpret both references to Israel as applying to the Jewish people. Therefore, in this passage, the name Israel is applied to two different parties: the Messiah and the nation. Also, just because Isaiah used the term "servant" to refer to the Jewish people in Chapter 41, it does not mean that he can't use the term to refer to someone else later in the book.

---

[308] Rabbi Singer 1:92-97.

In the Abrahamic Covenant, G-d promised Abraham a number of things. Three of the main ones included 1) Abraham's descendants becoming a great nation who would be the people of G-d, 2) a land for the Jewish people, and 3) G-d's blessing upon all the families of the earth through Abraham and his descendants. All of the things G-d promised were straightforward and clear, except for one. Namely, G-d was not clear about how He was going bless the entire world through Abraham and his descendants. That particular covenantal promise was conspicuous by its lack of detail, but it would to be fleshed out later in the Tanakh. The four Servant Songs in Isaiah (Isa. 42:1-9; 49:1-13; 50:4-11; and 52:13–53:12)[309] tell us how G-d would bless the whole world through the Jewish people. It would be through one special Jewish person, the Messiah. He would die for the sins of all, Jew and Gentile alike.[310]

We all need forgiveness from G-d, and Jesus came for all. In the words of Paul:

> For I am not ashamed of the gospel, for it is the power of G-d for salvation to everyone who believes, to the Jew first and also to the Greek.[311]

Many centuries later, Jesus came to me in my heart. It was unmistakable. I was lost, and He said, "I'm here." Then He brought some Christians into my life, and I heard the Bible. It was my moment to decide, and I said yes to Jesus.

Today, Jesus is waging campaigns all over the world in an effort to reach the lost. He is using different techniques in different lands to reach as many people as will receive His gift of forgiveness. He is waging campaigns in surprising places like China, Indonesia, Iran, Haiti, Saudi Arabia, and many, many more.

---

[309] F. Duane Lindsey, *The Servant Songs* (Chicago: Moody Press, 1985) xi.

[310] Isa. 52:15; 53:5-6.

[311] Rom. 1:16.

In Revelation Chapter 7, we are shown a glimpse of heaven. In verse 9, it says,

> After these things I looked, and behold, a great multitude, which no one could count, from every nation and *all* tribes and peoples and tongues, standing before the throne and before the Lamb, clothed in white robes, and palm branches *were* in their hands....[312]

So too, the Jews are portrayed in Isaiah Chapter 54 as being an enormous group of people who will be redeemed by the L-rd at the end of time.

G-d is so good.

Thank you Jesus.

* * * * *

Jesus spoke of His mission being for the sake of the Gentiles as well as for the Jews:

> And when they had come together, they were asking Him, saying, "L-rd, is it at this time You are restoring the kingdom to Israel?" He said to them, "It is not for you to know times or epochs which the Father has fixed by His own authority; but you shall receive power when the Holy Spirit has come upon you; and you shall be My witnesses both in Jerusalem, and in all Judea and Samaria, and even to the remotest part of the earth."[313]

---

[312] Actually, this multitude of Gentiles will only come from the harvest of souls occurring during the Great Tribulation. The total number of Gentiles from around the globe who will be with G-d in eternity will be far greater.

[313] Acts 1:6-8.

These words were spoken by Jesus, in His resurrected state, to the apostles.[314] So began a new stage in G-d's plan in which Christians would reach out first to the Jews with the message of Jesus, but then to all mankind. Jesus told them that the length of time for this period was up to G-d and was not for them to know. But common sense tells us that it would take a long time for Christians to travel to the remotest parts of the earth to provide everyone with an opportunity to hear the message of Jesus in their own tongue. As of today, it has been close to two millennia, and Christianity still has not reached every people group on earth with the gospel message. One of the prophetic signs Jesus gave by which we can tell that the end of time is drawing near is that the Christian message of salvation will be available to every tribe and tongue across the earth.[315] Christian mission agencies are working hard right now to reach this goal. These agencies are targeting unreached people groups across the globe, translating the Bible into their languages, and sending missionaries to them. The missionaries are tasked with establishing indigenous churches, even if some of those churches have to operate underground.

*   *   *   *   *

It is fair to ask why G-d has allowed the Jewish people to suffer so much for such a long time. We do not fully know the answer to this question. But certainly, part of the answer is that He wants people all over the world to find Him and be with Him in eternity.

---

[314] Acts 1:2. The apostles consisted of His disciples whom He was sending out in this moment. Their mission was to take His message of salvation across the Gentile world. Later, some others, including Paul, would be added to their numbers.
[315] Mt. 24:14.

11

A TWO-STAGE PLAN

In rocket science, propelling a rocket to the moon is quite a feat. Of course, a large quantity of fuel is required to launch a rocket up into space, propel it to the moon, and bring it back. Scientists have designed multi-stage rockets in order to accomplish this feat. The idea is simple enough: it takes more fuel to propel a heavier object, like a truck, than a lighter object, like a compact car. Therefore, once the fuel for the first stage is used up, the large fuel tank drops away. In this way, the weight of the rocket is reduced, and less fuel is needed to complete the trip. The rocket used in the 1969 Apollo 11 mission was a three-stage rocket.

So too, G-d designed a multistage plan to achieve His mission of rescuing humanity. The Apollo 11 mission lasted eight days, but G-d's mission is going on 4,000 years and counting. Yet, both missions are incredible feats. G-d's mission entails sending His people to the ends of the earth with a message of forgiveness in order to reach as many people for eternity as possible.

The first stage consisted of G-d reaching out to one man, Abraham, and forging a bond with him and his descendants after him. The idea was for Abraham's descendants to know G-d well, and for the rest of the world to be able to see Him as they gazed upon the positive difference He made in their lives. Of course, relationships require the willing participation of two parties. Unfortunately, the Jews were not always willing participants, which stunted the relationship. Nonetheless, there were Gentiles who learned of G-d through the Jews. For example, in the Tanakh we see Rahab, the queen of Sheba, Nebuchadnezzar, and Cyrus all being introduced to G-d through Jewish people.[316]

In the first stage, the Jews were to be stationary. They were to remain in the land of Israel, and they were not supposed to conquer any land beyond the borders G-d prescribed for them. In addition, they needed to follow G-d's ways and form a just society. They were also supposed to deal honorably and humanely with those in need as well as with foreigners. G-d was physically present in the Temple in Jerusalem, and He would bless them both nationally and individually.[317] Furthermore, He would protect them from any and all foreign invaders. They just needed to honor the covenant they made with Him by following the Law.

Nowhere in the Tanakh were the Jews called to be missional or to travel abroad and tell the Gentiles about G-d. In this regard, the Jews listened well, for they never sent out missionaries. Nor did they ever seek to conquer foreign nations, even during the height of their power under King Solomon.

The Tanakh speaks about the Gentile nations as well. In some instances, it speaks about specific foreign nations, but in other instances, the Gentile nations are referred to collectively. Such terms as *neighbors, nations, peoples, ends of the earth,* and *coastlands* are used to refer to the Gentile peoples. The terms *coastlands* and *ends of the earth* can be used to refer to both distant lands where people dwell or the peoples themselves. We still speak the same way today. For example, when referring to the Europeans and Americans, a newscaster

---

[316] Josh. 2:1-21; 6:17-25; 1 Kin. 10:1-13; Dan. 2:46-49; 3:24-30; Ezra 1.
[317] Deut. 28:1-14.

may begin a sentence by saying, "The west stands opposed to..." When the terms *coastlands* and *ends of the earth* are used, the passage is addressing those who live in the farthest corners of the earth as opposed to Israel's neighbors in the Middle East.

Today, the Hebrew word *gôy* (pl. *gôyim*) is used to refer to Gentiles, and it is sometimes used in a derogatory sense. In the Tanakh, however, this word is used to refer to a nation, and it is neutral. G-d's assessment of specific Gentile nations was revealed by what He said about them in various passages, as opposed to by using the word *gôy*. In fact, the word is even used in some instances to refer to the Jewish people. But generally, in the Tanakh, *gôy* is used to refer to a Gentile nation, and *gôyim* is used to refer to a number of Gentile nations.

When the Tanakh speaks of the ends of the earth, usually one of two subjects is being addressed. First, the passage might be referring to the return of the Jews from the ends of the earth at the end of time. Second, the passage might be about G-d's judgment of all the Gentile nations at the end of time. But there are also some passages in which G-d is dealing with the nations positively. These passages have to do with G-d's salvation extending to Gentiles all the way to the ends of the earth. For example:

> He [G-d] says, "It is too small a thing that You should be My Servant to raise up the tribes of Jacob and to restore the preserved ones of Israel; I will also make You a light of the nations so that My salvation may reach to the end of the earth."[318]

The meaning of this passage is straightforward. Yet, the passage is incomplete. It is like finding a fragment of a letter. You learn something, but you do not have the full context. There is a reason why G-d only gave a partial piece of information in this passage. We will examine this subject in Volume 4.

---

[318] Isa. 49:6.

The point is that there needed to be a second stage in G-d's plan in order to reach out to the ends of the earth. This does not diminish the wisdom of G-d's plan in the first stage. For, G-d placed the Jews in Israel, and Israel is the pivot point between Europe, Asia, and Africa. They were always in the middle of everything in the ancient world. For example, on one occasion, Cleopatra manipulated Mark Antony to gain control over part of Judea.[319] Hence, the Jews were in the perfect place to provide a witness of G-d to the ancient world. Of course, their witness did not reach the Incas in Peru or the Aborigines in Australia. Hence, G-d needed to include a second stage in His plan to be able to give everyone on earth a chance to find Him.

As noted in the last chapter, the "Servant" mentioned in the passage above cannot be the Jewish people because the Servant raises up "the tribes of Jacob" and restores "the preserved ones of Israel." Rather, the Servant is the Messiah, whose mission includes being a light to the nations so that "salvation may reach to the end of the earth." Of course, Jesus never traveled beyond Judea, let alone to the ends of the earth. But He did set in motion a plan for that to take place after He left this world. He trained His disciples in theology; He showed them by example how to live a godly life; He sent them out on training missions; and He called them to be apostles in His final instruction to them.[320] In other words, He called them to take His message of forgiveness out to the Gentile world and to raise up followers who would further advance the spread of His message.[321] In Jesus' words to His disciples,

> "...but you will receive power when the Holy Spirit has come upon you; and you shall be My witnesses both in Jerusalem, and in all Judea and Samaria, and even to the remotest part of the earth."[322]

---

[319] Josephus, *Antiquities* 15:4:1 (92-95.)
[320] Mk. 6:7-13; Lk. 10:1-20.
[321] Mt. 28:18-20.
[322] Acts 1:8.

Including His call on them to be missionaries, He also stated that they would each receive the power of the Holy Spirit. This is significant. For, in the days of the Tanakh, the Holy Spirit came upon the prophets and rested upon the Jewish kings, but following Jesus' visit, every Christian would be filled with the Holy Spirit! In the Apollo 11 journey, an enormous amount of fuel was expended in the first two stages simply to lift the rocket and set it free from the earth's gravitational pull. But in the third stage, less fuel was required to propel the rocket through space. In G-d's plan, more power is provided in the second stage to take the message of Christ out to the ends of the earth.

The Apollo 11 mission was brief, but G-d's plan is taking a very long time. The reason for this is that we are not openminded. G-d tries to overcome our walls, but He does not employ coercion or violence, as we would. Rather, He uses love, kindness, patience, and truth.[323] But this takes time, for we humans are a stubborn lot. Also, for some unknown reason, G-d has chosen to use flawed humans as His representatives, and we have failed spectacularly in this role. In fact, both the Jews and the Christians have failed most of the time, slowing the progress of His mission. For example, the Jews' rebellion in the wilderness caused a 40-year delay in G-d's program.

In the next three chapters, we will examine both the biblical record of the early Christian movement and the historical record of Christianity over the last 2,000 years.

---

[323] Rom. 2:4.

12

THE FIRST CENTURY CE

Jesus was beloved. No one had ever met a person like Jesus. He had the compassion of G-d. Some of the most well-known stories in the New Testament are of Jesus healing people on the street. Not only did He heal their infirmities, but He also gave them love and acceptance, healing the wounds in their hearts.

Jesus is also well known for giving speeches to large crowds about G-d's love for people. Another of His main activities was spending time with His disciples and getting them ready for their role once He was gone. In this regard, Jesus taught them the Tanakh, performed miracles in front of them, modeled godly living, had a personal relationship with each of them, and sent them out on trial runs to gain experience in telling people about Him.[324]

Then He was crucified. Three days later, He rose from the dead.

Following His resurrection, He physically appeared to His disciples and followers on multiple occasions over a period of

---

[324] Mt. 10; Mk. 6:7-13; Lk. 9:1-6; 10:1-20.

40 days.[325] He appeared to them to objectively prove that He had risen from the dead, and to spend a little more time with them to prepare them for what lay ahead. Then He ascended into the sky, passed through a cloud, and was gone from sight.[326] Just before Jesus left, He had the following interaction with His disciples:

> Now He said to them, "These are My words which I spoke to you while I was still with you, that all things which are written about Me in the Law of Moses and the Prophets and the Psalms must be fulfilled." Then He opened their minds to understand the Scriptures, and He said to them, "Thus it is written, that the Christ would suffer and rise again from the dead the third day, and that repentance for forgiveness of sins would be proclaimed in His name to all the nations, beginning from Jerusalem. You are witnesses of these things. And behold, I am sending forth the promise of My Father upon you; but you are to stay in the city until you are clothed with power from on high."[327]

Jesus was crucified on Passover, which fulfilled the foreshadowing of the very first Passover. In that event, G-d delivered the Jews from not only their enemies but also from their sins.

Passover is one of the three Jewish pilgrimage festivals—along with Shavuot, the Feast of Weeks, and Sukkot, the Feast of Booths. Shavuot takes place seven weeks and a day after the Feast of Firstfruits, which takes place two days after Passover. The Greek name for Shavuot is Pentecost, which means fiftieth.

---

[325] Acts 1:1-3; 1 Cor. 15:3-8.
[326] Acts 1:9-11.
[327] Lk. 24:44-49.

Another Jewish name for this festival is Hag HaKatzir, which means the Feast of Harvest. The purpose of this festival is to celebrate the beginning of the summer harvest.[328]

Hence, Jewish pilgrims were in Jerusalem on Passover and again, 52 days later, on Shavuot. These pilgrims came from all over the known world, where they had been scattered in the centuries leading up to this event. These Jews spoke foreign languages, but they still worshipped G-d.

Prior to ascending into heaven, Jesus told His disciples to sit tight in Jerusalem until the Holy Spirit came upon them, for the Holy Spirit would empower them to carry out their mission. So, the disciples, along with some others (about 120 in all), did as they were told. While they waited, they prayed. They also replaced Judas, who had committed suicide after he betrayed Jesus.[329]

Then it happened. On Shavuot, a sound like a "violent, rushing wind" filled the room where they were, and "tongues of fire" appeared above each of them.[330] The Holy Spirit not only came, but He came in dramatic fashion! In that moment, Jesus' followers were miraculously able to speak in foreign languages. Again, there were Jews from all over the known world who were in Jerusalem on that day for the festival. At the sound of the wind, a great number of people went out into the streets and assembled together in a large group. Jesus' followers went out to meet them and told them about Jesus. Even Jews who could not speak Aramaic heard the message, because Jesus' followers were speaking in different languages.[331] Then Peter gave a strong speech to a very large crowd about Jesus' crucifixion. Not only was it an amazing moment, but the outcome was amazing as well. Three thousand Jewish people received Jesus as their

---

[328] Ex. 23:16.

[329] Acts 1:15-26.

[330] Acts 2:1-4.

[331] Aramaic was the language that was spoken in Judea at that time. Acts 2:5-11.

L-rd and savior on the spot, and the number of Jesus' followers grew 26 times bigger in the blink of an eye![332]

Thus, not only did Jesus' crucifixion fulfill the ultimate meaning of Passover, but so too, the ultimate meaning of Shavuot (Pentecost) was fulfilled 52 days later. For, there was a tremendous harvest of souls on that day.

As the days went by, the Christian movement continued to grow. Jesus had told them there would be a great harvest, and He was right.[333] Many people at that time were ready to hear the message of salvation through the blood of Jesus. They knew they had sinned, the message made sense, and the evidence was strong. So, they accepted Him as their L-rd and savior. Some of them were the sinful outcasts of society, and some of them were religious, but once they received Jesus in their hearts, that distinction went away. Almost all of them began to follow Jesus wholeheartedly, and it looked the same for everybody. His personal love for each of them changed them, and His mission became their mission. It fulfilled them, and it propelled them.

Hence, the early Church did not have a clergy/laity type of structure. Rather, it was a movement. In fact, in the first days following Shavuot, the new Christians formed a tight-knit community, and the mood was electric. Miracles were happening, and people were experiencing G-d's direct love and the peace that comes with knowing you are going to heaven. The citizens of Jerusalem were witnesses to this burgeoning new movement, and many of them turned to Jesus for the forgiveness of their sins too. They did not see it as a rejection of Judaism but rather as the fulfillment of their faith as it is laid out in the Tanakh.

However, not all of the Jewish people looked favorably on the new movement. In particular, the Jewish religious leaders were dismayed that this was happening. They had Jesus executed to put a stop to this nonsense, but lo and behold, the Church was growing exponentially. Sadly, they chose the same tactic to try to squelch the growth of this movement, and they

---

[332] Acts 2:14-42.
[333] Jn. 4:34-42.

had its leaders thrown in jail.[334] When that did not work, they started executing the leaders.[335] The first to be murdered was a man named Stephen. Saul, a zealous pharisee who would later become the apostle Paul, got involved and headed up the effort to stomp out the Christian movement:

> And on that day a great persecution began against the church in Jerusalem, and they were all scattered throughout the regions of Judea and Samaria, except the apostles. *Some* devout men buried Stephen, and made loud lamentation over him. But Saul *began* ravaging the church, entering house after house, and dragging off men and women, he would put them in prison.
>
> Therefore, those who had been scattered went about preaching the word. Philip went down to the city of Samaria and began proclaiming Christ to them. The crowds with one accord were giving attention to what was said by Philip, as they heard and saw the signs which he was performing. *For in the case* of many who had unclean spirits, they were coming out *of them* shouting with a loud voice; and many who had been paralyzed and lame were healed. So there was much rejoicing in that city.[336]

Hence, most of the Christians were driven out of Jerusalem. But the net result wound up being the spread of the gospel message to Jewish people living throughout Judea and the Samaritans. So, the Church grew even more.

The Jewish pilgrims who came from all over the known world to celebrate Shavuot and wound up finding Jesus stayed on in Jerusalem. They stayed on because their lives changed, and because the new Christian movement was so alive. But at

---

[334] Acts 4:1-22; 5:17-18.
[335] Acts 6:8-7:60.
[336] Acts 8:1b-8.

some point, perhaps when the persecution started, they went home. When they did, they took Jesus with them, and the gospel began to spread far and wide throughout the Roman Empire. For, these new Christians were ready-made missionaries as they were native speakers of the languages of many of the Roman provinces.

In the above passage, the word for *scattered* in verses 1 and 4 is the Greek word *diaspīro*. *Diaspīro* comes from the verb *spīro*, which means "to sow," as in sowing seed.[337] In fact, this is the word used by Jesus in His famous parable of the sower and the soils.[338] Thus, the Jewish leaders' attempt to stop Christianity at its beginning backfired. They did not contain the fire; rather, it spread outside the confines of Jerusalem to Judea, Samaria, and farther away, to cities in which Jews were living throughout the Roman Empire. Using Jesus' metaphor, these young Christians sowed the seeds of G-d's offer of reconciliation across the Roman Empire, and a great harvest of souls followed.

Not long after the persecution began, an amazing thing happened. The chief persecutor, Saul, was not satisfied with most of the Christians leaving Jerusalem, so he decided to pursue them abroad. But Jesus pursued him.

Next in the book of Acts, the story shifts to Peter as G-d showed him in a revelation that animals and birds that were unlawful to eat had become clean. Peter did not know what to think of that, but then the Holy Spirit directed his path to the house of Cornelius. Cornelius was a Roman centurion who lived in Caesarea Maritima. Although not a Jew, he was a G-d-fearing man, and as Peter entered his house, Peter was greeted by a group of Gentile people who were open to G-d. Prior to this time, Christians were exclusively Jewish, except for the Samaritans. Once he entered the room and spoke to Cornelius, Peter understood the vision. Then he could see that Jesus came for all, the Jews and the Gentiles. So he told them about Jesus,

---

[337] Walvoord and Zuck, eds., *The Bible Knowledge Commentary*, New Testament Edition (Wheaton IL.: Victor Books, 1983) 372.
[338] Mk. 4:3-20.

and they received Him as their savior. In that moment, the Holy Spirit came upon everyone in Cornelius' house, and Peter had them baptized. When Peter traveled back to Jerusalem, he reported to the apostles what had happened. From that point on, they understood that their mission included taking the message of Christ to the Gentiles as well as to the Jews.

It took an event of this caliber to convince the Jewish Christians because, prior to this event, it was inconceivable to them that Gentiles could have their sins forgiven and become Christians. Their whole lives, they had heard that Gentiles were their enemies and were unclean. Therefore, G-d had to orchestrate this event so the Jews could understand that the time had come in His plan for the Gentiles to be included among His people. After all, it only makes sense that G-d's plan to save humanity would include everyone, Jews and Gentiles. Also, Eve was the mother of all humanity, both Jews and Gentiles, and G-d had made promises to her. Namely, He promised her that a great hero would come through her offspring who would do battle with Satan and overcome him.[339] The context of G-d's conversation with Eve was the future of humanity. That future included punishment, but it also included deliverance through this hero who would one day come. But it does not delineate that this hope would apply only to a tiny fraction of Eve's descendants. Today, the Jews make up only approximately 0.2% of the world's population. In other words, only one out of every 500 people today is a Jew. G-d is bigger than that. Also, G-d made a lot of promises to Abraham regarding his descendants, the Jews, and one that included the Gentiles. Namely, G-d said to Abraham, "in you all the families of the earth shall be blessed."[340] What could this all-encompassing promise to both the Jews and the Gentiles be? Jesus dying for the sins of the world fulfills it resoundingly.

Previously, Jesus had alluded to His disciples about the Gentiles.[341] But their disdain for the Gentiles was so ingrained

---

[339] Gen. 3:9-21.
[340] Gen. 12:3b.
[341] Jn. 10:16.

that they did not get it.[342] Therefore, G-d used Peter as His instrument to open the door of Christianity to the Gentiles. After this event, not much more is written about Peter in the book of Acts, which is the story of Christianity in the first century CE. Rather, the story shifts back to Paul in Acts Chapters 13 through 28.

Paul reached out to both Jews and Gentiles on his journeys around the Roman Empire, but most of his impact was among the Gentiles. In fact, Paul called himself an "apostle of Gentiles."[343] In addition, when the Jews revolted against the Romans in 66 CE, the Jewish Christians received a vision and left Jerusalem. Other Jews considered their flight to be treasonous. Four years later, in 70 CE, the Romans overran Jerusalem, and there was a bloodbath. But from the moment the Christian Jews fled, very few Jews would become Christian from then on, and Christianity would go on to be almost exclusively Gentile.[344]

Paul would go on to make three notable missionary journeys. On the first journey, he and Barnabas departed from Antioch, which was near the Mediterranean coast in Syria. They traveled to the island of Cyprus and then to the southern part of the province of Galatia, which is today central Turkey. There, many people were saved, and Paul established churches in multiple cities. This journey started around 46 CE,[345] and it is recorded in Acts Chapters 13 and 14.

After this journey was over, Paul and Barnabas argued over one of their helpers, John Mark, who had deserted them in the midst of the journey. Therefore, they split up into two teams and went their separate ways. Paul's second missionary journey is recorded in Acts 15:36 through 18:22. He went with Silas on

---

[342] Yet, once they understood that G-d's plan included reaching out to the Gentiles, they embraced it and gave glory to G-d (Acts 11:18.)

[343] Rom. 1:5; 11:13; Gal. 2:7-8.

[344] Bruce L. Shelley, *Church History in Plain Language* (Nashville: Thomas Nelson Publishers, 1982, 1995) 22-23.

[345] J.J. Brimson, B.A., Ph.D., J.P. Kane, Ph.D., et al, eds., *New Bible Atlas* (Leicester, England: Inter-Varsity Press, 1985) 80.

this journey. They left Antioch and traveled overland to the province of Galatia to check on the new churches. They were joined by Timothy in southern Galatia. From there, they traveled to the coast and then sailed west to the province of Macedonia, where Paul evangelized and established churches in the cities of Philippi and Thessalonica. These cities are located in modern-day Greece. Then they sailed south along the coast to the province of Achaia, which is today southern Greece. There, Paul evangelized in Athens and spent two years establishing a church in the city of Corinth. Then he and his band sailed east to the province of Asia (western Turkey) where they briefly stopped in the city of Ephesus and left behind two coworkers, Priscilla and Aquila.[346]

Paul's third missionary journey began in 53 and lasted until 58 CE.[347] It is recorded in Acts 18:23 through 20:38. On this trip, he again traveled overland to Galatia, where he checked on some of the churches he had established on his first missionary journey. In the latter part of this journey, he would likewise visit the churches he had established in the provinces of Macedonia and Achaia on his second journey. But in between, he would spend three years in Ephesus. There, he would evangelize and establish a church. Ephesus was on the coast of the Aegean Sea. It was a pagan center and the home of the temple of the goddess Artemis. G-d blessed Paul's efforts, which reverberated throughout the province. In fact, many people came to Christ, and they held a massive book burning of their occultic books.[348] Furthermore, so great was Paul's impact for Christ that the pagan idol industry suffered a loss. Of course, financial loss is a strong motivator, and sure enough, the decrease in idol sales led to a riot. It was following this riot that Paul left Ephesus to visit the churches in Macedonia and Achaia.[349]

There are a number of references to Paul in these chapters in Acts that are noteworthy. Prior to Jesus reaching out to him,

---

346 Ibid.
347 Ibid.
348 Acts 19:19-20.
349 Acts 19:23-41.

he was driven, religious, and controlling. Many years later, in these chapters, he was still driven. Indeed, he changed world history. But, other than that, he became a completely different man. No longer was he controlling. People did not have to do what he said, "or else." He told them the truth, but their choices were up to them. In addition, he was motivated by love for other people in a way that he was not before. We see this in his relationships. He was always surrounded by close friends.[350] He was not a harsh taskmaster but a man who loved people, and they loved him. After Paul visited the churches in Macedonia and Achaia, he set sail for Jerusalem. Along the way, he stopped in Ephesus to say one final goodbye to the leaders of the church. This event was recorded as follows:

> "And now, behold, bound by the Spirit, I am on my way to Jerusalem, not knowing what will happen to me there, except that the Holy Spirit solemnly testifies to me in every city, saying that bonds and afflictions await me. But I do not consider my life of any account as dear to myself, so that I may finish my course and the ministry which I received from the L-rd Jesus, to testify solemnly of the gospel of the grace of G-d. And now, behold, I know that all of you, among whom I went about preaching the kingdom, will no longer see my face. Therefore, I testify to you this day that I am innocent of the blood of all men. For I did not shrink from declaring to you the whole purpose of G-d. Be on guard for yourselves and for all the flock, among which the Holy Spirit has made you overseers, to shepherd the church of G-d which He purchased with His own blood...."
>
> When he had said these things, he knelt down and prayed with them all. And they

---

350 Acts 20:4.

began to weep aloud and embraced Paul, and repeatedly kissed him, grieving especially over the word which he had spoken, that they would not see his face again. And they were accompanying him to the ship.[351]

G-d is so good to us. His love changed Paul into a better man. Paul was no longer a religious fanatic. These people were precious to him.

Surely Paul was right. He had heard the Holy Spirit, and great affliction lay in store for him. But through it all, G-d would continue to use him to spread the word of Christ.

When he got to Jerusalem, a riot ensued, and the people wanted to string him up, but Roman soldiers prevented it. From that point on, he underwent a series of hardships that resulted in him being moved to Rome, awaiting trial before the emperor. Once in Rome, he waited two years to see Emperor Nero, who in the end had Paul executed. But during those two years, he continued to evangelize. Though incarcerated, he still was in contact with people, whom he told about Jesus. Specifically, he was in contact with members of the Praetorian Guard, who were guarding him. While imprisoned, he also wrote multiple letters that are in the New Testament. One of them is his letter to the Philippian Christians. Here are a few verses from Chapter 1:

> Now I want you to know, brethren, that my circumstances have turned out for the greater progress of the gospel, so that my imprisonment in the cause of Christ has become well known throughout the whole praetorian guard and to everyone else, and that most of the brethren, trusting in the L-rd because of my imprisonment, have far more courage to speak the word of G-d without fear....[352]

---

351 Acts 20:22-28, 36-38.
352 Phil. 1:12-14.

In these verses, we see that G-d's work was not impeded. Paul was able to lead many of his guards to Christ, and it appears that through them, the message of Christ spread throughout "the whole praetorian guard and to everyone else." The Praetorian Guard was an elite order of guards who had influence with people in high places throughout the city. Indeed, the L-rd works in mysterious ways, and He put Paul in the perfect place to make a big impact in Rome. In addition, Paul's positive attitude emboldened other Christians to stand strong in their faith despite the horrific persecution that was taking place under Nero. In fact, both Paul and Peter were executed around the same time, in the mid-60s CE, during Nero's reign of terror.[353]

One of the lies of history is that the Romans were civilized. That is what happens when you are in power for multiple centuries. Propaganda prevails, and many of your sins get erased from the historical record. But if we look closely, even what slipped through the cracks is enough to give us an idea of their extreme violence and cruelty. For example, Nero murdered his wife and mother. Imagine what he did to Christians. Among other heinous acts, he had Christians "smeared with pitch and used as living torches to illuminate *his*...nocturnal festivals."[354] Who in their right mind would go to such an event?

Fortunately, Roman persecution was not continuous, but rather intermittent. Nonetheless, persecution was so odious that it commanded every Christian's attention. Indeed, even if there was a lull, the threat of persecution was always there. Every individual Christian's life was in danger.[355] Yet, Jesus had promised His followers that He would be with them every step of the way as they proceeded forward to carry out His mission. And so He was, but not in the way they would have thought, for He did not strike down their oppressors. In the New Testament

---

[353] Shelley 40-41.

[354] Robert Payne, Ancient Rome (New York, NY: J. Boylston & Company, Publishers, 1966) 170.

[355] 2 Tim. 3:12.

book of 1 Peter, Peter addressed the Christians in four provinces located in what is today, Turkey, who were facing persecution. He called on them to bond together in love; to draw close to G-d; to follow Jesus' example; and of all things, to give "honor to the king!"[356] In other words, they were not to rebel in any way, but rather to patiently go through this horrific ordeal. After all, that is exactly what Jesus did. Why was this G-d's way for them? This was G-d's way because G-d is wise, and although each of their lives was in danger, the movement as a whole was not in danger. It turns out that as these Christians patiently endured this injustice with the Holy Spirit's help, their neighbors saw it and were impressed. Anyone can rebel, but to patiently face a violent death for what you believe is very hard to do. Hence, their neighbors listened to their message and realized that they too wanted an eternity founded on love. In fact, many received Jesus as their savior and joined the fold.[357]

In the end, all of the apostles were killed for their faith except one—John. He lived to a ripe old age, albeit his later years were spent in prison. He lived into the 90s CE, which is when G-d used him to write the last book in the New Testament, Revelation.

Not only Paul, but also Peter, John, and James wrote epistles in the New Testament. The epistles were letters that were written to churches by the apostles to offer words of encouragement, correction, and theological clarification. As you read through the book of Acts and the epistles, what you see is that Christianity in the first century consisted of a number of individual churches that were connected to their apostles but not to each other, at least not in any institutional sense. Thus, as problems would arise, such as persecution, heresy, or division in a church, the apostles would travel to that church or send a letter to help them.[358]

---

[356] 1 Pet. 2:13-24; 4:7-12; 5:6-7.

[357] Tragically, violent persecution against Christians still persists today, particularly in Africa and the Middle East. You can learn more about this at www.opendoorsus.org.

[358] In the case of Peter's letters, 1 Peter and 2 Peter, it is unclear if he

Needless to say, Jesus used the other apostles to do amazing things and reach the lost as well. He just did not have the entire story of the first century recorded in the New Testament because it is too much information. But He gave us the information we needed to know.

So, in the New Testament we have a concise version of the history of Christianity in the first century. The apostles were fearless. Once they established a church in a city, they would move on to the next city. Then it was up to the churches to continue to reach out to the lost in their cities and regions. The churches were filled with new Christians who were experiencing acceptance from G-d for the first time. It was life-changing, and they each saw with a clarity they never had before what is truly important in life. They studied the Bible together, and they formed tight-knit groups.[359] Some of the new Christians would become leaders in the churches. But they each played a real role. In other words, these churches operated as teams that Jesus could use to accomplish His will, and use them He did. Indeed, Jesus used the local churches to change the world in the first century.

*　*　*　*　*

Once the decades started to roll by following the deaths of the apostles and the first generation of Christians, as you might expect, the Church changed. The Church in the first century was a movement, but in the second century it morphed into a religious organization. On one level, we can see why that happened. One of the main problems the first-century churches faced was heresy. There were many bad actors who introduced heresies to try to alter the Christian message. Hence, the apostles' letters clarified exactly who Jesus is. This ongoing battle over truth was a major reason for the formation of the Catholic, or universal, Church. For, it seemed only natural that there should be a power structure with centralized leadership to

____

founded any of the churches these letters are addressed to.
[359] Acts 2:41-47; Col. 2:1-3.

protect the core beliefs of Christianity. Another change consisted of the Catholic Church becoming more liturgical than the early Church. Of course, both of these changes are very human—seeking structure and control and incorporating religious formalism. But this new version of the Church was not in line with Jesus' instructions in the New Testament. Furthermore, the results were not good, as the Church lost the dynamism it had in the first century.

Let's take a look at some of the passages from the New Testament that give instructions on how the Church is supposed to operate:

> **Mt. 28:18-20:** And Jesus came up and spoke to them, saying, "All authority has been given to Me in heaven and on earth. Go therefore and make disciples of all the nations, baptizing them in the name of the Father and the Son and the Holy Spirit, teaching them to observe all that I commanded you; and lo, I am with you always, even to the end of the age."

This passage is known as "the Great Commission." This is the role G-d has prescribed for both individual Christians and the Church as a whole to play. There are two main commands. The first one is baptizing people, which implies first telling them about Jesus so they have the opportunity to receive Him as their savior. The second one is discipling people, or in other words, teaching them the Bible and helping them to grow spiritually.

> **2 Cor. 5:18-20:** Now all these things are from G-d, who reconciled us to Himself through Christ and gave us the ministry of reconciliation, namely, that G-d was in Christ reconciling the world to Himself, not counting their trespasses against them, and He has committed to us the word of reconciliation.

> Therefore, we are ambassadors for Christ, as though G-d were making an appeal through us; we beg you on behalf of Christ, be reconciled to G-d.

This passage is one of many dealing with the subject of evangelism. Here we see that all Christians are to share their faith. Paul is using emphatic language in the last verse. There is nothing more important in life than for people to receive salvation so that they can go to heaven for eternity.

> **2 Tim. 2:1-2:** You therefore, my son, be strong in the grace that is in Christ Jesus. The things which you have heard from me in the presence of many witnesses, entrust these to faithful men who will be able to teach others also.

These two verses illustrate Christian discipleship. Here too, all Christians have a role to play in this work. Just as older Christians taught us the Bible, shared their lives with us, and encouraged us to take steps of faith, so should we extend ourselves to younger Christians whom G-d brings into our lives.

> **Rom. 8:1:** Therefore there is now no condemnation for those who are in Christ Jesus.

Indeed, G-d made it crystal clear in this statement that Jesus paid for all of our sins, those from before we received Him as our savior, and those we commit afterwards. His love and forgiveness are unconditional. G-d wants Christians to be secure in His love and not insecure.

> **1 Jn. 4:13-19:** By this we know that we abide in Him and He in us, because He has given us of His Spirit. We have seen and testify that the Father has sent the Son to be the Savior of the

world. Whoever confesses that Jesus is the Son of G-d, G-d abides in him, and he in G-d. We have come to know and have believed the love which G-d has for us. G-d is love, and the one who abides in love abides in G-d, and G-d abides in him. By this, love is perfected with us, so that we may have confidence in the day of judgment; because as He is, so also are we in this world. There is no fear in love; but perfect love casts out fear, because fear involves punishment, and the one who fears is not perfected in love. We love, because He first loved us.

Again, Christians are fully accepted by G-d and have no fear of losing their salvation. Furthermore, G-d pours His love into our hearts, which sets us free to be able to give love to others. In addition, G-d gives us His Spirit to enable us to love like Jesus did.

Jn. 13:34-35: "A new commandment I give to you, that you love one another, even as I have loved you, that you also love one another. By this all men will know that you are My disciples, if you have love for one another."

Jesus detested religious hypocrisy.[360] Therefore, Christians should abhor it as well. Rather, we should relate to each other with honesty and treat each other with grace and kindness. As non-Christians see this behavior, they will be drawn to Jesus as opposed to being repulsed by His followers. Not to mention, being involved in such a church is a breath of fresh air compared to what you experience in a church where people wear a fake smile.

---

[360] Mt. 23.

> **Jn. 14:16, 25-27:** I will ask the Father, and He will give you another Helper, that He may be with you forever…. These things I have spoken to you while abiding with you. But the Helper, the Holy Spirit, whom the Father will send in My name, He will teach you all things, and bring to your remembrance all that I said to you. Peace I leave with you; My peace I give to you; not as the world gives do I give to you. Do not let your heart be troubled, nor let it be fearful."

Jesus left, but He gave us instructions, and G-d gave us the Holy Spirit to help us.[361] In the 2,000-year period before Jesus, when G-d was working exclusively with the Jews, only their kings and prophets were filled with the Holy Spirit. But since the Day of Pentecost, the Holy Spirit has come upon every Christian.[362] He enables us to live godly lives and play our roles in the cause of Christ.

> **1 Cor 12:7-22:** But to each one is given the manifestation of the Spirit for the common good. For to one is given the word of wisdom through the Spirit, and to another the word of knowledge according to the same Spirit; to another faith by the same Spirit, and to another gifts of healing by the one Spirit, and to another the effecting of miracles, and to another prophecy, and to another the distinguishing of spirits, to another various kinds of tongues, and to another the interpretation of tongues. But one and the same Spirit works all these things, distributing to each one individually just as He wills.

---

[361] Jn. 16:7.
[362] Acts 10:44-48.

For even as the body is one and yet has many members, and all the members of the body, though they are many, are one body, so also is Christ. For by one Spirit we were all baptized into one body, whether Jews or Greeks, whether slaves or free, and we were all made to drink of one Spirit. For the body is not one member, but many. If the foot says, "Because I am not a hand, I am not a part of the body," it is not for this reason any the less a part of the body. And if the ear says, "Because I am not an eye, I am not a part of the body," it is not for this reason any the less a part of the body. If the whole body were an eye, where would the hearing be? If the whole were hearing, where would the sense of smell be? But now G-d has placed the members, each one of them, in the body, just as He desired. If they were all one member, where would the body be? But now there are many members, but one body. And the eye cannot say to the hand, "I have no need of you"; or again the head to the feet, "I have no need of you." On the contrary, it is much truer that the members of the body which seem to be weaker are necessary;...

The Holy Spirit gives every Christian a gifting, or an extraordinary ability. Each church is to function as a team in which every member has a role to play in which they utilize their gifting for the benefit of the church. The church is like a body where every part plays a vital role.

Eph. 4:11-13: And He gave some as apostles, and some as prophets, and some as evangelists, and some as pastors and teachers, for the equipping of the saints for the work of service, to the building up of the body of Christ; until

> we all attain to the unity of the faith, and of the
> knowledge of the Son of G-d, to a mature man,
> to the measure of the stature which belongs to
> the fullness of Christ.

Here is another passage where Paul speaks on the diversity of roles in a church. Yes, there are leaders and teachers, but they are not responsible to do the work of the church. Rather, their job is to help everyone else learn the Bible and become spiritually mature so that the members can do the work of the church. In fact, the goal of the leaders and teachers is for everyone to be a Bible expert.

Surely, this is the way the first century churches operated. There were no priests in the first century. The word *priest* is used 159 times in the New Testament. However, except for some references to Jesus, this word is used only in reference to the priests of first century Judaism.[363] Following the first century, the priesthood was introduced in the Church, and a clergy/laity model was established. From that point on, the priests were the theological experts, and the congregants played passive roles. Predictably, the progress of the spread of the gospel slowed down dramatically. We will cover this subject in the next chapter.

---

[363] Heb. 5:1.

13

THE CHRISTIAN AGE

The 1,700-year period of Christian history between the years 100 CE and 1800 CE was dominated by the Catholic Church. That is, of course, except for the Eastern Orthodox Church, which branched off from the Catholic Church in the mid-11th century.[364] They played a major role in Church history as well. However, we will mainly deal with the Catholic Church in this chapter, as it is beyond the scope of this book to cover the subject of Church history in its entirety.

The break between the two branches came in 1054 when Pope Leo IX served the Patriarch of Constantinople with a bull of excommunication.[365] Disagreements over theological issues and liturgical practices had been festering for centuries. But the

---

[364] Today, the Eastern Orthodox Church is made up of about 15 separate churches from mainly Eastern Europe but also Asia and the Middle East. For example, the Greek Orthodox Church and the Russian Orthodox Church are Eastern Orthodox churches (Bruce L. Shelley 42.)

[365] Eamon Duffy, *Saints and Sinners, a History of the Popes* (New Haven and London: Yale University Press, 1997, 2014, 2016) 116-117. A papal bull is an official document produced by the pope.

root issue was always a dispute over power in which the popes believed they were the highest authorities in the Church, but the patriarchs in the east disagreed. Finally, a few strong-willed men butted heads in 1054, and the breakup occurred.

In fact, the subject of Catholic history during this 1,700-year-long period is so extensive that we will not be able to cover it in any great detail. Rather, we will observe some of the main trends that took place and came to define the Catholic Church.

Trend Number One: The first trend consisted of the Church morphing into a hierarchical organization. In the first century, the Church was a movement of local churches established by the apostles. As problems would arise in the churches, including the introduction of heresies, the apostles would visit the churches or send an epistle to offer guidance and address any theological issues.[366] The people in the churches were very dear to the apostles. The churches would even send the apostles helpers, depending on their situations. It was these helpers whom the apostles would use to send messages, including the epistles, back to their churches.[367] But there was no centralized leadership or organized church structure. The local churches were doing G-d's work on their own with a helping hand from their founders when they needed it.

Everything changed in the second century. The apostles were all gone, and the Church became overwhelmingly Gentile. Persecution would rise and fall. But one thing would stay the same: heretics would continue to introduce false theological ideas into the Church. Inevitably, the heretics always undermined the same doctrine, the message of salvation through the blood of Christ.

---

[366] The apostles wrote the epistles, or letters, in the New Testament largely to deal with heresies. These letters clarify exactly who Jesus is and how to be saved, the two topics that heretics usually tried to alter.
[367] Homer A. Kent, Jr., *Philippians*, The Expositor's Bible Commentary, Vol. 11, gen. ed. Frank E. Gaebelein (Grand Rapids: Zondervan Publishing House, 1978) 135.

The Church would deal with the problem of heresy by having scholars address theological disputes, and by forming a centralized leadership structure to control the Christian message.[368] These scholars came to be known as the "Church Fathers." A partial list of these men would include Justin Martyr, Irenaeus of Gaul, Clement of Alexandria, Tertullian of Carthage, Origen, Jerome, and Augustine. They are still famous today for their writings and theological positions. Indeed, their positions influence our understanding of the Bible still today. As noted in the book, *God's Strategy in Human History,*

> The early church had the task of interpreting and elucidating the New Testament writings. What was implied often had to be made explicit. Sometimes new words (like "trinity") were coined. One of the earliest of these words was "free-will." The early church noted the Scriptures (such as Matthew 23:37) which indicated that man sometimes defied and disobeyed G-d's will.... We may not like the expression "free-will" for it is not used in the Bible, and was later misused by the Pelagians. But like "trinity," it was part of the early Christians' attempt to define apostolic teaching more clearly.[369]

As stated above, the other thing the early Church did to combat heresy was to form a hierarchical structure. The Christians creating the hierarchy were largely Romans, and if there was one thing Romans knew, it was how to set up and run an organization. Whether it was their army dominating on the battlefield or their prefects collecting taxes and maintaining order in the provinces, the Romans were very well organized.

---

[368] Duffy 9-10.

[369] Roger T. Forster and V. Paul Marston, *God's Strategy in Human History* (Wheaton, Illinois: Tyndale House Publishers, Inc., 1973) 243-244.

Hence, the Catholic Church was set up in a Roman way: a top-down structure with a supreme leader, the pope, and under him a group of bishops. The bishops were each the leader of a diocese, or the set of churches in a city.[370] Beneath the bishops were the priests, who were in charge of each of the churches.

But Rome's way was not G-d's way. The new Christians of the first century were on fire for the cause of Christ. First, Jesus forgave their sins and came into their hearts. No matter what they had done, His death was sufficient, and they were going to heaven. On top of that, G-d had a handpicked role for each of them to play. They each had a purpose. Needless to say, meeting G-d like this and receiving His love personally was life changing. G-d loved them so deeply that they started to love others. They were going to share this message of G-d's grace, even if it cost them their lives. Again, this was a movement that was powered by the Holy Spirit. The results were incredible. In the 60 years between the time of Jesus' death and the writing the book of Revelation, they spread the message of Jesus across much of the Roman Empire.

The problem in the second century was that the new, highly organized Church fostered a clergy/laity ethos. In a clergy/laity type of church, the priests are the experts and the paid professionals. The laity are the flock, and their role is passive. Unfortunately, the results were just what you would expect. The progress of the Great Commission slowed down considerably as the laypeople laid down their roles and became parishioners.

Beyond the changes to the structure and ethos in Christianity, there was another significant change that was introduced in the second century. Namely, Christianity became a religion. In the first century, there were no special clothes for the apostles, elders, and deacons. The elders, or overseers, and deacons were the two prescribed offices for local churches.[371] The elders were the leaders, and the deacons were team leaders

---

[370] At times, the bishops would relate to a pope in a collegial fashion as opposed to in a subordinate fashion.
[371] Acts 14:23; 1 Tim. 3:1-13; Titus 1:5-9.

of ministries within the churches. But they all dressed the same as everyone else.

Whenever Christians gathered in the first century, it was to pray, study the Bible, and share their lives with each other.[372] There were no scripted prayers, liturgical services, or sacraments. In the New Testament, only two rituals were prescribed: baptism and communion. In both cases, very few details were provided.[373] The reason for that is because these events are supposed to be heartfelt interactions between G-d and His children, not formulaic religious rites.

There were no popes in the first century. In fact, the word *pope* does not appear in the New Testament. There were also no bishops presiding over dioceses. Furthermore, there were no priests, except for Jesus.[374]

The introduction of popes, in particular, was a huge change in Christianity. Any history book on Catholicism will reveal how important the popes have been in Catholic history. Truthfully, it is all about the popes. The quality of their characters and the decisions they made shaped Catholicism. Of course, everybody knows that some were godly, while others were corrupt.

Interestingly, the basis for this office comes from a single statement Jesus made to Peter. Jesus said,

> "And I also say to you that you are Peter, and
> upon this rock I will build my church; and the
> gates of Hades shall not overpower it. I will give
> you the keys of the kingdom of heaven; and
> whatever you shall bind on earth shall be
> bound in heaven, and whatever you shall loose
> on earth shall be loosed in heaven."[375]

In this interaction, Jesus changed Peter's name from Simon to Peter. The name Peter is *Petros* in Greek, and it means

---

[372] Acts 1:12-14; 2:40-47.
[373] Mk. 1:4-5; Lk. 22:14-20; Acts 2:37-38.
[374] Heb. 4:14-16; 7:23-28.
[375] Mt. 16:18-19.

"rock." What Jesus was communicating was that, with His help, Peter's character would change. Peter had a heart for G-d, and he loved Jesus. But he often spoke too quickly and got himself into trouble. Hence, Jesus was telling him that he was going to become a rock, or in other words, a man of respectability and a leader. And Peter did. He was a key leader of the Church in the first century. Indeed, he was the key leader on the day of Pentecost and in the earliest days of Christianity. But he was never the bishop of Rome or the pope, at least not according to the New Testament. Rather, evidence suggests that there wasn't a bishop in Rome until the middle of the second century.[376]

In the New Testament, the word translated as either "bishop" or "overseer," depending on the translation, is the Greek word *episkopos*. This word is used interchangeably with the Greek word *presbuteros*, which is translated as "elder."[377] Again, in the first century, there were no bishops in the sense that we think of them today.[378] There were just local church leaders. In fact, Peter did not refer to himself as a bishop but as a *sumpresbuteros*, meaning a co-elder.[379]

In terms of the last part of Jesus' statement, based on the context, the word *keys* is metaphorical. Jesus is referring to the battle being waged over the souls of men in the heavenly places. His point is that Peter's prayers would be authoritative in the heavens above to hold the forces of darkness back from blinding the eyes of human beings. Jesus has a plan to reach the lost, and in His plan, He uses people to play important roles, like Peter. In Jesus' words, "the gates of Hades shall not overpower it (the Church)." The question is, do these two verses prescribe an ongoing succession of supreme leaders in the Catholic Church, or is the Papacy essentially a human invention?[380]

------

[376] Richard P. McBrien, *The Church* (New York, NY: HarperCollins Publishers, 2008) 98.

[377] E.g., in Titus 1:5-9.

[378] McBrien 44.

[379] 1 Pet. 5:1.

[380] McBrien 41-42.

Trend Number Two: The second profound change in Catholic history took place when the Church gained a measure of governmental power.

Following the apostles, the Church would continue to undergo persecution. The level of persecution rose and fell depending on the emperor. Then, an amazing thing happened; Constantine came along. He was the first emperor who bowed to Jesus. His reign impacted Christianity in two ways, one good, and one bad. The good impact was that the hellish persecution ended.

On the bad side, in the early 300s, Constantine opened a door to the halls of power in the Roman Empire, and the Church walked through it. This choice by the Church to wield governmental power would lead to spiritual decline and even calamity. It started innocently enough as Constantine "gave the rights and duties of magistrates to all the bishops in his empire. Many of the bishops carefully searched their consciences before they agreed to accept the post, for Christian tradition, centuries old, looked at the state and all of its work as being corrupt. But finally, with gratitude, they assented to the change and regarded it as a sign of the new era that was dawning."[381]

Rightly did they weigh this decision carefully, for power is an intoxicant. Of course, they made the wrong choice, and they probably knew it. As time would go by, the Church would throw caution to the wind and seek ever-greater levels of power. Sin would be the result, and damage was caused to the Church's witness for Jesus. In fact, the Church became distracted from their mission to take the message of Jesus to the world and instead pursued the same things governmental leaders pursue today—money, sex, revenge, and power. Indeed, the popes would go on to engage in power struggles both internally and

---

[381] Payne 252.

externally with the nations around them. Here are a few examples of their internal power struggles:

> Leo (Pope Leo III (795–816)) however, had more pressing problems than an overweening king on the doorstep. Hadrian's long pontificate had ensconced a number of his relatives and supporters in the Roman administration, who may have resented the arrival of a parvenu pope with no pedigree.[382] Strong factional rivalries developed in the city, and during a procession of exorcism and blessing round the city in April 799 a crowd led by Pope Hadrian's nephew Paschalis set upon the Pope and tried to blind him and rip out his tongue. This was an attempt to secure the Pope's deposition by making him unfit for office, but the job was botched, and Leo recovered both sight and speech. He fled to the protection of Charlemagne at Paderborn.[383]

Following is an example of a good pope engaged in a power struggle with a corrupt generation of Catholic clergy:

> Leo IX (Pope Leo IX (1049–54)) determined to take the papacy out beyond Italy, and to make it the spearhead of a general reform. In a whirlwind pontificate of five years he travelled to Germany, France and northern Italy. Wherever he went he held a series of great reforming synods, which attacked the evils of simony, lay investiture and clerical marriages....
>
> In one week, Leo had asserted papal authority as it had never been asserted

---

[382] The reign of Pope Hadrian I extended from 772 CE to 795 CE.
[383] Duffy 94.

before. Bishops had been excommunicated and deposed, a powerful and prestigious archbishop summoned to explain himself in Rome, and the whole system of payments for promotion within the Church had been earth-shakingly challenged. And Rheims[384] was only the beginning. Leo launched an all-out attack on the financial traffic in ecclesiastical appointments, from village priests up to bishops and archbishops, deposing the guilty and even reordaining priests ordained by such bishops, for simony[385] at the time was held to be a heresy which invalidated the sacraments celebrated by the simoniac.[386]

Here are a couple typical examples of the machinations of the popes as they competed for power with the kings of the surrounding nations and entangled themselves in European politics:

It is to East Francia that (Pope) John XII turned when Berengar II threatened the Papal States.[387] East Francia was dominated by a small number of duchies, including the Duchy of Saxony in the north, to which the elected kingship of East Francia had passed in the early tenth century.[388] Before long the Saxons

---

[384] Rheims was the site of a synod held by the pope in the mid-11th century in which he inaugurated a purge against simoniac bishops.
[385] Simony is the sale of spiritual items such as offices for money or property.
[386] Duffy 114-115.
[387] The Catholic Church once ruled a territory comprised of part of Italy called the Papal States. Berangar II was the king of Italy.
[388] East Francia was the eastern portion of what had once been Charlemagne's empire. Its territory roughly corresponds to that of

were the strongest power in Europe. Otto I of Saxony had succeeded his father, Henry, becoming the second king of Germany, and now John XII sent him a beguiling offer; in exchange for assistance, John XII would crown him Roman Emperor.

In 961 Otto I heeded the call by the pope, invaded Italy, captured Berengar and exiled him to Germany where he died a few years later. John XII kept his promise, crowning Otto I Roman Emperor in 962. From then on, the Roman Empire was forever linked with the German crown and German emperors also automatically inherited the Italian throne. Otto reciprocated with a famous decree—The *Diploma* or *Privilegium Ottonianum*—in which he guaranteed the independence of the Papal States, confirmed and extended the temporal power of the papacy and pledged to defend the Church's rights and possessions.[389]

and,

...even by the standards of the period Urban (Pope Urban VIII (1623–44)) carried nepotism to new heights. His favoritism to his family cost the papacy 105,000,000 scudi, and in old age would torment Urban with well-justified fears that he had squandered the patrimony of the Church. His nephews drew him into a disastrous war at the end of his pontificate with their hated rival Odoardo Farnese, who held the papal fief of Castro.[390] This cynical war,

---

modern-day Germany.

[389] Christopher Lascelles, *Pontifex Maximus* (United Kingdom: Crux Publishing Ltd., 2017) 103.

[390] This fiefdom was located in central Italy.

undertaken to grab Farnese's possessions on a flimsy pretext, ultimately drew Venice, Tuscany and Modena into an anti-papal league, left the Papal States devastated, the papal coffers empty, and the ambition of Urban to assert an unchallenged secular power in Italy in shreds.

The war of Castro was not the only political catastrophe of Urban's pontificate, for his Francophile sympathies led to a steady alienation between the papacy and the Habsburgs in Spain and the empire.[391] Urban understood the need for the Pope to preserve neutrality between Catholic nations, and genuinely struggled to do so. He was convinced, however, that Habsburg dominance in Italy was a greater danger to the papacy than any threat from France, and this assumption, coupled with his natural sympathy for France, consistently skewed his policy....

The same pro-French sympathies colored Urban's involvement in the Thirty Years War. Here again his intentions were basically good, for he wanted to settle the rivalry between Richelieu's France and Spain and the Habsburg empire, in the interests of a concerted front against Protestantism. It was a hopeless task.[392] France worked to inflame the Pope's fears of Spanish ambition in Italy, and Spain took a high moral line on Urban's failure to condemn Richelieu's alliance with Protestant Sweden—as Philip IV wrote to the Pope in 1635, 'I trust that...your Holiness will deal with the King of France, who has allied himself with the

---

[391] The Habsburgs were one of the most powerful dynasties in the history of Europe.

[392] Cardinal Richelieu was a high official in both the Catholic Church and the French government.

Protestants, as the duty of a Pope demands.'[393]
The failure of the Pope to achieve peace between
the Catholic parties to the Thirty Years War was
an eloquent—and for the papacy an ominous—
indicator of the increasingly marginal place of
religious considerations in determining the
politics of Europe.[394]

Trend Number Three: The third trend is really just a continuation of the second one: the Church's accumulation of power. The difference is that there was a marked increase in both the level and amount of sin that was sanctioned by the popes. During this time, Jesus was shown a seat in the back of the Church. For example, His name was mentioned at the beginning and end of official documents, but only in a perfunctory way. In the middle of the documents, where the heart of the matter was being discussed, He was nowhere to be found. The mission of the popes became the preservation of the Catholic Church, as opposed to the declaration of the gospel message to the unreached peoples of the earth. Obviously, this shift was a mistake that zapped the Church's ability to advance the gospel. This is why Jesus exhorted His followers:

> "Abide in Me, and I in you. As the branch
> cannot bear fruit of itself unless it abides in the
> vine, so neither can you unless you abide in Me.
> I am the vine, you are the branches; he who
> abides in Me and I in him, he bears much fruit,
> for apart from Me you can do nothing."[395]

Once the shift in focus had gone on long enough, a different form of fruit ripened as the corruption and power struggles of the popes and clergy eventually led to programs of great evil. These programs included the Crusades, the Inquisition, and

---

[393] Philip IV was the king of Spain.
[394] Duffy 233-234.
[395] Jn. 15:4-5.

witch hunting. The Crusades began in 1095 and lasted approximately 300 years. The next program was the Inquisition, which began around 1230 and lasted approximately 600 years. The final one was witch hunting, which began around 1400 and lasted approximately 375 years. Thus, all told, this period lasted around 735 years. Thankfully, these programs took place prior to the Industrial Age. Therefore, in terms of the Inquisition and witch hunting, the crimes of the Church could not be perpetrated on the European citizenry rapidly by utilizing modern technology. An apt metaphor for this 600-year-long period would be "a slow-motion holocaust." The level of heinous evil was the same, but the element of mass production was missing. It took place one victim at a time.

1. <u>The Crusades</u>

The Crusades were a series of holy wars that were fought to liberate Palestine from the Muslims. The first one was initiated by Pope Urban II in 1095. By 1099, the Crusaders had taken Jerusalem. Then the Europeans established a province along the coast on the eastern side of the Mediterranean Sea.[396] But the Muslims regrouped and started fighting back. In 1187, under the leadership of Saladin, the Muslims seized control of Jerusalem and the First Crusade was over.[397]

In all, seven major crusades would be launched by the popes, in which Crusaders would be sent out from Europe to take the Holy Land. The First Crusade was the most successful. Some of the wars were ill conceived and poorly conducted. In particular, the Second, Fourth, Fifth, and Seventh Crusades were disasters.[398] The last time the Europeans were in control of Jerusalem was 1244. Their last stronghold in the Middle East, the port city of Acre, fell in 1291.

---

[396] Shelley 189.
[397] Saladin was the sultan, or king, of Egypt and Syria.
[398] Blech 366-368.

So why should this series of wars be characterized as a "program of great evil?" After all, wars between nations were common in those centuries. First, let's consider the appropriateness of popes initiating wars. By this time, the popes had become the rulers of a group of territories within the Italian Peninsula that formed a country named the Papal States. Thus, the popes were supreme leaders of both the Catholic Church and a nation. The Papal States was in existence between 754 and 1870.[399] That is very impressive. It lasted over a millennium, and a very turbulent millennium at that. Hence, it makes sense that the popes would, on occasion, initiate wars with other nations.

However, what does the New Testament say about this part of Catholic history? Jesus had much to say about the kingdom He started when He came 2,000 years ago. Jesus' kingdom was to be a spiritual kingdom as opposed to a political or physical kingdom. For example, we see this in His exchange with the Roman prefect, Pontius Pilate:

> Therefore Pilate entered again into the Praetorium, and summoned Jesus and said to Him, "Are You the King of the Jews?" Jesus answered, "Are you saying this on your own initiative, or did others tell you about Me?" Pilate answered, "I am not a Jew, am I? Your own nation and the chief priests delivered You to me; what have You done?" Jesus answered, "My kingdom is not of this world. If My kingdom were of this world, then My servants would be fighting so that I would not be handed over to the Jews; but as it is, My kingdom is not of this realm." Therefore Pilate said to Him, "So You are a king?" Jesus answered, "You say *correctly* that I am a king. For this I have been

---

[399] Gustav Schnurer, "States of the Church," *The Catholic Encyclopedia* (New York: Robert Appleton Company, 1912,) on CD, Kevin Knight, ed. http://www.newadvent.org/cathen/14257a.htm 2009.

born, and for this I have come into the world, to testify to the truth. Everyone who is of the truth hears My voice." Pilate said to Him, "What is truth?" And when he had said this, he went out again to the Jews and said to them, "I find no guilt in Him."[400]

Although Pilate was an ungodly man, he understood what Jesus was saying. Jesus was not here to establish an earthly kingdom or nation. Pilate was not threatened by Him and sought His release. However, the Jewish people went along with their leaders and called for Jesus to be crucified, and Pilate could not dissuade them. Though he had the power to override them, it was in Pilate's best interest not to get in a conflict at that time. So, he took the coward's way out and ordered Jesus to be crucified.[401]

To further reinforce this point of Jesus' kingdom being a spiritual kingdom, recall that in the Tanakh, G-d made an important promise to Abraham about the land that would be given to his descendants.[402] In fact, to some degree, the whole Tanakh is centered on this promise in which G-d gave the land of Israel to the Jews. Of course, eventually He removed them from the land, only to bring the tribes of Judah and Benjamin back after 70 years. But the point is that the New Testament is fundamentally different. For, G-d did not promise Christians a land of their own in the New Testament.

Furthermore, Jesus was categorically opposed to violence in the New Testament. Nowhere do we see Jesus calling for His followers to commit acts of violence. Christians are called to advance the cause of Christ through acts of love, not acts of

---

[400] Jn. 18:33-38.
[401] Mt. 27:20-26.
[402] Gen. 12:1-3, et al.

physical force or war. On the night of Jesus' arrest, Peter drew his sword and cut off a man's ear. Here was Jesus' response:

> But Jesus answered and said, "Stop! No more of this." And He touched his ear and healed him.[403]

The Church was given a mission, but it was not to become a nation and engage in international politics, including fighting wars. The achievement of nationhood violated Jesus' plan for the Church, and in fact, it only harmed the Church's ability to carry out the Great Commission. This was certainly the case with the Crusades.

The Crusades were to be "holy wars." What is the distinction between a "holy war" and any other war? The distinction includes a few facets. First of all, the Crusaders believed it was G-d's will for them to vanquish the Muslims and remove them from the Holy Land. Second, the popes employed a new way to finance these wars. Namely, they offered spiritual benefits instead of cash as pay to the soldiers. Third, the Crusaders each wore crosses that were made of cloth and sewn onto their clothes.[404] Finally, the Crusades were supposed to be fought with nobility. This means the Christian soldiers were not to pillage the towns they conquered or rape anyone. Rather, Urban and the following popes called for Augustine's model of war to be followed.[405]

> Augustine had laid down the principles of a "just war": It was conducted by the state; its purpose was the vindication of justice, meaning the defense of life and property; and

---

[403] Lk. 22:51.

[404] Duffy 136.

[405] Augustine was a famous theologian and bishop from the fourth century.

its code called for respect for noncombatants, hostages, and prisoners.[406]

The problem was that the Crusaders did not behave this way at all. In those days, both Jews and Arabs were living in Jerusalem. The Catholics viewed Jewish people with disdain. So, when the Crusaders broke into Jerusalem, the Jews were subjected to war crimes alongside the Arabs:

> In 1099, the crusaders, marching under the sign of the cross, stormed into Jerusalem to claim the city for Christ. Again the streets of the city ran with blood as the crusaders slaughtered more than forty thousand people and set fire to mosques and synagogues. In one particular situation, 969 Jewish men, women, and children were herded into a synagogue and set ablaze by crusaders. As the people screamed and burned alive, the crusading warriors stood outside and sang, "Christ, We Adore Thee."[407]

Unfortunately, this was not an isolated incident. So outrageous was the behavior of these soldiers, in the name of Christ, that close to 1,000 years later, their deeds are still recalled. Today, whenever ISIS, Hamas, or some other Muslim terrorist organization commits an act of great evil, the minute Christians denounce the violence, the Muslim world immediately says, "What about the Crusades?" They are right; Christian history is no better. Of course, it is not about winning an argument, but rather, it is about winning people to Jesus, and the Crusades have hampered that effort.

---

[406] Shelley 188.
[407] John Hagee, *Attack on America* (Nashville: Thomas Nelson Publishers, 2001) 42.

2. The Inquisition

As bad as the Crusades were, the Inquisition was worse. The Inquisition began as a response to heresy. In the 1100s and early 1200s, three episodes of heresy proved to be injurious to the Church. The first two were internal in which dissenting factions called on the Church leadership to divest itself of worldly power and return to the poverty and simplicity of the early Church. But the Church leadership was not interested. Yet, the two movements were attracting followers. Furthermore, the first movement executed a successful coup and held onto power for a surprising ten years.[408] But the worst of the three movements was the third one. It was an external movement that originated amongst a group of people in Albi, France, known as the Cathari. They espoused a mystical form of Christianity that resembled Gnosticism.[409] They believed in Jesus but denied that He ever lived as a human being on earth.

Once the Albigensian movement was underway and growing rapidly, the Church had enough. It was at that point they decided to take a strong stand and put an end to this trouble. First, they initiated a crusade in which they launched an invasion of southern France in order to wipe out the Cathari. This phase was successful, but the pope went further and initiated a second phase to remove any and all remaining pockets of Cathari. This second phase was the beginning of the Inquisition. The popes saw this practice as a tool to be used to rid themselves of the scourge of heresy. But they did not see that the cure was worse than the disease. In setting up and conducting the Inquisition, the popes and the inquisitors were guilty of evil comparable to that of the great monsters of history. Instead of bringing glory to Jesus, they elicited a response of revulsion and set back their mission immeasurably. They should have simply dealt with the heresy in the way the apostles

---

[408] The first two movements were led by Arnold, an abbot of Brescia, Italy, and Peter Waldo, a wealthy merchant from France, respectively.
[409] The Gnostics were heretics who caused trouble in the Christian churches during the first century.

did in the first century. Namely, the apostles prayed for the young Christians scattered about the Roman Empire, wrote letters to them clarifying the truth, and called on them to hold fast to their faith in Jesus.[410] Paul also called on the church leaders to disallow false teachers from teaching in their churches.[411]

But these methods were not sufficient in the eyes of the fed-up popes, and so began a 600-year-long period of terror. The Inquisition spread quickly across Europe. By 1255, the Inquisition was already underway in Sicily, France, Germany, Belgium, Spain, and Italy.[412] Here is a rundown of the steps that were taken at the beginning of the Inquisition:

> In 1215 the Fourth Lateran Council, under Innocent III's leadership, provided for the state's punishment of heretics, the confiscation of their property, excommunication for those unwilling to move against the heretic, and complete forgiveness of sins for those cooperating.
>
> In 1220 the pope took the Inquisition from the hands of the bishops and turned it over to the newly formed Dominicans and nine years later the Synod of Toulouse systematized inquisitorial policies, leaving the alleged heretic with virtually no rights..... The "trial" was secret, and the accused had to prove his innocence ... without the benefit of counsel or knowledge of his accusers.
>
> The final, significant step came in 1252. Pope Innocent IV authorized torture as a

---

[410] Col. 1:23.

[411] 1 Tim. 1:4.

[412] Joseph Blotzer, "Inquisition," *The Catholic Encyclopedia* (New York: Robert Appleton Company, 1910) on CD, Kevin Knight, ed. http://www.newadvent.org/cathen/08026a.htm 2009.

means of getting information and confessions from accused heretics....

Canon law, it is true, forbade a cleric from shedding blood.... He could only hound, and interrogate, and torture the prisoner. If he found the unfortunate person guilty of heresy he turned him over to civil authorities, usually for burning at the stake.

It was an ugly business, but almost everyone, after Augustine, agreed that saving the body by amputating a rotten limb was the path of wisdom. Clearly the Church of Rome was the body and the heretic the rotten limb.[413]

Here is the text from the papal bull, in which Pope Innocent IV limited, but sanctioned, torture in the examination of heretics:

The head of state or ruler must force all the heretics whom he has in custody, provided he does so without killing them or breaking their arms or legs, as actual robbers and murderers of souls and thieves of the sacraments of God and Christian faith, to confess their errors and accuse other heretics whom they know, and specify their motives, and those whom they have seduced, and those who have lodged them and defended them, as thieves and robbers of material goods are made to accuse their accomplices and confess the crimes they have committed.[414]

---

[413] Shelley 211-212.
[414] Pope Innocent IV, *Ad Extirpanda*, Law 25, https://www.documentacatholicaomnia.eu/01p/1252-05-15,_SS_Innocentius_IV,_Bulla_'Ad_Extirpanda',_EN.pdf (accessed April 14, 2025).

Torture was not an option, but rather, it was mandated to be used against anyone who was accused of being a heretic but claimed to be innocent! The only limits placed on the torture were that the victims could not be killed or have their arms or legs broken.

However, a person could avoid torture by coming forward and confessing that they are a heretic. Furthermore, those who chose this option were not subjected to any severe punishment but instead had to perform acts of penance, such as going on a pilgrimage.[415] (These provisions were not in Innocent's bull, but they were normal parts of the Inquisitorial process.)

In the next section of the bull, Innocent wrote:

> And the house, in which a male or female heretic shall be discovered, shall be levelled with the ground, never to be rebuilt; unless it is the master of the house who shall have arranged the discovery of the heretics. And if the master of the house owns other houses in the same neighborhood, all of the other houses shall in like manner be destroyed, and the goods that shall be found in the house and the others related to it shall be dispersed to the populace, and shall belong to whoever carries them off, unless the removers shall be appointed by law. Above all, the master of the house, besides incurring eternal infamy, must pay the government or locality fifty pounds Imperial in coin; if unable to pay, he shall suffer life imprisonment....[416]

This command sounds eerily like the pressure the Nazis put on the citizenry of Europe as they rounded up the Jews. If anyone tried to hide Jewish people, that person would also be sent to a concentration camp. In this case, anyone trying to hide

---

[415] Blotzer "Inquisition."
[416] Pope Innocent IV Law 26.

a heretic would be subject to having all of their possessions taken and their house leveled to the ground. In addition, it was illegal, in perpetuity, for another house to be built on that site. On top of that, a stiff fine was levied, and if the person who tried to hide the heretic was unable to pay the fine, then they would suffer life imprisonment.

Bear in mind, the pope devised these practices and wrote these words. In the entire bull, Jesus is never mentioned, and no Bible verses are quoted. Evidently, Innocent and all the succeeding popes were unconcerned with Jesus' will in dealing with heretics. Those who have read Jesus' teachings know where He stood on these practices. He was opposed to injustice and torture. In the words of Jesus,

> "The Spirit of the L-rd is upon Me, because He anointed Me to preach the gospel to the poor. He has sent Me to proclaim release to the captives, and recovery of sight to the blind, to set free those who are oppressed...."[417]

and,

> "Blessed are those who mourn, for they shall be comforted. Blessed are the gentle, for they shall inherit the earth. Blessed are those who hunger and thirst for righteousness, for they shall be satisfied. Blessed are the merciful, for they shall receive mercy."[418]

Jesus' heart is with the oppressed, not the oppressors.

For six centuries, not a single pope wrote a bull reversing this evil system. In fact, a number of popes during this period had been inquisitors earlier in their careers. It is hard for us to comprehend just how sick and evil the Inquisition was. In short, the Catholic Church set up torture chambers and utilized the

---

[417] Lk. 4:18.
[418] Mt. 5:4-7.

rack, sleep deprivation, waterboarding, and the strappado[419] to coerce confessions.[420]

3. <u>Witch Hunting</u>

This large-scale program was actually a part of the Inquisition. The difference was that the Church was trying witches instead of heretics. The inquisitors were formally sanctioned to try witches in 1484 by Pope Innocent VIII in his papal bull, "Summis Desiderantes." Here are the opening lines of the bull:

> Innocent, bishop, servant of the servants of God, Ad futuram rei memoriam. Desiring with supreme ardor, as pastoral solicitude requires, that the catholic faith in our days everywhere grow and flourish as much as possible, and that all heretical depravity be put far from the territories of the faithful, we freely declare and anew decree this by which our pious desire may be fulfilled, and, all errors being rooted out by our toil as with the hoe of a wise laborer, zeal and devotion to this faith may take deeper hold on the hearts of the faithful themselves.[421]

This introduction to the papal bull describes well the pope's determination to stamp out witchcraft. He pictures himself as a hardworking farmer who would work tirelessly to rid the Catholic Church of the weeds of "heretical depravity" that threatened to spread and cause great damage among the faithful. Surely, over the next three to four centuries, no stone

---

[419] The strappado method of torture consisted of tying the victim's hands behind their backs, and then hoisting and suspending them in the air by their wrists.

[420] Lascelleles 153; Blotzer, "Inquisition."

[421] Pope Innocent VIII, *Summis Desiderantes*, https://en.wikisource.org/wiki/Summis_desiderantes (accessed April 19, 2025).

would be left unturned in Europe in the effort to rid witchcraft from their midst.

Witches were considered to be heretics. But they were distinct in that they drew power from demons in order to commit diabolical acts against their neighbors, or so it was believed. They were typically thought to be women. Some of the most common crimes witches were accused of committing included causing hailstorms to damage others' crops; causing others' dairy cows to produce little, or their own to produce much; causing acrimony in a marriage so that another might swoop in as a lover; having sex with demons; causing miscarriages; stealing infants to kill and eat; and luring others to become witches.[422]

In the premodern world, man's understanding of science and nature was practically nonexistent. This lack of knowledge led to superstitious thinking, which in turn led to people judging their neighbors and blaming them for their problems. Thus, things like bad weather, poor harvests, and miscarriages were thought to be caused by their enemies, whom they deemed to be practicing witchcraft. This toxic way of thinking spread like wildfire amongst the population of Europe, including the popes and most of the clergy.[423] In fact, the Catholic Church viewed witchcraft as such a grave threat that they spared no expense in their attempt to ferret out any and all potential witches.

Only the flimsiest pretext was needed to summon someone to appear before the inquisitor. After all, the Church believed that witches operated in secrecy. Therefore, the Church contended that there would seldom be any solid evidence. The inquisitors often used torture to elicit "confessions" from those

---

[422] Heinrich Kramer and James Sprenger, *Malleus Maleficarum*, (www.forgottenbooks.org: Forgotten Books, 1486, translated by Montague Summers in 1928, republished by Forgotten Books in 2008) 111-112, 159-163, 175, 226, 238-239, 318-319, 398, 425.

[423] So backward was the thinking of the Catholic leadership that they even believed witches could fly on broomsticks (Kramer and Sprenger 175.)

who maintained their innocence. In the end, the Church convicted a multitude of peasants who would typically either be burned at the stake or imprisoned for the rest of their lives.

Following in the wake of Innocent's papal bull, two inquisitors who were experienced in trying witches co-wrote an exhaustive manual that would set the stage for this large-scale program of witch hunting.[424] The name of their manual was *Malleus Maleficarum*, or *The Hammer of Witches*. Following are some quotes detailing how the torture was to be carried out:

> And here, because of the great trouble caused by the stubborn silence of witches, there are several points which the judge must notice, and these are dealt with under their several heads.
>
> And the first is that he must not be too quick to subject a witch to examination, but must pay attention to certain signs which will follow. And he must not be too quick for this reason: unless G-d, through a holy Angel, compels the devil to withhold his help from the witch, she will be so insensible to the pains of torture that she will sooner be torn limb from limb than confess any of the truth.
>
> But the torture is not to be neglected for this reason, for they are not all equally endowed with this power, and also the devil sometimes of his own will permits them to confess their crimes without being compelled by a holy Angel....[425]

and,

---

[424] Kramer and Sprenger 39, 44-45; Herbert Thurston, "Witchcraft," *The Catholic Encyclopedia* (New York: Robert Appleton Company, 1912,) on CD, Kevin Knight, ed. http://www.newadvent.org/cathen/ 15674a.htm 2009; Blech 371.

[425] Kramer and Sprenger 341.

> The next step of the Judge should be that, if after being fittingly tortured she refuses to confess the truth, he should have other engines of torture brought before her, and tell her that she will have to endure these if she does not confess. If then she is not induced by terror to confess, the torture must be continued on the second or third day, but not repeated at that present time unless there should be some fresh indication of its probable success.[426]

These are examples of how to use torture to elicit a confession from an alleged witch. In the first quote, we see that the Church considered it to be evidence that a woman was a witch if she was able to maintain her innocence while being tortured. The thinking was that the devil was enabling her to resist. (Never once in this long manual is the thought entertained that maybe the woman was innocent and was fighting for both the truth and her life.) Therefore, the ordained Catholic judges were encouraged to not grow weary, but to press on with more torture. The judges were instructed in the second quote to use their judgment whether to continue the torture that day or wait until the next day. Furthermore, they had other means of torture at their disposal which they could use either to threaten the accused, or to employ, if need be.

One may ask, how often was this hideous practice employed, and how many suspected witches were burned at the stake? Needless to say, the data is poor, and we do not know the answers to these questions with a high degree of certainty. However, we can say that in this large manual on how to try witches, it is not the case that torture was only permitted under the most extreme circumstances. Rather, witchcraft was presented as a grave threat to Catholicism, and torture was presented as a viable tool to be used as need be. So surely, a very

---

[426] Kramer and Sprenger 346.

large number of women were victimized by the Catholic Church during this period.

Here is a quote from the Catholic Encyclopedia regarding the number of victims:

> The arguments, for example, which three hundred years ago convinced our fathers of the existence of witches and sent millions of them to the torture and the stake, make no impression on our more enlightened minds.[427]

It should be noted that the Catholic Encyclopedia is a pro-Catholic source, so you would not expect them to err on the high side. Nonetheless, "millions" sounds high. It makes sense that this many cases could have been opened over such a long period of time. But hopefully there were fewer tortures and even fewer executions.

Jesus was tortured. Then He was executed. So too, in the case of this grave crime against humanity, justice was denied.

Power corrupts.

* * * * *

Another serious, long-term Catholic issue was the sale of indulgences to finance wars and the construction of the Vatican. Oddly enough, it was this issue that ultimately led to the Reformation. Simply put, indulgences were a kind of "get out of jail free card" to reduce or eliminate one's stay in purgatory. Catholics believe that if you turn to Jesus, you will be forgiven and go to heaven. But before you get there, you must first suffer in purgatory in order to pay the debt you owe to G-d for your sins. They believe you can do penance in this life to reduce your stay in purgatory, or you can buy an indulgence.[428]

---

[427] Joseph Wilhelm, "Protestantism," *The Catholic Encyclopedia* (New York: Robert Appleton Company, 1911,) on CD, Kevin Knight, ed. http://www.newadvent.org/cathen/12495a.htm 2009.
[428] Lascelles 145-147.

The popes of the Renaissance made a lot of money for the Catholic Church by selling indulgences. Obviously, wherever large sums of money are being handled, corruption grows. The sale of indulgences was no different, and in fact, it was "riddled with corruption."[429] But along came a "wild boar" of a man named Martin Luther.[430] Luther was born a peasant, yet his family believed in education. On his way back to college to study law, a bolt of lightning knocked him to the ground.[431] He took it as a sign from G-d and decided to become a monk. The results of this course change were quite different in some ways, but not very different in others. He remained poor, and he still studied, but instead of studying law, he studied the Bible.

Luther was a flawed man. He was boorish, abrasive, and dogmatic. But he was also a man of integrity and a critical thinker, and he had a spine of steel. Luther received his doctorate in theology, and he went on to teach the Bible at the University of Wittenberg in Germany. In the course of his studies, he came to see that the Catholic Church had added requirements to the gospel message presented in the Bible.[432] Namely, in the Bible, salvation is presented as a free gift which was paid for by Jesus' death on the cross.[433] Hence, Luther opposed the role of the sacraments in salvation, the presumption that a priest had any authority to absolve a person's sins, and the idea that indulgences contributed anything towards salvation.[434] Luther's root issue was that the Catholic Church had veered away from the Bible in its theology and practices. He believed that the Bible took precedence over Church tradition and papal statements.[435] In 1517, he wrote his famous 95 Theses, challenging the practice of selling indulgences. Sparks flew between Luther and Pope Leo X, and the pope excommunicated him and ordered his writings to

---

[429] Duffy 200.
[430] Shelley 237.
[431] Ibid., 238.
[432] Ibid., 239-241.
[433] Ibid., 239; Kittelson 109, 114.
[434] Shelley 240-241; Kittelson 113-114.
[435] Lascelles 204.

be burned. But it was too late, Luther's message resonated with people, and the Reformation took off.[436] Of course, the Reformation resulted in Protestantism, which quickly spread across Europe.[437]

Some of the positive changes coming from the Reformation included a new emphasis on the Bible in which people began to read the Bible for themselves; a return to the Biblical message of salvation through Jesus' work on the cross alone; and the establishment of a less hierarchical church that more closely resembled the Church of the first century.[438] However, not all that was wrong with Catholicism was corrected by the Protestants. For example, Luther continued to espouse anti-Semitism and witch hunting. Sure enough, these sinful practices remained in Protestantism.[439]

*　*　*　*　*

A key question is, how well did the Catholic Church and Protestant churches do in carrying out the Great Commission during this 1,700-year-long time period? Unfortunately, the answer is, not very well.

Of course, the damage to the cause of Christ that resulted from the Church's massive sinful programs is incalculable. It is impossible to say how many people around the world recoiled in disgust as they witnessed the Catholic Church perpetrate acts of violence in the name of Christ.

In terms of the Church evangelizing, or taking the gospel message to the ends of the earth, the results were weak for most of those 1,700 years. It took up to about 1200 CE for the Church to reach the areas in Europe and around the Mediterranean Sea that the apostles did not get to in the first century. Specifically,

---

[436] Duffy 200, 203-204.

[437] Ibid., 207; Johann Peter Kirsch, "The Reformation," The Catholic Encyclopedia (New York: Robert Appleton Company, 1911,) on CD, Kevin Knight, ed. http://www.newadvent.org/cathen/12700b.htm 2009.

[438] Duffy 201; Shelley 241-243.

[439] Lascelles p. 205; Thurston, "Witchcraft."

Catholicism spread to Germany, France, the British Isles, Scandinavia, and northern Africa, among others.[440] Following that, the spread of the gospel slowed down until the late 15th century, when the Age of Exploration began. The Catholic Church tagged along with the explorers and established churches among the indigenous peoples in the newly discovered lands. For their part, the Protestants started getting involved in missions in the 18th century. But it was not until the 19th century that missions work really took off amongst the Protestant churches.[441]

*   *   *   *   *

Almost everything written thus far in this chapter has been negative. Yet, there were some positives too. But we only have a chapter to cover 17 centuries and will not be able to go into those. If this chapter was about another subject, such as the earth's surface, we would not be identifying any beautiful objects in nature such as wildflowers or ponds surrounded by cattails. Rather, we would only be examining landforms that are visible from a high altitude, such as mountain ranges, large rivers, and deserts. Unfortunately, all of the major features of Church history during this period were negative. But that does not mean there were no wildflowers and scenic ponds during this period. Surely there were some good popes and times during these centuries. For example, one of the popes we cited was a reformer—Leo IX. He fought to stem the tide of moral decay that was occurring in the Church in his days. In a sense, these 17 centuries were like the divided kingdom period in ancient Israel. In this era of Catholic history, the leadership was generally bad, sin abounded, and the witness of the Church for Jesus was impotent. However, every now and then a godly pope would be selected who would fight against sin and corruption. But overall, the Church failed in its G-d-given mission during these centuries.

---

[440] J. Herbert Kane, *Christian Missions in Biblical Perspective* (Grand Rapids, Michigan: Baker Book House Company, 1976) 258.
[441] Kane 260.

I understand that this evaluation of Catholic history is unflattering. Please know that my goal in writing this chapter is not to bash the Catholic Church. My goal is to tell the true story of what happened during this period.

Needless to say, not everyone will agree with these conclusions. In his encyclical, *Mit Brennender Sorge*, written in 1937 in the days leading up to WW II, Pope Pius XI castigated the Nazis for their anti-Catholic policies. In point 34, the pope issued the following defense of Catholicism:

> You are often told about the human deficiencies which mar the history of the Church: why ignore the exploits which fill her history, the saints she begot, the blessing that came upon Western civilization from the union between the Church and your people?[442]

Evidently, the pope was hearing criticism of Catholic history. Thus, he issued this retort. Unfortunately, this statement was tangential to the pope's main argument in this encyclical, and he did not offer any specifics about Catholic history to support it.

Again, my goal in this chapter is not to denigrate anyone; it is to portray Christian history accurately. And the truth is that the Church's overall record is bad. Having said that, I feel compelled to recognize that the Church's record is not reflective of the way many Catholics I know live their lives. Of course, none of them are perfect, but they each have a sincere faith and are doing their best to follow Jesus. For example, my sister-in-law's mother is Catholic, and she has a heart of compassion. I value her and appreciate her sincere concern for the difficulties that my children have had to face. My father is 95 as I write this chapter, and he just finished a week in the hospital. He has some Catholic friends whom he has known for years. They live in a different city, but he is still in touch with them. Along with some other members of their church, they have been praying

---

[442] Pope Pius XI, *Mit Brennender Sorge* (Rome: Libreria Editrice Vaticana, 1937) 34.

regularly for my dad. I appreciate their prayers greatly and admire their faith. I also have a friend who is an Irish Catholic. He has a heart for those in need. A number of years ago, he found a home in a church named after St. Francis of Assisi in which they emphasize serving the poor. Year in and year out, they quietly obey Jesus by looking out for the needs of "the least of these."[443] I could go on. Thank G-d, for He is able to bypass sinful Christian leaders and personally reach people in their hearts. He does this both to reach the lost and to guide His children. I have no doubt that He has reached a myriad of people down through the ages, even during the darkest days of Church history.

---

[443] Mt. 25:31-46.

14

CHRISTIANITY IN THE MODERN AGE

Art blossomed in the Renaissance period, and humanity turned to reason in the Age of Enlightenment. But it was really the freedom won by the colonists in the American Revolution, and the prosperity generated by the Industrial Revolution, that launched the world into the Modern Age.

Prior to the American and French Revolutions, the European peoples had suffered under feudalism for multiple centuries. But finally, sweet freedom came, and the creativity of the masses was unleashed. Rapid developments in science and industry followed, and the world would never be the same. The two revolutions took place in the late 1700s. The Industrial Age began about the same time. For simplicity's sake, we will say the Modern Age began in 1800.

Ever since then, societal change has accelerated. Our lives have been affected tremendously both by technology and a shift in cultural values. Instead of working primarily on farms or in the trades, many of us now sit at computers and perform our work using software. We drive cars instead of riding horses. We can fly a plane from one coast to the other in under six hours instead of going by wagon train, which could take months. Today, we have the world's knowledge at our fingertips on our smartphones. No longer do we need to go to the library and perform a tedious search of the books and magazines available at that particular library.

Another major change in the modern world has to do with warfare. There will never be another 100 Years' War. Gone are the days of rifles that fire one round.

Yet, the change in morality has affected us on an even deeper level. For example, divorce went from practically unheard of to commonplace. The effects stemming from this change in the lives of parents and children are incalculable. Moral values like patience, self-control, and honesty have diminished. One indicator of how well our society is doing is the rise in school shootings. People blame guns, but Americans had guns long before these events began. Why didn't people shoot their classmates then? Few people consider the possibility that school shootings are to a large degree a side effect of the changes in our moral fabric. Perhaps the most glaring aspect of our moral descent has come in the area of sexuality. One hundred years ago, a person would have been deeply ashamed to lose their virginity before marriage. Now it is just the opposite; it is considered embarrassing if you remain a virgin into adulthood. Of course, sex is G-d's idea. He gave it to us as a gift to make marriages special and to bring babies into the world. The more sex is engaged in outside of marriage, the more people damage their souls. Indeed, it is a systemic problem as children are exposed to sexual content at a very early age in our schools today. Beyond that, imagine the damage that pornography on the internet has caused.

Surely, there have been some good changes as well. For example, our society has gone out of its way to provide access and assistance to handicapped people so that they can experience a meaningful life. Perhaps the greatest change has come in the area of racism. Once an everyday, accepted part of life, racism is now disdained and is slowly fading away. Another positive change is the improvement in women's rights in the modern world.

Needless to say, all of our lives are so very different from how they would have been if we were born in the 1700s. Of course, these far-reaching changes have affected Christianity as well.

On one hand, the message of Christianity has not changed at all. We are still sinners who stand guilty before G-d, and people can still accept Jesus' death on the cross as a payment for their sins. On the other hand, church structures, practices, and beliefs have been influenced by the modern world. In both the Catholic Church and the mainline Protestant churches, there have been some good changes and some bad ones.

In the Catholic Church, they felt the heat. For instance, it was long held that the popes were infallible. But eventually, that stance became untenable. First, there were all the morally repugnant statements written down by the popes over the centuries. Then science entered the picture. Galileo was sentenced to imprisonment for the rest of his life for putting forward that the earth revolves around the sun.[444] Once modern science definitively proved the pope wrong, the Church had to address it. The Church responded by stating that not all of the popes' statements are infallible. Rather, only when the popes issue ex cathedra statements are they speaking infallibly.[445] Ex cathedra statements are official pronouncements made by the popes that deal with matters of faith and morality. The Catholic Church also held a council named Vatican II, starting in 1962, to deal with other such criticisms of Catholicism. Reforms coming out of Vatican II included, among others, using local languages as opposed to Latin during church services and rescinding their former, anti-Semitic position that the Jews were responsible for Jesus' death.[446]

During the Modern Age, the Catholic Church has struggled with some major scandals. One has to do with Pope Pius XII

---

[444] Duffy 234-235.
[445] McBrien 103-104.
[446] Duffy 361-362.

during World War II. He was the wrong man for the moment. Pius was a cartoonishly weak man. Though he was apprised of what was going on in the death camps, he refused to condemn the evil. Opportunity after opportunity fell in his lap in which he could have redeemed himself by calling out the genocide, but each time he stood down. For example:

> In November 1941 Pius XII would learn ... about the unfolding mass murder of Europe's Jews when Father Pirro Scavizzi, an Italian military chaplain, gave him a bloodcurdling account on his return from the Eastern front....
>
> Scavizzi delivered an impassioned letter from a Polish priest.... the priest said that the Poles could not understand what they termed the Vatican's "crime of silence." He begged the pope to make his voice heard.[447]

and,

> On September 22, 1942, Roosevelt's envoy, Myron Taylor met again with the pope, this time handing him a report documenting German atrocities. "It is widely believed," Taylor told him, "that Your word of condemnation would hearten all others who are working to save these thousands from suffering and death."[448] He coupled this appeal with a long memo, addressed to Cardinal Maglione, containing reports of the ongoing slaughter of Poland's Jews. It painted a horrifying picture:

---

[447] David I. Kertzer, *The Pope at War* (New York: Random House, 2022) 215-216.

[448] Taylor memo given to Pius XII , September 22, 1942, FDR Library, psfa 4942, p. 40. The original is found at ASRS, AA.EE.SS., Pio XII, parte 1, Germania, posiz. 742, ff. 16r-19r.

Liquidation of the Warsaw Ghetto is taking place. Without any distinction all Jews, irrespective of age or sex, are being removed from the Ghetto in groups and shot. Their corpses are utilized for making fats and their bones for the manufacture of fertilizer.... Jews deported from Germany, Belgium, Holland, France, and Slovakia are sent to be butchered.... Caravans of such deportees being transported in cattle cars are often seen.

Taylor's memo concluded, "I should much appreciate it if Your Eminence could inform me whether the Vatican has any information that would tend to confirm the reports contained in this memorandum. If so, I should like to know whether the Holy Father has any suggestions as to any practical manner in which the forces of civilized public opinion could be utilized in order to prevent a continuation of these barbarities."[449]

Although a note in the recently opened secretariat files shows that the pope read this memo immediately, he was slow to respond....

On October 10 Cardinal Maglione finally handed the pope's response to Tittmann [the US representative to the Vatican]. The statement, unsigned, acknowledged that reports of "severe measures taken against non-Aryans" had also reached the Holy See from other sources, "but

---

[449] Taylor memo to Maglione, September 26, 1942, FDR Library, psfa 4942, pp. 138-139. The Italian translation of the memo is found at ASRS, AA.EE.SS., Pio XII, parte Extracta, Germania, Extracta, posiz. 742, Ebrei, ff. 21r-23r, along with a note "Il Santo Padre ne ha preso visione" (The Holy Father has seen it), f. 14r.

that up to the present time it has not been possible to verify the accuracy thereof." The pope had accepted Monsignor Dell'Acqua's advice. Best to offer the Allies no confirmation of the reports of the Nazis' mass murder of Europe's Jews and risk having the Vatican invoked in confirming the Allies' charge. In fact, best not even to use the word "Jews" at all.[450]

So, Pius lied, refused even to name the Jews as the victims, and would not sign his name to his statement. The main reason for his behavior is that he was a coward. The stated reason is because he was afraid that if he spoke out against the Nazis, Hitler would persecute the Catholics in Germany and in the other lands he controlled.[451]

The other major scandal taking place in the Catholic Church in the Modern Age is the epidemic of pedophiliac assaults in which priests have been preying on the boys in their churches. Despite a multi-decade cover-up, the staggering numbers of guilty priests and their victims are becoming clearer. This scandal extends back to at least 90 years ago.[452] It spans multiple dioceses and even continents.

Like the large-scale scandals of the past, first and foremost, innumerable victims have suffered irreparable damage. Another victim is Jesus' good name, as the Catholic Church has again repulsed the people of the world with its conduct.

---

[450] David I. Kertzer 239-243. Tittmann to Hull, October 10, 1942, NARA, RG 59, CDF 1940-44, 740.00116, box 2917, pp. 2, 3; also published in FRUS 1942, vol. 3, pp. 777-78. The Vatican copy is found at ASRS, AA.EE.SS., Pio XII, parte Extracta, Germania, posiz. 742, f. 27r. Over the next many months, Monsignor Bernardini, the nuncio in Bern, would pass along to the Vatican a series of documents from Jewish organizations detailing the extermination of the Jews of Central and Eastern Europe. AAV. *Arch. Nunz. Svizzera*, b. 221, fasc. 626, ff. 93r-120r.

[451] David I. Kertzer 84, 236.

[452] Ibid., 8, 63-64.

Yet, there has also been a good witness of Jesus presented by the Catholic Church in the Modern Age. Namely, Mother Teresa could not have done a better job of presenting the love of Jesus to the world. Her goal was simply to love and care for those in need. As a young nun, she moved to India, where she was called by G-d to care for the poor. She obeyed, and for the rest of her life, this angel gave up her life in service to some of the poorest people on earth. G-d blessed her efforts, and many other nuns followed her example and joined her. She founded the Missionaries of Charity, and over the years they have sent out teams of sisters to serve the poor in cities all over the world.

In Matthew 25, Jesus said:

> "Then the King will say to those on His right, 'Come, you who are blessed of My Father, inherit the kingdom prepared for you from the foundation of the world. For I was hungry, and you gave Me *something* to eat; I was thirsty, and you gave Me *something* to drink; I was a stranger, and you invited Me in; naked, and you clothed Me; I was sick, and you visited Me; I was in prison, and you came to Me.' Then the righteous will answer Him, 'L-rd, when did we see You hungry, and feed You, or thirsty, and give You *something* to drink? And when did we see You a stranger, and invite You in, or naked, and clothe You? When did we see You sick, or in prison, and come to You?' The King will answer and say to them, 'Truly I say to you, to the extent that you did it to one of these brothers of Mine, *even* the least *of them*, you did it to Me.'[453]

Mother Teresa followed these words, and in so doing, she bore witness to Jesus' heart of compassion for the poor.

---

[453] Mt. 25:34-40.

Similar to the Catholic Church, the mainline Protestant denominations have both represented Jesus well at times and misrepresented Him at other times. One alarming problem in the Protestant denominations has been the movement amongst some of the pastors away from belief in the Bible. For example, in their book, *Are We Living in the End Times?*, authors Tim LaHaye and Jerry B. Jenkins wrote:

> What would you think of an Episcopal bishop who loudly championed the views that:
>
> * the resurrection of Christ was not a real event but a legend
> * there was no empty tomb, no angels, no appearances
> * no reasonable person could believe in the literal interpretation of the Bible
> * the virgin of a literal Bible—the virgin of annunciation, Bethlehem, and the manger—"will have to go"
> * the church should actively endorse and even celebrate homosexual behavior, as well as heterosexual liaisons outside of marriage
>
> John Shelby Spong, the Episcopal bishop of Newark, New Jersey, has enthusiastically promoted all of those heretical views in his many controversial books. In his latest work, *Why Christianity Must Change or Die*—which he says is the summation of his life's work—he insists that the first-century ideas that shaped the New Testament are hopelessly outdated and provincial and must be discarded if Christianity is to survive in the modern world....[454]

---

[454] Tim LaHaye and Jerry B. Jenkins, *Are We Living in the End Times?*

Spong fundamentally disagrees with the Bible. In 1 Corinthians, Paul wrote:

> ...if there is no resurrection of the dead, not even Christ has been raised; and if Christ has not been raised, then our preaching is vain, your faith also is vain.[455]

Bishop Spong released his book in 1999. But in the above passage from 1 Corinthians, we see that there have always been opponents of Jesus, even in the first century. Needless to say, if you take Jesus out of the Christian message, then you are left with nothing. The problem is that Bishop Spong is not alone. There are many other Protestant seminary professors and pastors who believe as he does.[456] He is just the only one brazen enough to state his beliefs so clearly. The result of the influx of unbelieving leaders in the modern Protestant churches has been a decrease in both membership and relevance.

Yet, there have also been times in the Modern Age in which the Protestant churches have done a laudable job representing Jesus. Two big ones include abolition and the evangelistic movement started by Billy Graham. The abolitionist movements in England and America were both largely Christian movements. In England, the Quakers led the way and were joined by some big names from the Anglican Church, William Wilberforce and John Newton, as well as John Wesley from the Methodist Church. This movement's efforts led to the passage of the Slave Trade Act in 1807 and, eventually, to the ending of this atrocious human institution within the British Empire. In America, Quakers were again at the forefront of the abolitionist movement dating all the way back to the late 1600s. Of course, slavery finally ended in America when the North defeated the South in the Civil War. Certainly, the Christians who were the driving forces of these movements were on the right side

---

(Wheaton, Illinois: Tyndale House Publishers, Inc., 1999) 68.
[455] 1 Cor. 15:13-14.
[456] LaHaye and Jenkins 74-78.

of history. They brought glory to Jesus, whose heart is with the downtrodden.[457]

Billy Graham was a Southern Baptist. He was given a gift by G-d to be able to captivate a stadium full of people. Specifically, he taught them the message of forgiveness through the blood of Jesus. For over six decades, he filled stadiums and led a multitude of people to salvation. But it was even better than that. Prior to each event, his team spent months in each city training volunteers from local churches to meet and invite the new Christians to their churches. Only G-d knows how much these new believers' lives changed and how many people they went on to reach for Jesus.

*   *   *   *   *

Unsurprisingly, while society was rapidly changing, G-d was at work as well. Specifically, He moved in the second half of the 20th century, and new churches formed that were quite different from the Catholic and Protestant churches. In fact, to some degree, the new churches resemble the local, dynamic churches of the first century. Correspondingly, there has been a great harvest of souls in America. In addition, there has been a renewed emphasis on foreign missions, which has resulted in tremendous growth in the number of Christians in both developed countries, like China, and countries in the third world.

In the 1960s, young people in America protested the Vietnam War, listened to rock music, and experimented with drugs and sex. And one more thing, many of them found Jesus. Of course, it is no surprise that Jesus loved the hippies, for He loves everyone. The 2023 movie, *Jesus Revolution*, tells the story of this revival among the youth of California.[458] In the movie, a middle-aged pastor, Chuck Smith, ministered to the young people who were coming to Christ in droves.

---

[457] Luke 4:18-19.

[458] *Jesus Revolution*, directed by Jon Erwin, (2023; Hollywood, CA: Kingdom Story Company/Lionsgate,) Prime Video.

Contemporaneous to what was happening in California, all over America, G-d was inspiring other people to start churches. These churches were unaffiliated with any of the mainline denominations or each other. They arose amongst suburbanites, people in the inner cities, and both blacks and whites. Each of these churches is culturally different and unique. But they have all moved away from ritualistic services. Rather, they teach the Bible, emphasize the message of salvation through the blood of Jesus, and are pro-Israel. They have also moved away from the clergy/laity model. Instead, like the first-century churches, they teach the importance of every member playing their role to advance the cause of Christ. The results have been similar all over the country. There has been a great harvest of souls as people are meeting Jesus and falling in love with the Bible. People are hungry for a church experience like this, in which they study the Bible and follow Jesus together. These churches are known as "Megachurches" because they have grown so large. Christians who go to these churches are called Evangelicals. Jesus is their savior, and G-d has changed their lives, so how could they not then tell other people about what they have found?[459]

Maybe you know someone who goes to one of these churches, and you are thinking that they are not perfect, and neither is their church. Of course, you are correct—they are imperfect. Yet, hopefully they are making an effort to follow Christ. For, G-d is gracious, and He uses imperfect people who are trying to do His will. G-d also works with them to help them grow, which He does with imperfect churches as well.

The other very positive development during the Modern Age is the dramatic change in missions. In fact, there have been two main changes: the methodology employed by missionaries on the mission field and the zeal of the missions community to reach every people group on earth.

---

[459] It should be noted that there are also other churches and denominations included in the Evangelical movement, such as the Baptist Church.

Missions work following the first century was fundamentally flawed. For example, during the Age of Exploration, the Catholic Church worked in conjunction with the Spanish and Portuguese rulers who were conquering and exploiting the indigenous peoples. Obviously, these unions reduced the missionaries' effectiveness to some degree. The missionaries did build hospitals and schools to care for the local people and educate them. Certainly, these efforts were noble. But it was also standard practice for the missionaries to introduce their languages and cultures to the native peoples for their betterment. The problem with that practice is that it is arrogant. After all, who are we to tell other people that they should change their language or clothing to be the same as ours and to adopt our culture as though our way of life is superior?

Thankfully, this flaw was addressed over the course of the 20th century. The practice of cultural imposition was seen for what it was—unnecessary and offensive. It had been holding earlier missionaries back from greater success. Therefore, it became taboo among missionaries, who instead started to wear the clothes of the peoples they were living amongst. As Paul says in 1 Corinthians:

> For though I am free from all *men*, I have made myself a slave to all, so that I may win more. To the Jews I became as a Jew, so that I might win Jews; to those who are under the Law, as under the Law though not being myself under the Law, so that I might win those who are under the Law; to those who are without law, as without law, though not being without the law of G-d but under the law of Christ, so that I might win those who are without law. To the weak I became weak, that I might win the weak; I have become all things to all men, so that I may by all means save some.[460]

---

[460] 1 Cor. 9:19-22.

Hence, cultural differences were seen as irrelevant. After all, why would you put an unnecessary obstacle in front of people, making it more difficult for them to come to Christ? The goal is for them to know Jesus and go to heaven, not to learn to live like a Westerner. Furthermore, this change in methodology enabled the new, indigenous Christians to more easily evangelize the rest of their people. For, the new Christians did not have to change their external appearance, but rather continued to look and speak like everyone else in their nation. Sure enough, this new philosophy has led to greater results.

In the Catholic Church, these matters were addressed early in the 20th century when Pope Benedict XV wrote the encyclical *Maximum Illud*. In *Maximum Illud*, he laid out a strategy in which indigenous people would be trained as clergy, and they would become the spiritual leaders of their people.[461] Furthermore, Benedict directed the missionaries to only represent Jesus and not to be involved in seeking a profit for their home nations.[462]

The Holy Spirit has moved substantial numbers of Christians in the Modern Age to approach the Great Commission with the same passion and commitment that the Christians in the first century had. These missionaries are Catholics, Protestants, members of the new megachurches, and new, indigenous converts.

In 1910, in Edinburgh, Scotland, a group of missions-minded Christians gathered to consider world evangelization. Given the modern technological advances of that day, they felt it might be possible to fulfill the Great Commission and evangelize the entire world within their lifetime.[463] Two world wars and the Great Depression shattered their goal. Nonetheless, the Holy Spirit continued to work in the hearts of Christians. In 1974, in

---

[461] Pope Benedict XV, Maximum Illud (Rome: Libreria Editrice Vaticana, 1919) points 14-16.
[462] Pope Benedict XV points 19-20.
[463] Matt Bennett, "3 Eras Shape Modern Missions," October 11, 2023, https://abwe.org/blog/3-eras-shape-modern-missions (accessed May 5, 2025).

Lausanne, Switzerland, another conference was held in which this goal was brought back to life.[464] Ever since, this goal has burned in the hearts of an army of likeminded Christian workers who have devoted their lives to its accomplishment.

In Lausanne, Ralph Winter taught that the Greek word *ethne* should not be translated as *nations* but as *people groups*.[465] These groups are not political nations but rather sociolinguistic groups, of which there are typically multiple per nation. By designating the peoples of the earth in such fashion, Winter accomplished two objectives. One, he clarified the mission given by Jesus to the Church, and, two, he ignited the Christian world by showing them the finish line they needed to reach. This word is found in Matthew 24:14, in which Jesus says:

> This gospel of the kingdom shall be preached
> in the whole world as a testimony to all the
> nations, and then the end will come.

The accomplishment of this goal is one of the "signs" Jesus gave in His famous speech, the Olivet Discourse, and it will take place shortly before Jesus returns to earth at the end of time. The word *nations* in this verse is the Greek word *ethne*. Hence, Jesus was saying that when Christians have penetrated every people group on earth with the gospel, the end will come. This is the mission of the Church. Winter's message was well received. The Christians left the conference and set about accurately dividing up humanity into these groups. Once they did that, then it was time to strategize the best way to evangelize each unreached people group. Unreached people groups are defined as groups with "few, if any, indigenous believers, missionaries, Bibles, Christian resources, or churches."[466] Then

---

[464] Ibid.

[465] Ibid.

[466] Joshua Project, "Global Mission Trends," https://view.officeapps.live.com/op/view.aspx?src=https%3A%2F%2 Fjoshuaproject%2Enet%3A443%2Fassets%2Fmedia%2Fppt%2FGlob

it was time to go to work. It was a daunting task, but it had a definable workload. Ever since, interdenominational mission agencies have been diligently working to send out mission teams to all of the different people groups, including both the unreached people groups and the ones in which there is already some level of Christian witness.

Of course, it is not just about making the gospel available to everyone on earth; it is about reaching people for eternity. Another change in methodology that missionaries have been implementing in modern times is letting go of things like establishing churches that are extensions of Western churches. Also, the new churches don't need to look like they do in our culture. For example, in Iran, it is a capital offense to convert from Islam to Christianity. So, missionaries cannot just get a visa, rent a building, put a cross on it, and start handing out Bibles. Rather, Bibles must be smuggled into the country. Furthermore, G-d is working directly in Iran. He is touching peoples' hearts, appearing to people in dreams, and arranging encounters in which people who are open to Jesus wind up bumping into Christians at work or on a bus.[467] As they meet and start to talk, the Holy Spirit nudges the Christian to mention Jesus. Then, the open person hears the message and receives Him as their savior, either on the spot or not long thereafter. The problem is that the new Christian cannot go to a church to begin to learn the Bible. Instead, missionaries meet with just one or two new Christians to teach them the Bible, and this is the model for churches today in Iran. After all, Jesus said, "For where two or three have gathered together in My name, I am there in their midst."[468] The obvious advantage of these tiny churches is safety, as the Iranian government has been torturing and putting to death those who are caught evangelizing. But the other advantage is that these churches are successful. Jesus is

---

alMissionTrends%2Epptx&wdSlideId=389&wdModeSwitchTime=177 6707564351 (accessed April 20, 2026) Presentation - slide 25.

[467] VOM (The Voice of the Martyrs), *Iran: Desperate for God* (Bartlesville, OK: Living Sacrifice Book Company, 2006) 7-8, 60, 137-138, 141.

[468] Mt. 18:20.

precious to the new Christians, and they are hungry to both learn the Bible and follow its direction. In a relatively short amount of time, they go on to share their faith, and then they become the teachers in new two- or three-person churches. This model leads to exponential growth in the spread of the gospel. Historically, missions work, in which church buildings were constructed and parishes were established, produced only incremental growth.

There is another significant development that is taking place today. Namely, there is one final people whom G-d is reaching out to—His people, the Jews! He set them aside for the better part of 2,000 years while He worked primarily with Gentile Christians. But Daniel predicted that after a gap of time, G-d would one day use them again as His representatives on earth. Specifically, He will use them for the final seven years of human history.[469] Today we are seeing signs that the end of history is drawing near, and we are starting to see Jewish people coming to Christ. These Jews believe in Jesus as their savior, but they also still follow the Law and observe the practices of Rabbinic Judaism, at least to some degree. This movement, which is known as Messianic Judaism, began in the 1800s.[470] But it really started gaining steam in the 1970s, when "significant numbers" of Jewish people started to place their faith in Jesus.[471] Albeit, the vast majority of Jewish people today still do not believe that Jesus is the Messiah.

*　　*　　*　　*　　*

Praise G-d! He turned the Christian Church around in the Modern Age. The megachurches resemble the dynamic local churches of the first century. Indeed, that is their goal. Evangelical Christians love the Bible. They believe that every Christian has an important role to play in the cause of Christ,

---

[469] Dan. 9:24-27.
[470] Richard Harvey, *Mapping Messianic Jewish Theology* (Bletchley, Milton Keynes, England: Paternoster, 2009) 3.
[471] Ibid., 2.

and G-d is using them to reach the lost, both here at home and overseas.

Of course, the question remains the same for evaluating how well the Church has done in these centuries. Namely, how well has the Church carried out the Great Commission? The answer is, thanks to G-d's help, much better than it did during the previous 17 centuries.

Christian missions have been very successful in Africa, Latin America, and Asia. For example, in 1976 in Africa, it was estimated that 20,000 people a day were accepting Jesus as their savior![472] As of 2020, approximately 67% of the world's Christians resided in Africa, Latin America, and Asia, as opposed to only 33% in North America and Europe.[473] In addition, there has been tremendous growth in the number of Christians in China, which is opposed to G-d, and in Iran and Indonesia, which are opposed to Christianity.[474]

Yet, there is still much work left to be done to fulfill the Great Commission. Currently, 60 percent of all non-Christians live in unreached people groups, and they have little to no chance of hearing the gospel message right now.[475] Furthermore, 96% of all missionaries today go to reached people groups, for example in Africa or South America, as opposed to unreached people groups.[476] A big part of the problem is that a large percentage of the unreached people groups are in Muslim countries and India, where it is dangerous and illegal to evangelize.[477] Herein lies one

---

[472] Kane 261.

[473] Joshua Project, "Global Mission Trends," (accessed April 20, 2026) slide 40.

[474] Joshua Project, "Global Mission Trends," (accessed April 20, 2026) slides 12-14.

[475] Joshua Project, "Clarifying the Remaining Task," https://media.joshuaproject.net/public/assets/media/handouts/clarif ying-the-remaining-task.pdf (accessed April 20, 2026) Infographic.

[476] Joshua Project, "Frontier Peoples Overview," https://media.joshuaproject.net/public/assets/media/handouts/fronti er-peoples-overview.pdf (accessed April 20, 2026) Infographic.

[477] Joshua Project, "Global Mission Trends," (accessed April 20, 2026) slide 28; Joshua Project, "Why India,"

additional similarity between first-century Christians and Christians today. Namely, just as the Romans brutally persecuted the Christians of the first century, so too, missionaries today may have to face violent persecution on a large scale. Yet, Jesus calls on Christians to be willing to make this sacrifice.[478] Jesus was incredibly brave, and now He is calling on His people to be brave.

---

https://media.joshuaproject.net/public/assets/media/handouts/why-india.pdf (accessed April 20, 2026) Infographic.
[478] Lk. 9:22-23; Jn. 15:18-20; Acts 7:54-8:3; 2 Cor. 11:23-18; 2 Tim. 3:10-12; 1 Pet. 4:12-14.

15

THE REGATHERING
OF THE JEWS

Jacob treasured the promises G-d made to Abraham regarding the Jewish people. An important part of G-d's promises has to do with the plot of land He picked just for them. In Jacob's day, it was known as Canaan. Jacob grew up there, but after he tricked his father by posing as his brother, he had to run away. So, he left and went to stay with his uncle in Mesopotamia. However, he returned many years later and lived in the land that was promised to him and his descendants. Eventually, when he was quite old, he had to leave again. This time he was forced out by a famine. He went to Egypt, where he stayed until he died. On his deathbed, Jacob called on his sons to bury his remains in the land of Canaan in a cave that Abraham had purchased many years before.[479] And so they did.

Like his father Jacob, Joseph valued the things of G-d above all else. He too wanted to leave Egypt and return to Canaan. But he became old, and he knew it was not to be. He could tell that

----

[479] Gen. 49:30; 50:13.

the Jews were going to be stuck in Egypt for a long time. Yet he had faith that G-d's will would be done and that the Jews would return to their land one day. After all, G-d is faithful to His promises. Therefore, Joseph charged his family to take his remains with them and bury him in the Promised Land once they were able to leave Egypt. A few centuries later, at the first Passover, they finally left. Moses made sure to take Joseph's bones with them.[480] In fact, for the next forty years, they transported Joseph's remains until Joshua laid his bones in the ground for good in Shechem.[481]

Wisely, Jacob and Joseph trusted that G-d would fulfill His promises. Of course, they had no idea that their descendants would go on to rebel so badly on more than one occasion that they would be removed from the land.[482] Joseph died approximately 3,750 years ago. No one from that day would have ever believed the future that lay in store for the Jews. But we know what they have endured down through the ages. In fact, their mere existence today is so improbable that it is proof of G-d. In the Modern Age, we have witnessed the hand of G-d acting on behalf of the Jews, as He has started the final regathering! Surely, the complete fulfillment of all of G-d's promises to the Jews cannot be too far in the future.

Down through the ages, the Jews' existence in their land has been impacted by either foreign occupation or threats of war. Their experience has fallen far short of the glorious promises that G-d made to Abraham, Isaac, and Jacob. For example, on his way out of Canaan the first time, Jacob was given the following prophetic dream by G-d:

> And he had a dream, and behold, a ladder was
> set on the earth with its top reaching to heaven;
> and behold, the angels of G-d were ascending

---

[480] Gen. 50:24-25; Ex. 13:19.

[481] Josh. 24:32.

[482] The Northern Kingdom was exiled by Assyria in 722 BCE, and the Southern Kingdom was exiled by Babylonia in 586 BCE and Rome in 70 CE.

and descending on it. And behold, the L-rd stood above it and said, "I am the L-rd, the G-d of your father Abraham and the G-d of Isaac; the land on which you lie, I will give it to you and to your descendants. Your descendants shall also be like the dust of the earth, and you shall spread out to the west and to the east and to the north and to the south; and in you and in your descendants shall all the families of the earth be blessed. And behold, I am with you, and will keep you wherever you go, and will bring you back to this land; for I will not leave you until I have done what I have promised you.[483]

Indeed, G-d is faithful. He was always with Jacob, and He did bring Jacob back to the Promised Land. So too, He will bring all of the Jewish people back to their land one day, and He will establish them in peace from that time on and forevermore.

*   *   *   *   *

In Volume 2, we discussed how the Jews of the Southern Kingdom received a great number of warnings leading up to their first exile but precious few leading up to the second one. Perhaps one of the reasons the postexilic Jews were given fewer warnings is because they should have known better after their first downfall. The older people who returned from Babylonia lived through all of the misery, including the siege, the horrendous march to Babylon, and the seventy years of captivity. It was awful. But then, just as the prophet Jeremiah had predicted, G-d restored the Jews to their land. Therefore, the Jews should have been listening to their new prophets carefully at this point. But alas, half a millennium would go by without G-d speaking through any new prophets after Malachi, and, sure enough, the Jews would forget the messages of the prophets who wrote in the aftermath of the Babylonian exile.

---

[483] Gen. 28:12-15.

Thus, when Zechariah wrote, "And I took my staff, Favor, and cut it in pieces, to break my covenant which I had made with all the peoples,"[484] the Jews should have been very concerned and remained mindful of this warning. But by the time Jesus showed up, these words had long since been forgotten. The Jews were not cautious. They were not seeking G-d's will, and they rushed to judgment concerning Jesus. The results have been 2,000 years of misery. G-d promised Jacob that He would always be with him wherever he went, but G-d has not been with the Jews to protect them while they have been in the Diaspora. Indeed, it has been just as Zechariah prophesied—G-d's favor was removed from them!

However, G-d has also promised the Jews multiple times through the prophets that, ultimately, He will restore them. And so He will. He will be faithful to His word, just as He was to His promises to Jacob. For example, in another prophecy in Zechariah, G-d says:

> 'Behold, I am going to save My people from the
> land of the east and from the land of the west;
> and I will bring them *back*, and they will live in
> the midst of Jerusalem, and they will be My
> people and I will be their G-d in truth and
> righteousness.' [485]

Imagine, the Jews failed G-d so seriously that He cast them out of their land and withdrew His protection from them. But at the end of time, He will come back for them out of faithfulness to His promises to Abraham. Ezekiel prophesied about it this way:

> The hand of the L-rd was upon me, and He
> brought me out by the Spirit of the L-rd and set
> me down in the middle of the valley; and it was
> full of bones. And He caused me to pass among

---

484 Zech. 11:10.
485 Zech. 8:7-8.

them round about, and behold, *there were* very many on the surface of the valley; and lo, *they were* very dry. And He said to me, "Son of man, can these bones live?" And I answered, "O L-rd G-d, Thou knowest." Again He said to me, "Prophesy over these bones, and say to them, 'O dry bones, hear the word of the L-rd.' Thus says the L-rd G-d to these bones, 'Behold, I will cause breath to enter you that you may come to life. And I will put sinews on you, make flesh grow back on you, cover you with skin, and put breath in you that you may come alive; and you will know that I am the L-rd.' "

So I prophesied as I was commanded; and as I prophesied, there was a noise, and behold, a rattling; and the bones came together, bone to its bone. And I looked, and behold, sinews were on them, and flesh grew, and skin covered them; but there was no breath in them. Then He said to me, "Prophesy to the breath, prophesy, son of man, and say to the breath, 'Thus says the L-rd G-d, "Come from the four winds, O breath, and breathe on these slain, that they come to life." ' " So I prophesied as He commanded me, and the breath came into them, and they came to life, and stood on their feet, an exceedingly great army.[486]

What an absolutely amazing experience this ancient man had. Somehow, Ezekiel was there, walking in the midst of these bones. He watched this bizarre scene and even heard the sound of the great rattling produced by this trove of bones as they danced to find their mates!

As is the case with some of Daniel's prophecies, these words were not given for those living at that time, but rather for those

---

[486] Ezek. 37:1-10.

of us who are alive now, as the time of the end draws near. What an apt description this prophecy is of the regathering of the Jewish people to their land in the Modern Age. These bones were very dry. They had been there for a long time. Now we know that they were there for 2,000 years. Of course, it would take a miracle for them to reattach, have flesh grow around them, and have a living soul indwell them. They could not do this on their own. Only G-d could cause this to happen. That is the point. All throughout the Diaspora, the Jews were at the mercy of their Gentile hosts, and the Gentiles could not have treated them any worse if they tried. The Jews were powerless for the most part to assert their will and reinhabit their land. But G-d was not powerless, and when the time was right, He began the regathering.

Ezekiel's vision of the dry bones is fairly well known, though some of you may be reading it for the first time. If so, you may wonder how we know this vision is portraying the regathering of the Jews to Israel at the end of time. We know this because Ezekiel goes on to interpret the vision in the following verses:

> Then He said to me, "Son of man, these bones are the whole house of Israel; behold, they say, 'Our bones are dried up, and our hope has perished. We are completely cut off.' Therefore prophesy, and say to them, 'Thus says the L-rd G-d, "Behold, I will open your graves and cause you to come up out of your graves, My people; and I will bring you into the land of Israel. Then you will know that I am the L-rd, when I have opened your graves and caused you to come up out of your graves, My people. And I will put My Spirit within you, and you will come to life, and I will place you on your own land. Then you will know that I, the L-rd, have spoken and done it," declares the L-rd.'"[487]

---

[487] Ezek. 37:11-14.

This is a prophecy for the "whole house of Israel" as opposed to individual Jews. It is about the restoration of the nation, not the physical resurrection of individuals. In this prophecy, Ezekiel quotes the whole house of Israel as saying, "Our bones are dried up, and our hope has perished. We are completely cut off." Surely this has been the sentiment of the Jewish people over the last 2,000 years. Certainly, in the first half of the 20th century, they were without hope. Only the power of G-d could deliver them from their enemies and place them back in their land. Thus, G-d gave Ezekiel this vision of an event only He could cause to happen. In the beginning of this chapter in Ezekiel, when G-d first showed him these bones lying on the ground, He asked Ezekiel if they could come to life. Needless to say, Ezekiel was cautious, and he said, essentially, "What do I know, G-d? You are the one who knows."[488] Later, in verse 14, Ezekiel quoted G-d, who said that such an event would be evidence, causing people to "know that I, the L-rd, have spoken and done it." In other words, the Jews returning to their land and re-forming as a nation would be as unrealistic as ancient bones coming together, taking on flesh, and resuscitating. For, to have your capital destroyed, a large portion of your population killed, and the remainder sent into exile was a death sentence for a people in the ancient world. But Ezekiel was right, and in 1948, the world witnessed the return of the Jews to their land. Except for the Jews, no other nation from the ancient world survived this treatment. Only they were able to retain their national identity while in exile all those years. All the other nations the Romans dismantled are extinguished. Surely, this miracle is strong evidence that the Jews are the people of G-d.

On the inside of the Yad Vashem entryway is inscribed part of verse 14 of Ezekiel 37. Here is the translation they use: "I will put my breath into you and you shall live again, and I will set

---

[488] Ezek. 37:3; cf. Isa. 55:3, 8-11. Ezekiel was wise. He understood that when it comes to the things of G-d, he did not know everything, and he needed to listen to G-d. For G-d's thoughts are higher than ours. So too, we should not be certain of ourselves regarding theology, but rather we should learn to listen to what G-d has to say.

you upon your own soil…" Surely there could be no better verse to encapsulate the hand of G-d delivering the Jews from their hellish exile.

The museum is a long, thin triangular prism that is laid out chronologically. At the beginning, there is a triangular screen on which home movies of the Jews are played. These movies were shot before anti-Semitism started heating up in Europe. There was anti-Semitism, but it was at a level that was survivable, and the Jews made the best of their situation. Though the Jews were doing their best, including not forgetting G-d and building strong, loving families, they were not fully free, and they were not home.

But then things took a turn for the worse. The level of anti-Semitism really started to ramp up in Germany. Eventually, Hitler and his minions came up with the Final Solution. They did their best to accomplish the work of the devil, but in the end, G-d mercifully brought the curtain down on Hitler and the Third Reich. Then the world debated the plight of the Jews in the UN, with many standing opposed to them. But G-d had His way, and His people started to come back to their land.

Although the Third Reich was over, anti-Semitism was still alive. Be that as it may, time was of the essence, and the Jews hurriedly cobbled together a government. Even though they were far from ready, they raised the curtain on their revived nation on May 14, 1948. This was the best day the Jews had in 2,000 years.

Inconceivably, the next day was another really bad day. On May 15, they were simultaneously attacked from every side by Egypt, Jordan, Syria, Lebanon, and Iraq. There were also Palestinian fighters and some Saudi Arabian soldiers who joined the enemy coalition. What is more, the Jewish army was not fully formed when the attack was launched. The Jews had virtually no chance for survival. But in reality, the coalition of Arab nations had no chance. For, G-d had renewed His favor over the Jews, and to Him, this coalition of attackers was but a gnat. Thus, although the Arabs proclaimed that they would utterly destroy the "Zionist entity" within ten days,[489] the war ended up dragging on into 1949. In the end, the war proved to be a disaster for the Arabs, as the Jews had increased the original territory they were allotted by the UN by 60%.[490]

That was the hand of G-d. Furthermore, the hand of G-d has been on display on other occasions since 1948. For example, the Six-Day War in 1967 was a stunning victory. It was akin to David defeating Goliath when that pompous Gentile failed to recognize G-d and His people.

In Yad Vashem, the far end of the long, narrow museum is not a concrete wall or a screen. Rather, as mentioned in an earlier chapter, the end wall is a large triangle made of glass with a doorway opening onto a veranda. It represents freedom. It is a picture of the end of the very long, very dark night the Jews spent in exile. G-d has brought the Jews back into their land, and He has been protecting them.

Of course, He is not finished. Their return in 1948 was only the beginning of the end. We know G-d is not done yet because 1) the Jews are hated and not living in peace; 2) only a segment of the Jewish people have returned from exile;[491] and 3) there is still more prophecy left to be fulfilled regarding the end of time.

So, life is a struggle for the Jews today as they have multiple enemies seeking their demise. But one day, G-d will give the Jews a new lease on life. Indeed, the final phase of the regathering will not just be a return to Israel, but to Eden. Nature will be restored, and war will be over forever. Furthermore, as it says in Jeremiah 31, there will be a new covenant, and the Jews will be transformed in such a way that they will be able to keep G-d's Law from their hearts. It will be natural for them to do so. G-d will be there with them, and they

---

[489] Mordecai Naor, *The Twentieth Century in Eretz Israel*, A Pictorial History, trans. Judith Krausz (1998) (Tel-Aviv: Am Oved Publishers Ltd., 1996) 265.
[490] John F. Walvoord, *Armageddon, Oil and the Middle East Crisis* (Grand Rapids, MI: Zondervan Publishing House, 1990) 79.
[491] Ezek. 39:28.

will each know Him.[492] In Ezekiel Chapters 36 and 37, G-d spoke words that are similar to those in Jeremiah:

> "For I will take you from the nations, gather you from all the lands, and bring you into your own land. Then I will sprinkle clean water on you, and you will be clean; I will cleanse you from all your filthiness and from all your idols. Moreover, I will give you a new heart and put a new spirit within you; and I will remove the heart of stone from your flesh and give you a heart of flesh. And I will put My Spirit within you and cause you to walk in My statutes, and you will be careful to observe My ordinances. And you will live in the land that I gave to your forefathers; so you will be My people, and I will be your G-d."[493]

> "On the day that I cleanse you from all your iniquities, I will cause the cities to be inhabited, and the waste places will be rebuilt. And the desolate land will be cultivated instead of being a desolation in the sight of everyone who passed by. And they will say, 'This desolate land has become like the garden of Eden; and the waste, desolate, and ruined cities are fortified *and* inhabited.' Then the nations that are left round about you will know that I, the L-rd, have rebuilt the ruined places *and* planted that which was desolate; I, the L-rd, have spoken and will do it."[494]

and,

---

[492] Jer. 31:31-34 (30-33.)
[493] Ezek. 36:24-28
[494] Ezek. 36:33-36.

"And they shall live on the land that I gave to Jacob My servant, in which your fathers lived…. And I will make a covenant of peace with them; it will be an everlasting covenant with them. And I will place them and multiply them, and will set My sanctuary in their midst forever. My dwelling place also will be with them, and I will be their G-d, and they will be My people. And the nations will know that I am the L-rd who sanctifies Israel, when My sanctuary is in their midst forever."[495]

The biblical prophecy of the end of time appears surreal to us today, but one day it will be reality. We can count on it, for G-d has promised it, and He is faithful.

Isaiah wrote of the final phase of the regathering that:

. . . the ransomed of the L-rd will return, and come with joyful shouting to Zion, with everlasting joy upon their heads. They will find gladness and joy, and sorrow and sighing will flee away.[496]

Truly the Jews have known pain, but one day they will know joy. Specifically, they will know the joy that Adam and Eve experienced in the Garden of Eden. In fact, G-d's peace and joy will infuse their souls.

Take heart and keep trusting G-d. His plan is underway. No one can stop it, and the end is not far away.

---

[495] Ezek. 37:25-28.
[496] Isa. 35:10.

16

THE 70TH WEEK

In Volume 2, we studied Daniel 9:24-27, in which G-d laid out a timeline for the Jewish people stretching all the way to the end of history. In the text, there is a conspicuously obvious gap in the timeline between the death of the Messiah and the coming of the Roman prince who will commit an abomination in the Jewish Temple. Of course, one of the things that jumps out in this prophecy is that there will be a Temple at the end of time. Therefore, the Temple must be rebuilt at some point between now and the occurrence of this event. The Roman prince will be the antichrist. He will seek to rule the world, and he will achieve an unparalleled level of success in that goal. Then he will cause a world war and bring the earth to the brink of destruction.[497]

Daniel tells us that the final phase of history will be a seven-year period in which G-d will again work with the Jews. For, He will have ended His work with the Church by this point. Daniel did not tell us how long the gap of time would be in which G-d would be taking a break from working with the Jews. This gap has been so long now that some foolish Christians have

---

[497] Mt. 24:22; Rev. 13:7.

surmised that G-d is done working with the Jews. They should read this passage in Daniel 9. They should also read 2 Peter in the New Testament, where it is implied that it would not be a brief interlude, but rather, it would be a very long period until the end comes.[498]

The amount of suffering the Jews have endured over the last 2,000 years is beyond comprehension. Inexplicably, Christians have participated in the persecution of the Jews. It is not surprising when Gentiles behave like predatory animals towards the people of G-d, but we do not expect to see Gentile Christians engaging in such evil. But as we noted in Chapter 9 when we discussed the beginning of the Diaspora, they did. In fact, the record of both Catholics and Protestants is deplorable. For example:

> Pope Innocent III (1198-1216) had written that the guilt of the Jews for the crucifixion of Jesus consigned them to perpetual servitude, and, like Cain, they were to be wanderers and fugitives.
>
> The five thousand Jews of England were expelled in 1290; they were taken in by the dukes of central France. The Jews of France, which was then a relatively small circle-shaped kingdom, were repeatedly expelled and allowed to return—until they were finally expelled in 1394; many wandered to Spain.[499]

Unfortunately, the Jews got caught up in the notorious Spanish Inquisition in which they were some of the primary targets. Prior to the Inquisition, the Jews were treated poorly in Spain and were coerced to convert to Catholicism. The Inquisition was utilized to ferret out any Jews who had claimed to convert but were secretly practicing Judaism. Indeed, in a 12-year period in the latter part of the 15ᵗʰ century, more

---

[498] 2 Pet. 3:3-9. Cf. Ezek. 37:2.

[499] Chaim Potok, *Wanderings: Chaim Potok's History of the Jews* (New York: The Ballantine Publishing Group, 1978) 413.

than 13,000 Spanish Jews were found guilty and burned at the stake.[500]

> With the fall of Muslim Spain there came the hunger for religious unity and the wish to see an end to the faces of strangers. Spain had fought a five-hundred-year-long war against Islam. It wanted itself purified of dross. On March 31, 1492, an edict of expulsion directed against the Jews was signed in Granada. On May 1 of that year Spain began to expel all Jews who would not accept Christianity. About one hundred seventy thousand left the land. They were wandering through Europe, Portugal, North Africa, Turkey. Tens of thousands accepted baptism. The last Jew left Spain on July 31, 1492, the seventh day of the Hebrew month of Av. Spain was officially empty of Jews. Pope Innocent III had triumphed. All the Jews were wanderers, lost in a vast enchanted world.[501]

Needless to say, the quotations above from Chaim Potok's book, *Wanderings*, are concise and do not fully convey the scope of the injustice and hatred the Jews bore as they lived as foreigners for centuries in Europe and around the world. At the heart of much of the bigotry and persecution was the Catholic Church. Indeed, it is hard for the Jews to accept Jesus as their savior because of the awful things Christians have done in the past.

Of course, it was not just the Christians who mistreated the Jews of the Diaspora. The Jewish people were also treated poorly by the secular European and Russian governmental leaders and by the emerging Muslim Empire. Heinous crimes were perpetrated by all of these parties against the Jews. For example, Muhammad expelled two Jewish communities from

---

[500] Ibid., 415.
[501] Ibid., 415-416.

the city of Medina and then executed the men from the third community. These poor men were accused of betrayal and sentenced to death. In fact, approximately eight hundred Jewish men from the third tribe were beheaded and buried in a large mass grave.[502] Muhammad then distributed their wives, children, and possessions among the Muslims. He kept one of the wives, who was named Rayhana,[503] for himself. Needless to say, Muhammad's hatred for the Jews has echoed down through the centuries, and his crimes against them are still being perpetrated by his followers today.

The mistreatment of the Jews reached its zenith in the European anti-Semitism of the 19th and 20th centuries, culminating in the Holocaust. It was so awful that many Jewish people asked, Where is G-d?

The answer is that G-d despised every racial insult and every drop of blood that was exacted from each Jewish victim. But He had accepted the Jews' decision—made 2,000 years ago—when they chose to reject Jesus. Unfortunately, the consequences of their choice have been horrific, as they have been subjected to two millennia of oppression, violence, and mindless hatred. However, regardless of their choice, G-d made unilateral promises to Abraham,[504] and one day He will return to the Jews and shepherd them again. Indeed, one day, G-d will make everything right. In the words of the disciple John in the book of Revelation, "He shall wipe away every tear from their eyes; and there shall no longer be *any* death; there shall no longer be *any* mourning, or crying, or pain; the first things have passed away."[505]

But according to the Jewish prophets of both the Tanakh and the New Testament, prior to the very end of history, sin and

---

[502] Ergun Mehmet Caner and Emir Fethi Caner, *Unveiling Islam* (Grand Rapids, Michigan: Kregel Publications, 2002) 52.

[503] Muhammad Husayn Haykal, *The Life of Muhammad* trans. Ismail Ragi A. al Faruqi (Indianapolis, IN: American Trust Publications, 1976, 1993) 315-316.

[504] Gen. 15.

[505] Rev. 21:4. Cf. Isa. 25:8, 35:10.

carnage will become unchecked and will occur all over the world. The suffering will be great for both Jews and Gentiles alike. This seven-year period is called the Tribulation, with the final three and a half years being called the Great Tribulation.[506] Additionally, Jesus foretold that the years leading up to the final seven year period would be increasingly difficult for humanity in terms of such things as natural disasters, famine, disease, and war.[507] The apostle Paul foretold that as the end draws near, society will become increasingly godless, with the result being that sin will flourish, decency will abate, and the world will become an inhospitable place to live and raise a family.[508] Jesus said that the years leading up to the final period will be like the birth pangs of a woman in that the suffering around the world will become more frequent and grow in intensity. Then the final apocalyptic period will come, in which oppression, violence, chaos, and fear will overwhelm virtually everyone alive at that time.[509]

In the Tanakh, Isaiah describes the final days of history similarly:

> Behold, the L-rd lays the earth waste, devastates it, distorts its surface, and scatters its inhabitants. And the people will be like the priest, the servant like his master, the maid like her mistress, the buyer like the seller, the lender like the borrower, the creditor like the debtor. The earth will be completely laid waste and completely despoiled, for the L-rd has spoken this word. The earth mourns *and* withers, the world fades *and* withers, the exalted of the people of the earth fade away. The earth is also polluted by its inhabitants, for they transgressed laws, violated statutes, broke the everlasting

---

[506] Mt. 24:21.
[507] Mt. 24:1-14.
[508] 2 Tim. 3:1-15.
[509] Mt. 24:8.

covenant. Therefore, a curse devours the earth, and those who live in it are held guilty. Therefore, the inhabitants of the earth are burned, and few men are left....

Terror and pit and snare confront you, O inhabitant of the earth. Then it will be that he who flees the report of disaster will fall into the pit, and he who climbs out of the pit will be caught in the snare; for the windows above are opened, and the foundations of the earth shake. The earth is broken asunder, the earth is split through, the earth is shaken violently. The earth reels to and fro like a drunkard, and it totters like a shack, for its transgression is heavy upon it, and it will fall, never to rise again.[510]

This is a prophecy of the very final days of history. It will be a time of judgment. Perhaps G-d's judgment will include features such as earthquakes and other natural disasters. But certainly also, His judgment upon the earth will be that He will leave us to our own devices. Apparently, we will ask Him to leave, and He will oblige. We already see the seeds of this today in America as G-d and His values are not welcome here anymore.

Paul wrote that G-d has provided mankind with a restraining agent that holds back lawlessness. But in the final period, He will remove this influence, and lawlessness will proceed unabated.[511] Theologians have posited that the restraining agent is the Holy Spirit working through Christians. Hence, once G-d stops working through the Church as a force for good in society, evil will rise.[512]

The final days of history will be a time like no other. Throughout history there has been a social order in which everyone has a position in society. For example, you are either

---

[510] Isa. 24:1-6, 17-20.

[511] 2 Thess. 2:1-10.

[512] Walvoord and Zuck 719.

an employee or a company owner, an ordinary citizen or a government official, and so on. But when the end comes, there will be no order. It will be chaos, as people will be revolting against authority.

The pollution Isaiah is referring to is not literal pollution. Although, it is quite possible that people will continue to abuse the earth going forward, leading to an ecological disaster at the end of time. But Isaiah is predicting that a state of moral pollution will pervade the earth. He is speaking of the decay of honesty, chastity, and respect. People will give themselves over to their baser instincts, which will lead to the downfall of society.

Finally, there will be war. In World War I, the battlefields were alien landscapes the world had never seen before. The acres of land between the two enemy sides were devoid of foliage, pockmarked by craters from explosions, and littered with corpses and barbed wire. At the end of history, such barren landscape will be present all over the world, or as Isaiah says, the earth's surface will be distorted. Further, the earth will be "shaken violently" and "broken asunder." In other words, there will be nuclear war, and it will be massive. The death toll will be astronomical. In the words of Isaiah, it will reach a point where very few people will be left. In fact, Jesus will return just in time to prevent the total annihilation of all life on the planet![513]

Throughout history, G-d has been at work to accomplish His will. What is He going to be doing during the final phase of human history? Part of the answer, as we have already noted, is that He will stop providing a buffer to keep evil from spiraling out of control. It is similar to a decision some terminal cancer patients make when they stop treatment. Many patients choose to undergo chemotherapy to prolong their days, but some patients forgo that therapy to shorten their misery. That is what G-d is going to do. He is going to refrain from intervening and from saving us from ourselves.

---

[513] Mt. 24:22.

However, G-d will be working with humanity on another level. Namely, G-d will continue His work to reach the lost on an individual basis.[514] Yet, there will be a change. Both the Tanakh and the New Testament indicate that He will stop working with the Christian Church and instead renew His work with the Jews. For example, in the beginning of the book of Revelation, Jesus dictated letters to John for seven Christian churches in the ancient world. But after Revelation Chapter 3, there are no further references to Christian churches in the remaining nineteen chapters. Rather, we see G-d dealing with the Jews, and we also see the focal point on earth shifting to Jerusalem. At the end of the book of Revelation, Jesus returns to earth to fulfill all of the remaining Messianic prophecies from the Tanakh. As we saw in Volume 2, according to Daniel 9:24-27, G-d was going to work with the Jews for seventy additional sets of seven years in order to accomplish His goals in history. The final, unique set of seven years will be the end of human history. This set of seven years is the topic of the book of Revelation.

Daniel's prophecy also gives other details that line up with the book of Revelation.[515] Namely, Daniel introduces a character who would later be defined in great detail by the book of Revelation. One day this man of darkness will come and fulfill all of the predictions in the Bible. He is the antichrist, and we have seen his type before. He will resemble Antiochus Epiphanes IV, Herod the Great, Caligula, Stalin, Hitler, and many others who have wrought tyranny and violence down through the ages. Only, he will be worse in that he will have our modern-day technology at his disposal to control the masses and punish his political enemies. In fact, it is even worse than that, for he will traffic with the devil as his program of evil moves forward.[516] He will throw the world into a state of turmoil. Indeed, the upheaval the world experienced during World War II will seem small in comparison. This statement

---

[514] Rev. 6:9-11; 7:9-17.

[515] Dan. 9:26-27; Rev. 13.

[516] Rev. 12:1-4; 2 Thess. 2:5-10.

sounds like hyperbole. Yet, according to the Bible, the final seven-year period will be the hardest time ever for mankind:

> 'Alas! for the day is great, there is none like it; and it is the time of Jacob's distress, but he will be saved from it.'[517]

and,

> Now at that time Michael, the great prince who stands *guard* over the sons of your people, will arise. And there will be a time of distress such as never occurred since there was a nation until that time; and at that time your people, everyone who is found written in the book, will be rescued.[518]

This period will be tremendously difficult for the Jews. One of the awful things the Jews will be subjected to will be a repeat of the abomination of Antiochus Epiphanes IV.[519] In fact, according to Daniel, Antiochus is a type of the antichrist. Here is a synopsis from the historian Josephus of Antiochus' crimes against G-d and His people:

> Now Antiochus, upon the agreeable situation of the affairs of his kingdom, resolved to make an expedition against Egypt, both because he had a desire to gain it, and because he contemned the son of Ptolemy, as now weak, and not yet of abilities to manage affairs of such consequence; so he came with great forces to Pelusium, and circumvented Ptolemy Philometer by treachery, and seized upon Egypt. He then came to the places about Memphis; and when he had taken

---

[517] Jer. 30:7.

[518] Dan. 12:1.

[519] Dan. 11:29-35.

them, he made haste to Alexandria, in hopes of taking it by siege, and of subduing Ptolemy, who reigned there. But he was driven not only from Alexandria, but out of all Egypt, by the declaration of the Romans, who charged him to let that country alone....

King Antiochus returning out of Egypt for fear of the Romans, made an expedition against the city of Jerusalem; and when he was there, in the hundred and forty-third year of the kingdom of the Seleucidae, he took the city without fighting, those of his own party opening the gates to him. And when he had gotten possession of Jerusalem, he slew many of the opposite party; and when he had plundered it of a great deal of money, he returned to Antioch.

Now it came to pass after two years in the hundred and forty and fifth year,... that the king came up to Jerusalem, and pretending peace, he got possession of the city by treachery; at which time he spared not so much as those that admitted him into it, on account of the riches that lay in the temple; but, led by his covetous inclination (for he saw there was in it a great deal of gold, and many ornaments that had been dedicated to it of very great value,) and in order to plunder its wealth, he ventured to break the league he had made. So he left the temple bare, and took away the golden candlesticks, and the golden altar [of incense], and table [of shew-bread], and the altar [of burnt-offering];... and by this means cast the Jews into great lamentation, for he forbade them to offer those daily sacrifices which they used to offer to G-d, according to the law. And when he had pillaged the whole city, some of the inhabitants he slew, and some he carried captive, together with their wives and children, so that the multitude of those captives that were taken alive amounted to about ten thousand.... And when the king had built an idol altar upon G-d's Altar, he slew swine upon it, and so offered a sacrifice neither according to the law, nor the Jewish religious worship in that country. He also compelled them to forsake the worship which they paid their own G-d, and to adore those whom he took to be gods; and made them build temples, and raise idol altars, in every city and village, and offer swine upon them every day. He also commanded them not to circumcise their sons, and threatened to punish any that should be found to have transgressed his injunction. He also appointed overseers, who should compel them to do what he commanded. And indeed many Jews there were who complied with the king's commands, either voluntarily, or out of fear of the penalty that was denounced. But the best men, and those of the noblest souls, did not regard him, but did pay a greater respect to the customs of their country than concern as to the punishment which he threatened to the disobedient; on which account they every day underwent great miseries and bitter torments; for they were whipped with rods and their bodies were torn to pieces, and were crucified while they were still alive and breathed. They also strangled those women and their sons whom they had circumcised, as the king had appointed, hanging their ʿsons about their necks as they were upon the crosses. And if there were any sacred book of the law found, it was destroyed,...[520]

---

[520] Flavius Josephus, *The Antiquities of the Jews by Josephus,* Book 12, Chapter 5, Paragraphs 2-4, William Whiston, trans., 1737,

Antiochus wanted to be great, but in reality, how very small he was. He thought he could defeat his Greek countrymen who were ruling Egypt. But then a bigger fish, the emerging Roman Empire, put him in his place. Predictably, he left to save his skin, but his ego was wounded. So, he looked for someone weaker to take it out on in order to reinvigorate his image. But just as the fool failed to take note of the Romans when he attempted to take over another land, now he failed to take note of G-d as he perpetrated acts of violence and evil against His people. The godly Jews did not acquiesce despite the savage punishment they were forced to endure. Eventually, the Maccabees rose up and fought their Greek overlords and, with G-d's help, overcame them.

So too, at the end of time, a man will arise and repeat the same acts of evil against the Jews. Just as Antiochus profaned the Temple by sacrificing pigs upon the altar, and just as he demanded that the Jews stop worshiping G-d and instead worship the false Greek gods, so too, this future man of darkness will make similar demands of the Jews. Only, the antichrist will proclaim himself to be G-d and demand that the Jews bow down to him![521]

Just as Josephus wrote of Antiochus using treachery, the book of Revelation foretells that the antichrist will use deception to gain power.[522] Of course, this is to be expected. He will be like his leader, Satan,[523] and he will tell noxious lies that both attack G-d's character and lead to the ruin of those who fall sway to his deception. The surprising aspect of his deception will be how brazen his lies will be. Daniel put it this way: he will "magnify himself above every god and will speak monstrous things against the G-d of gods."[524] Apparently, this master of

---

https://dn720706.ca.archive.org/0/items/theAntiquitiesOfTheJews_5 07/TheAntiquitiesOfTheJews-flaviusJosephus.pdf (accessed April 8, 2026.)

[521] Dan. 9:27; 11:36; 2 Thess. 2:3-4; Rev. 13:11-15.

[522] Rev. 13:11-15.

[523] Rev. 13:1-6.

[524] Dan. 11:36.

lying will speak such outrageous lies that people will fall for them. He will even go so far as to demand the worship of every human being on earth. Furthermore, in our modern era, he will have the databases and tracking devices needed to reach his tentacles across the entire earth and enforce his demands.[525]

It is no surprise that the antichrist will be a megalomaniac who will magnify himself and seek to rule the world. Men such as this have popped up throughout history. We saw multiple examples of such men in the 20th century. Perhaps Hitler was the best example from the 20th century of what the antichrist will be like. The antichrist, too, will be a man of war.[526] Hitler was trying feverishly to develop nuclear weapons. If he had obtained them, he would have launched them to save his skin. The antichrist will have them.

The book of Revelation also speaks of a helper of the antichrist who will tap into satanic power and perform supernatural signs to give credence to the antichrist's bold claims.[527] Of course, the antichrist will also use persecution to root out those who know who the real G-d is and who will not bow their knees to him.[528] These brave men and women will be following in the footsteps of "those of the noblest souls" who would not submit to Antiochus' threats of violence and bow their knees to his false gods. Thus, the antichrist will use fear as well as economic oppression to shepherd the bulk of humanity into complete subservience.[529] Daniel is telling us that we can identify him by looking at the life and deeds of Antiochus Epiphanes. Daniel made it clear that they are two different men, albeit they are similar. Daniel prophesied that Antiochus would arise out of the Greek Empire, which he did, and that the antichrist will arise out of a revived version of the Roman Empire, which he will. Daniel portrays them both as "little

---

[525] Rev. 13:16-18.
[526] Dan. 11:38-39; Rev. 13:4.
[527] Rev. 13:11-15.
[528] Rev. 12; 13:5-7.
[529] Rev. 13:16-18.

horns" that arise out of the two different empires.[530] How apropos; they are both little men who are intensely selfish, uncaring, and cowardly.

So, we will be able to identify the antichrist in that he will be the leader of a revived Roman Empire. Presumably, it will be made up of the descendants of the Romans. Perhaps the antichrist himself will be Italian and come from the city of Rome.

The antichrist's character will be the opposite of Jesus' in every way. He will be ambitious, and he will be violent.[531] He will hate G-d and persecute His people. In the words of John in Revelation 13:

> And there was given to him a mouth speaking arrogant words and blasphemies; and authority to act for forty-two months was given to him. And he opened his mouth in blasphemies against G-d, to blaspheme His name and His tabernacle, *that is*, those who dwell in heaven. And it was given to him to make war with the saints and to overcome them; and authority over every tribe and people and tongue and nation was given to him.[532]

G-d will allow this evil to take place, but only for a time— forty-two months. These are the three and a half years of the Great Tribulation. They will be the final three and a half years of history, and they will be hellish.

Here is another detail about the antichrist from Daniel:

> "And he will show no regard for the gods of his fathers or for the desire of women, nor will he

---

[530] Dan. 7:7-8; 8:5-14.
[531] Dan. 7:8; Rev. 13:11-15.
[532] Rev. 13:5-7.

show regard for any *other* god; for he will
magnify himself above *them* all.[533]

Again, only G-d can see the future, and here, Daniel, who lived during the days of the Babylonian Empire, appears to be foretelling the moral state of our day. Daniel says this man will show "no regard for the desire of women." While it is possible that Daniel is telling us that the antichrist is imitating Christ in being celibate, it is more likely that he is telling us that the antichrist will not be straight. The antichrist will detest and blaspheme G-d. Therefore, how appropriate it would be for him to reject G-d's gift of marriage. G-d created Eve for Adam. She was beautiful and the perfect match for him in every way. So too, every wife is nothing short of a beautiful gift from G-d to her husband. But a growing portion of society does not agree with the Bible on this issue today. Views on sexuality started to change during the "sexual revolution" of the 1960s, and they have continued to evolve ever since. Thus, it appears that the antichrist will fit right in with today's values and be gay, or possibly even a pedophile.

Daniel's statement that the antichrist will "put a stop to sacrifice and grain offering" and commit an abomination[534] is given more definition by Paul's statement that this man will "take his seat in the temple of G-d, displaying himself as being G-d."[535] Again, the Temple will be rebuilt by this point in time. Of course, the Temple was leveled to the ground by the Romans 2,000 years ago, and two mosques have been erected on the Temple Mount in the intervening years. Today it is inconceivable that the two mosques would ever be removed so that the Temple could be rebuilt, or that the Muslims would allow the Jews to rebuild their Temple adjacent to the Dome of the Rock. Yet, the prophets say that the Temple will be rebuilt. Perhaps war will erupt between the Arabs and the Jews one day and the mosques will be destroyed in the midst of the battle.

---

[533] Dan. 11:37.
[534] Dan. 9:27.
[535] 2 Thess. 2:4.

In the book of Ezekiel, there is another prophetic detail that is hard to see ever taking place. In Ezekiel 38:11, it describes Israel at the end of history as a "land of unwalled villages."[536] In addition, this verse describes the Jews as "those who are at rest, that live securely, all of them living without walls, and having no bars or gates." Today, the Jews have many walls, both inside Israel and along their borders. These walls are necessary as a defense against terrorist attacks. The Jews also have David's Sling and the Iron Dome to protect themselves from missile attacks. It is unimaginable today to think that the Jews would ever surrender their defenses to someone else in light of the hatred and threats that have been issued against them. Yet, the prophets say that the day will come when the Jews disarm.

Could it be that the Jews and Arabs will engage in war to such an extent that the peace and safety of the world will be imperiled? If that were to happen, then the Jews will come under tremendous pressure from around the globe, thereby opening a door for the antichrist to come in and broker a deal. In this deal, he will promise to defend the Jews, but they will have to disarm. This outcome fits with the prophecy in Daniel 9:27, where it says that the antichrist will "make a firm covenant with the many for one week." Thus, the Jews will be forced to go along with the antichrist's deal, which will take place at the beginning of the seven-year period. In addition, it may well be that a provision will be included in this covenant which will grant the Jews the right to rebuild the Temple, for such a provision may be needed to entice the Jews to sign the agreement.

This scenario explains how the Jews could rebuild the Temple as well as why they would surrender their defenses to someone else. Certainly, we must not assume we fully understand what will happen, as we have not been given all the details of these future events. But perhaps we have a rough idea of what will happen, and once these events transpire, then we

---

[536] To be clear, this passage is describing Israel in the Tribulation period just before the final end of human history. It is not describing Israel in eternity when the Jews will permanently experience peace.

will understand exactly what the prophets were predicting. Of course, we can be sure that everything G-d has predicted will take place. For twenty long centuries it was unimaginable to think that the Jews would ever be sovereign over their land again, but then it happened in 1948. So too, the Temple will be rebuilt.

Needless to say, the Jews should be wary of entering into covenants with Gentile leaders. For example, in the early 620s CE, the three Jewish communities in Medina made a covenant with Muhammad. In the covenant, they ceded authority to him as he promised to bring peace and unity to the five groups of people living there: the three Jewish communities, his Muslim followers who were emigrating from Mecca to Medina, and the indigenous Arabs of Medina who were in the process of converting to Islam.[537] He was a shrewd politician, and he was making promises of religious freedom and equal rights under the law. So, the Jews went along with him.

Muhammad claimed that his religion was actually the same as Judaism. He said that Islam was a continuation of Judaism and Christianity, and that he was a new prophet of G-d. Muhammad incorporated a number of stories from the Tanakh in his message, but he made a lot of mistakes in his retelling of those stories.[538] He was also a Gentile. Hence, the Jews did not recognize him as their new prophet.[539] Muhammad did not like that.[540] As time went by and the Muslims in Medina grew in strength, he got rid of all three Jewish communities, one at a time, as they were each accused of scheming against him and committing treason.[541] Thus, the covenant the Jews made with Muhammad blew up in their faces. So too, the covenant the Jews will make with the antichrist will wind up being a disaster.

---

[537] Yahiya Emerick, *Muhammad* (Indianapolis, IN: Alpha books, 2002) 131-132; Haykal 179-183.

[538] Don Richardson, *Secrets of the Koran* (Ventura, California: Regal Books, 1999) 33-35; Caner and Caner 52.

[539] Emerick 42-146; Haykal 191-192.

[540] Richardson 33-35.

[541] Ibid., 35-37; Caner and Caner 52.

According to Daniel, all hell will break loose in the middle of the seven years.[542] It will be at that moment that the antichrist will declare his true intentions and perform his abomination. Jesus prophesied of this day and offers the following advice to the Jewish people:

> "Therefore when you see the ABOMINATION OF DESOLATION which was spoken of through Daniel the prophet, standing in the holy place (let the reader understand), then let those who are in Judea flee to the mountains; let him who is on the housetop not go down to get the things out that are in his house; and let him who is in the field not turn back to get his cloak. But woe to those who are with child and to those who nurse babes in those days! But pray that your flight may not be in the winter, or on a Sabbath; for then there will be a great tribulation, such as has not occurred since the beginning of the world until now, nor ever shall...."[543]

Jesus is saying to you to forget your possessions and just flee. For it is at this point that the antichrist, who hates G-d and Jesus,[544] is going to turn on every Jewish person who resists him spiritually. Certainly, do not bow to him, but do not stay and resist him either.

These events will play out just as the prophets have predicted. When you see them occur, it will be time to get out. G-d has decreed a limited amount of time for the antichrist to reign and commit atrocities. His day will end when Jesus returns and stops him. Until that day comes, G-d will provide a place for you to flee. It is in a "wilderness"[545] in the

---

[542] Dan. 9:27.
[543] Mt. 24:15-21.
[544] Rev. 12:4-5.
[545] Rev. 12:6, 14.

"mountains."[546] He will protect you there.[547] This place may be in the lands of "Edom, Moab and the foremost of the sons of Ammon," which Daniel noted will be spared from conquest by the antichrist.[548] These lands are in modern-day Jordan.[549] Pray to G-d, and He will lead you to where you need to go. Perhaps your experience will be similar to David's when he fled to the wilderness to escape King Saul.

When the day comes and Jesus ends the antichrist's reign of terror, He will then travel the globe and regather you back to your land from all the locations where you have been driven.[550]

*   *   *   *   *

I have been arguing in this four-volume set that it is stated, both implicitly in the Tanakh and explicitly in the New Testament, that the way to salvation is through the sacrifice of Jesus, which is necessary for the payment of our sins. However, in the final seven years there is an additional requirement. There is a work, and it must be performed in order to achieve eternity with G-d in heaven. Namely, you cannot bow your knee to the antichrist. You must resist, and you must do so by not taking his mark upon your forehead or the back of your right hand.[551] This will be very difficult as you will be persecuted, and it could even cost you your life. But it will lead to salvation in the next life. May you stay strong and never give in.

In the Garden of Eden, G-d gave Adam and Eve a free will choice: whether to stay with Him in paradise or reject Him and leave. The way they were given to exercise their choice to leave was to eat the fruit from one particular tree.[552] Once they did so, they went on to suffer the consequences, and there was no way

---

546 Mt. 24:16.

547 Rev. 12:13-17.

548 Dan. 11:41.

549 John F. Walvoord and Roy B. Zuck, *The Bible Knowledge Commentary*, Old Testament Edition (Wheaton, Illinois: Victor Books, 1985) 1372.

550 Isa. 11:11-12.

551 Rev. 13:16-18.

552 Gen. 2:16-17.

to take it back. Similarly, during the final period of history, each person will have a choice to make. Only, this time it will be Satan offering the choice. He will employ the antichrist to coerce people into making the wrong choice.[553] The way to exercise this choice will be to take the antichrist's tattoo upon your body. By taking his mark, you will be signifying your subservience to him. If you reject his mark, you will not be able to buy any food to eat. This choice, as well, will have consequences that you can never take back. Namely, those who bow to this man will be separated from G-d for eternity.[554]

*   *   *   *   *

As seen earlier in this chapter, one of the details about the end times that is clear in the prophecies of the Tanakh is that these days will be the worst time ever for the Jews. Sadly, great suffering is about to come upon you. Please remember the message of the book of Esther. Fearing for her life, Esther stepped forward to do the right thing and save her people, who were facing a sentence of genocide. For, her husband, King Ahasuerus, the ruler of the Persian Empire, had agreed to this sentence at the request of Haman, whom Ahasuerus had promoted to be the head over all the nobles. Haman had become enraged when a Jew named Mordecai would not bow to him.[555] The weak and impulsive king agreed to Haman's genocidal request, which, unbeknownst to him, included Esther.[556] Indeed, Mordecai was Esther's uncle, and he sent her a message, which said:

> "Do not imagine that you in the king's palace
> can escape any more than all the Jews. For if
> you remain silent at this time, relief and
> deliverance will arise for the Jews from another

---

[553] Rev. 13:15-18.
[554] Rev. 14:9-13; 20:4.
[555] Esth. 3:1-5; Dan. 3 (3:1-30.)
[556] Esth. 3:8-10.

place and you and your father's house will perish. And who knows whether you have not attained royalty for such a time as this?"[557]

Dear Jewish people, G-d knows who each of you is. He loves you, and He is watching you. No, He has not worked with your people in the way He worked with your forefathers for a very long time. But He will return and work with you again in the final phase of human history. His role for you will be that of witnesses to the world for Him. G-d has appointed each of you for such a time as this. Stand tall, and do not bow to this bully. Be brave and show the people of the world the way to G-d; do not go along with this man and allow him to put his tattoo from hell on your body.[558] G-d loves each individual Gentile, and He wants them to find eternity too.[559] The book of Revelation says that a great number of people around the world will find G-d at this time.[560] He is calling you to lead the way. Daniel put it this way: "And those who have insight will shine brightly like the brightness of the expanse of heaven, and those who lead the many to righteousness, like the stars forever and ever."[561]

Dear Jewish friends, I am so sorry. The awful suffering is coming again. Do not be surprised when you see it happen, for it will happen just as the ancient prophets foretold. Trust G-d. He will allow violence and evil, but only for a time. Certainly, He will not allow it to go on one minute longer than it has to in order for Him to accomplish all of His purposes.

---

[557] Esth. 4:13-14.

[558] Josephus tells us that during the days of the persecution of Antiochus, some of the Jews stood tall, but others caved. Daniel had earlier prophesied that it would be this way (Dan. 11:32-33.) So too, you will have to make an awful choice at the end of time. Be very careful not to give up eternity for continued life in this world. Cf. James Montgomery Boice, *Daniel* (Grand Rapids: Baker Books, 1989) 116-117.

[559] Rev. 14:6-7.

[560] Rev. 7:9-17. These Gentile believers will be persecuted and die as martyrs at this time, too (Rev. 6:9-11.)

[561] Dan. 12:3.

Some of you will escape to a safe place G-d has for you in the wilderness, but some of you will not escape. Know that when men spit words of hate in your faces, G-d will be there, and He will see you. He will hear every vile word, and He will see every blow that hits you. Your blood will cry out to Him like Abel's blood did all those years ago.[562] Know that there will be justice.

Some of you may live long enough to see Jesus coming in the sky, but some of you will not. Yet, one day, G-d will dry all of your tears.[563] Furthermore, according to the prophets, this will be the last time you ever suffer.[564]

Take heart, for G-d has been working throughout history to accomplish His plan to make everything right.[565] He will see it through, and one day His will shall be done on earth as it is in Heaven. When the final seven years begin, each day will pass, and in the end, G-d will send His Messiah to deliver you, and the nightmare will finally be over!

---

[562] Gen. 4:10.

[563] Isa. 25:8-9.

[564] Isa. 33:17-24.

[565] Dan. 9:24.

17

DANIEL 9:24

"Seventy weeks have been decreed for your people and your holy city to finish the transgression, to make an end of sin, to make atonement for iniquity, to bring in everlasting righteousness, to seal up vision and prophecy, and to anoint the most holy *place*...."

This sentence is the beginning of the four-verse prophecy we considered in Volume 2, Chapter 7. This is a transcendent prophecy that sets a timeline for the rest of G-d's dealings with the Jewish people throughout history. In this verse, it establishes that the Jews are G-d's people, and that He is going to use them to play an important role in His rescue plan for mankind. This verse also reveals the six goals of G-d's plan, which we will discuss in this chapter.

In the beginning of Daniel Chapter 9, we find him reading a prophecy from the book of Jeremiah in which G-d revealed to Jeremiah how long the Babylonian exile would last, namely 70 years. Daniel became excited as it was nearing the end of the

70 years, and he began to pray. Specifically, he prayed for the forgiveness of the sins of the Jewish people:

> And I prayed to the L-rd my G-d and confessed and said, "Alas, O L-rd, the great and awesome G-d, who keeps His covenant and lovingkindness for those who love Him and keep His commandments, we have sinned, committed iniquity, acted wickedly, and rebelled, even turning aside from Thy commandments and ordinances. Moreover, we have not listened to Thy servants the prophets, who spoke in Thy name to our kings, our princes, our fathers, and all the people of the land.... O L-rd, in accordance with all Thy righteous acts, let now Thine anger and Thy wrath turn away from Thy city Jerusalem, Thy holy mountain; for because of our sins and the iniquities of our fathers, Jerusalem and Thy people *have become* a reproach to all those around us. So now, our G-d, listen to the prayer of Thy servant and to his supplications, and for Thy sake, O L-rd, let Thy face shine on Thy desolate sanctuary. O my G-d, incline Thine ear and hear! Open Thine eyes and see our desolations and the city which is called by Thy name; for we are not presenting our supplications before Thee on account of any merits of our own, but on account of Thy great compassion. O L-rd, hear! O L-rd, forgive! O L-rd, listen and take action! For Thine own sake, O my G-d, do not delay, because Thy city and Thy people are called by Thy name."[566]

---

[566] Dan. 9:4-6, 16-19.

Following this very heartfelt prayer, G-d sent the angel Gabriel to Daniel to give him the prophecy in verses 24 through 27. The prophecy deals with the very things Daniel was praying about: sin and forgiveness, exile, and the destruction of Jerusalem, including the Temple. Daniel was praying for the restoration of the Jewish people from the Babylonian exile, but G-d gave him a prophecy that went far beyond his prayer. This prophecy deals with the restoration of humanity at the end of time. This prophecy also gives a timeline for Jewish history following the Babylonian exile. The timeline should be interpreted literally as opposed to symbolically, just as Jeremiah's prophecy of 70 years was fulfilled literally. Interestingly, the timeline includes the number 70. But Daniel is not calling for 70 years, but rather 70 sets of seven years. In other words, G-d was prophesying that He would work with the Jewish people for 490 more years to accomplish all His goals. In this prophecy, a few very important events are given, which will each play a prominent role in the completion of G-d's six goals. These events include the death of the Messiah, the destruction of Jerusalem and the Temple by the Romans, and a number of details about the final seven-year period and the evil world ruler who will arise at that time. We covered this information in Volume 2, including how there would be a gap of time between the 69th set of seven years and the 70th set, when G-d will return to working with the Jews at the end of history.

G-d can actually see the future, and the specific amount of time prophesied will be shown to be accurate. In addition, the six magnificent outcomes G-d prophesied in verse 24 will come to pass. Just as G-d set the Jews free from exile in Babylon, so too, He will set the Jews and all of humanity free from our groaning under the oppression of wicked world rulers, and from our imprisonment to our own sinful natures.[567] He already has set us free from the price of justice we each owe for our moral guilt. Here are the six goals:

---

[567] Ps. 51:5 (7;) Eph. 2:3.

1. The first goal is "to finish the transgression." The 70th week coincides with the final seven years of human history. It will be a unique period that will be worse than any time ever before in human history. War, disease, hunger, ecological disasters, and governmental oppression will be global. Sin and trauma will touch every person on earth. A number of grave transgressions and injustices have already taken place in history, and new ones will take place in the final period. The question is, Which one is being singled out in this verse?

Fortunately, the book of Daniel gives us a clue as it emphasizes a particular sin. This sin is mentioned in verse 27 in this prophecy, and it is called an "abomination." This sin will be committed by the man who is known as the antichrist. He will come to power as the head of a revived Roman Empire. Once again, the age-old dream of ruling the world will come to the fore. Only this time, the arrogant leader will succeed to a greater degree than has ever been accomplished before. But that still will not be enough to satisfy this evil man. He will go on to commit a very unique sin similar to the sin that took place following the days of Noah. In that event, which we have already covered in Chapter 2 of this book, the people were united and attempted to "build a tower whose top *will reach* into heaven" and make a name for themselves.[568] This was their childish attempt to take on G-d and cast off His authority. In the antichrist's case, not only will he seek to conquer the world, but he will also attempt to supplant G-d.

In history, Roman emperors made pretenses, sometimes strongly, about their divinity. This Roman Emperor will take it to the next level. In verse 27, Daniel prophesies that he will make a covenant with the Jewish people at the beginning of the seven-year period, perhaps as he is rising in power. But in the middle of the seven years, he will break the covenant and commit an abomination. We understand what this will look like based on the abomination committed by Antiochus Epiphanes IV, which Daniel also predicted.[569]

---

[568] Gen. 11:4.
[569] Dan. 11:31.

Antiochus could not stand either the G-d of the Jews or their religion, Judaism. He viewed their faith as an impediment to their Hellenization. Therefore, he forbade the observance of the Sabbath and the festivals, banned circumcision, and destroyed all known copies of the Tanakh. [570] The punishment for violating these policies was death. But he still was not done. After all this, he perpetrated the abomination in the Temple, which we discussed earlier.

Righteously did the Jews revolt, for they feared and honored G-d. It was not easy, and it took time, but in the end, G-d granted them victory. Daniel prophesied that at the end of time there will be a repeat of these events. The antichrist will both put a stop to the practice of Judaism and commit an abomination in the Temple.[571] His abomination will outdo Antiochus', as the antichrist will declare himself to be G-d and demand to be worshipped.[572] G-d will allow this blasphemous act to stand for three and a half years. It will be the greatest time of distress in all of history for the Jews. It is unimaginable to think that the horror the Jews will face will be worse than the cruelty they have already been subjected to by the Egyptians, Greeks, Romans, Catholics, and Germans. But Daniel says that it will be.[573] The prophet Jeremiah describes these days as follows:

> "For thus says the L-rd, 'I have heard a sound of terror, of dread, and there is no peace. Ask now, and see, if a male can give birth. Why do I see every man *with* his hands on his loins as a woman in childbirth? And *why* have all faces turned pale? Alas! for that day is great, there is none like it; and it is the time of Jacob's distress, but he will be saved from it.'..."[574]

---

[570] F. F. Bruce, *Israel and the Nations* (Grand Rapids: William B. Eerdmans Publishing Company, 1969, 1985) 145.
[571] Dan. 9:27.
[572] 2 Thes. 2:4.
[573] Dan. 12:1.
[574] Jer. 30:5-7.

In righteousness, the Jews will stand up and resist this evil man. In the end, G-d will see to their victory.

2. The second goal is to "make an end of sin." This is vitally important to our health and well-being. This is what Daniel's prayer in the beginning of Chapter 9 was all about. Not only do power-crazed world leaders sin, but so do all the rest of us. Our sins may not include committing acts of physical violence, but we each have hurt others, sometimes deeply. As well, we each have been wounded by the unrighteous words and deeds of others. We are demonstrably incapable of living righteously. The record of Jewish conduct documented over a 1,000-year period in the Tanakh proves this point. Jesus as well stated this fact in a way we could understand in the Sermon on the Mount:

> "You have heard that the ancients were told, "You shall not commit murder" and "Whoever commits murder shall be liable to the court." But I say to you that everyone who is angry with his brother shall be guilty before the court; and whoever shall say to his brother, "Raca"[575] shall be guilty before the supreme court; and whoever shall say, "You fool," shall be guilty *enough to go* into the fiery hell....
>
> You have heard that it was said, "You shall not commit adultery"; but I say to you, that everyone who looks on a woman to lust for her has committed adultery with her already in his heart."[576]

Here we see G-d's standard for righteousness. It includes not only our behavior but also what goes on in our hearts and

---

[575] Per the NASB Key Word Study Bible, raca is Aramaic for either empty-head or good for nothing. Spiro Zodhiates, Th.D., Executive Ed., *The Hebrew-Greek Key Word Study Bible*, New American Standard Bible (La Habra, CA: The Lockman Foundation, 1984, 1990) 1265.
[576] Mt. 5:21-22, 27-28.

minds. Jesus is right. What if you are very self-controlled and able to abstain from any outward wrong behaviors, but all the while you are harboring disgust and displeasure towards another person, or lustful thoughts towards a woman other than your wife? What if your true thoughts get revealed? The other person, or people, would feel insulted, hurt, and violated, and they would be right. Inner sins are visible to G-d and are just as wrong and unacceptable. Of course, the truth is that we are not capable of perfectly controlling our words and deeds. When we sin in our hearts, it will come out eventually.

Simply put, we are sinful, and we are all powerless to change our moral nature. We need G-d's help to be restored to moral wholeness. We need Him to eradicate sin by removing evil world leaders and their empires, and by removing it from within our hearts. This is the existence He designed us for, and this is the reality He will return us to at the end of the 70th set of seven years.

In the book of Jeremiah, Jeremiah quotes G-d, who is speaking about the end of time as follows:

> "I will make a new covenant with the house of Israel and with the house of Judah, not like the covenant which I made with their fathers in the day I took them by the hand to bring them out of the land of Egypt, My covenant which they broke, although I was a husband to them," declares the L-rd. "But this is the covenant which I will make with the house of Israel after those days," declares the L-rd, "I will put My law within them, and on their heart I will write it; and I will be their G-d, and they shall be My people."[577]

---

[577] Jer. 31:31-33 (30:32.)

Praise G-d. He will change the Jews' hearts, and He will restore their souls. Or as Daniel put it, He will "make an end of sin."

3. The third goal is to "make atonement for iniquity." This goal is the only one that has already been completed. It was accomplished in the early 30s CE, just as Daniel predicted it would be in verse 26, when he wrote that the Messiah will be cut off following the 69th set of seven years.

Surely Jesus showed up right on time, and He resoundingly fulfilled this goal when He was crucified. There He was, hoisted in the air, with spikes driven through His hands and His feet. He knew exactly when the goal was accomplished, at which point He said, "'It is finished!' Then He bowed His head and gave up His spirit."[578]

How could G-d come in the form of a man, teach spiritual truth, heal the sick, ignore the injustice of the Roman occupation, and then allow us to execute Him? How could that be His plan? It is shocking. It is not the plan we would have come up with. Yet, G-d says, "My thoughts are not your thoughts, neither are your ways My ways.... For *as* the heavens are higher than the earth, so are My ways higher than your ways, and My thoughts than your thoughts."[579] Why is this G-d's plan? This is His plan because there is no other way. This is how desperate our predicament is. This is the price of justice for our sins, and this is how great G-d's love is.

All along, G-d was communicating His plan. This is why G-d commanded Abraham to do the unthinkable— to place his only son, Isaac, on an altar as a sacrifice. This event foreshadowed that one day G-d would send Jesus to be a sacrifice. Only in Jesus' case, G-d did not put a stop to it.

This is why G-d had the Jews sacrifice lambs on the night of the very first Passover, even though the Jews were the victims of slavery and murder. It was a picture of how they were still guilty before G-d for their sins. They, too, needed a sacrifice to

---

[578] Jn. 19:30.
[579] Isa. 55:8-9.

pay the price of justice on their behalf. Of course, the lambs could not actually pay the price of justice for human sins. But Jesus could. Though being G-d Himself, He took on the form of a man, and then He lived an innocent life. Therefore, He actually could pay the price for the sins of another man. Furthermore, He could pay for the sins of all mankind because He was also G-d, and He had the infinite capacity needed to pay the price for all the sins committed throughout history. Indeed, this is why Isaiah prophesied that the Messiah would be a descendant of David, but also that His name would be "Mighty G-d."[580]

G-d was also communicating this message through Isaiah when he wrote Chapter 53. Though in hindsight it is a clear prediction of Jesus' first coming, it did not make sense before Jesus came and died on the cross. Again, this is not the plan we would have come up with, but now it makes sense. For example, here are verses 5 and 6 from Chapter 53:

> But He was pierced through for our transgressions, He was crushed for our iniquities; the chastening for our well-being *fell* upon Him, and by His scourging we are healed. All of us like sheep have gone astray, each of us has turned to his own way; but the L-rd has caused the iniquity of us all to fall on Him.

That is Jesus.

Furthermore, G-d was foreshadowing Jesus in the rituals of the Day of Atonement. In this annual festival, the sacrificial goat foreshadowed Jesus as a blameless sacrifice for sin. Additionally, the High Priest had to immediately get out of the Holy of Holies once he sprinkled the sacrificial blood on the Mercy Seat. Indeed, it was only a symbolic act. The price of justice for his sins was not actually paid, and he was not fit to be in G-d's presence. Had he not left right away, he would have perished in a ball of flames like Nadab and Abihu did.[581]

---

[580] Isa. 9:6-7 (5-6.)
[581] Lev. 10:1 ff.

The Hebrew word from Daniel that is translated "make atonement" is the verb *kāpar*. As we learned in Volume 1, the gold lid on top of the Ark of the Covenant is the *kappōret*. It is a noun that is derived from the verb, and it means a place of atonement or a mercy seat. But whereas the High Priest would apply the blood of a bull and a goat on the mercy seat once a year, Jesus presented His own blood before G-d in heaven one time for the sins of the world."[582]

Jesus' disciple Peter wrote, "For Christ also died for sins once for all, the just for the unjust, in order that He might bring us to G-d, having been put to death in the flesh, but made alive in the spirit."[583] This is the third goal of Daniel 9:24. It was performed solely by Jesus. It had to be. Through His act, justice has been served, and now we can be forgiven and come into G-d's presence for real.

4. The fourth goal is to "bring in everlasting righteousness." Wow! Certainly G-d's power and resources will be needed for this goal to be realized. What does this goal even mean? It is the flip side of the second goal. It is what society and life will look like free from sin. But this is beyond our ability to comprehend, as all we have ever known is sin. None of us is righteous, society is not righteous, and definitely, history is not righteous. We are self-protective. Our natural modus operandi is to advance our own interests. We hide our shame. We can be self-absorbed. Some of us are willing to hurt others. On the other hand, some of us are kind people who truly care about others. But, none of us are morally perfect. Even faithful Daniel confessed that he too was a sinner.[584]

Sometimes society goes to a bad place morally, where ungodly values become socially acceptable and a majority of the people go down the wrong path. Actually, this is not uncommon in history, even among the Jews. Jeremiah described such a

---

[582] Heb. 9:11-15.
[583] 1 Pet. 3:18.
[584] Dan. 9:20.

time in Judah, just before G-d allowed the Babylonians to ravage Jerusalem:

> For from the least of them even to the greatest
> of them everyone is greedy for gain, and from
> the prophet even to the priest everyone deals
> falsely. And they have healed the brokenness of
> My people superficially, saying, "Peace, peace,"
> but there is no peace.[585]

Here, virtually everyone in Judah had rejected the path of goodness to pursue selfishness—even the religious leaders. Indeed, they were the worst of all. They claimed to be speaking on behalf of G-d, but they were lying. They reassured the people that G-d was going to grant them peace, when in fact it was just the opposite.

In the New Testament, it is prophesied that human society will be in a similar place in the days leading up to the end of history:

> But realize this, that in the last days difficult
> times will come. For men will be lovers of self,
> lovers of money, boastful, arrogant, revilers,
> disobedient to parents, ungrateful, unholy,
> unloving, irreconcilable, malicious gossips,
> without self-control, brutal, haters of good,
> treacherous, reckless, conceited, lovers of
> pleasure rather than lovers of G-d; holding to
> a form of godliness, although they have
> denied its power....[586]

Some people believe we are approaching the end of time today. After all, one day it will arrive. But the point is that the fourth goal will lead to an existence that will be the opposite of the state of moral decay that society will be in prior to the end

---

[585] Jer. 6:13-14.
[586] 2 Tim. 3:1-5.

of time. Following the final seven years of history, G-d will deliver us from ourselves, and no one will live this way. We will all serve each other from our hearts. No one will be greedy. We won't love money; we will be lovers of G-d. We will have peace with Him, peace with others, and peace within our hearts. Imagine what it will be like to treat others with kindness from a pure heart. Thank G-d that one day we will experience righteousness. We cannot fully picture it now, but in that day, everyone in society will live righteously, and we will know joy. Malachi explains it like this: "But for you who fear My name the sun of righteousness will rise with healing in its wings; and you will go forth and skip about like calves from the stall."[587] In this verse, righteousness is pictured as the warm sun on a beautiful spring day in which the cows are released after a long winter's confinement in their stalls. They get to return to the pasture, and it is life-giving. They literally dance, jumping around the way they did when they were calves. It is wonderful, and so it will be one day for us.

5. G-d's fifth goal is to seal up vision and prophecy. This is reassuring. There is so much wisdom in the Bible, and yet there are a number of unanswered questions too. In fact, it was by design that G-d gave some prophecies with specific details and some with vague details. G-d did this for strategic reasons. It is like playing a card game in which you do not reveal your cards until the right moment. Only, this is not a game. For example, in the book of Jeremiah, Jeremiah places himself in history by giving the names of the kings who ruled at that time. He wrote a lot of prophecy, and a lot of it was about a coming catastrophic defeat for the Jews. He mentioned that the enemy would be from the north.[588] Then he got specific and revealed who the enemy would be—Babylon.[589] The book of Joel, on the other hand, is quite different. First of all, as opposed to being long, it is short. But beyond that, Joel never gives a historical marker

---

[587] Mal. 4:2 (3:20.)
[588] Jer. 10:22.
[589] Jer. 20:4.

that tells us when he wrote. Scholars today debate whether he wrote before or after the Babylonian exile. That makes it difficult to interpret his prophecy. Joel speaks of dark days and a great drought that will come upon the Jews. In addition, he mentions an army from the north, but he does not reveal their identity.[590] Hence, whereas Jeremiah ties himself down with specific details about people and events, Joel does not. There are clues in Joel that seem to indicate his prophecy pertains to the time of the end, but you cannot be certain about what he is prophesying. Again, this is all on purpose. G-d has a reason for revealing some details of history in advance while being unclear about others until the day comes for them to take place. Once they take place, then the prophecies make total sense.

According to the fifth goal, at the end of history, there will be no more prophecy or foreshadowing left to be fulfilled. It will all have come to pass, and it will all make sense. Furthermore, all the lies and subtle critiques questioning the goodness of G-d will be cleared up. We will meet G-d face to face,[591] and we will behold and understand His righteousness, justice, mercy, kindness, patience, and power.

There are some passages in the Bible that raise questions for which there are no ironclad answers. For example, why will animal sacrifices for burnt offerings, sin offerings, and guilt offerings be reinstituted at the end of time if Jesus' death paid for every sin ever committed?[592]

Certainly, this is an important question. Yet, this is the way G-d had the Bible written. In it, He has given us many clear answers, but not all the answers. He has given us enough information and evidence to trust Him, and that is what He is looking for from us—faith. Eve knew enough about G-d's goodness to trust Him, but she thoughtlessly broke His one and only rule anyway. At a minimum, she could have postponed her disastrous decision and gone to G-d to ask Him about the accusations the serpent raised against Him. After all, He gave

---

[590] Joel 2:20.
[591] 1 Cor. 13:12.
[592] Ezek. 40-45; Heb. 7:23-9:15; Rabbi Singer 2:94.

Eve her life. Then all He did was love her and tell her the truth. She owed Him that.

Thank G-d for His fifth goal, for one day we will have all the answers, and it will all make sense. In Chapter 12 of his book, Zechariah prophesies of the moment when the truth about Jesus will be revealed to the Jewish people:

> And I will pour out on the house of David and on the inhabitants of Jerusalem, the Spirit of grace and of supplication, so that they will look on Me whom they have pierced; and they will mourn for Him, as one mourns for an only son, and they will weep bitterly over Him, like the bitter weeping over a first-born.[593]

This verse is amazing. Zechariah is quoting G-d, who speaks of personally having been pierced by the Jewish people. Jesus will appear to the Jews at His second coming. The wounds will be manifest in His body, and the Jews will see them. Then all the confusion will be gone. They will know exactly how the Trinity works and that Jesus died for their salvation. They will grasp the price of justice that Jesus paid to set us free, and they will break down and weep for the pain He endured.

6. G-d's sixth goal is "to anoint the most holy place." This is referring to the Holy of Holies. This sacred place will be anointed, or reestablished. Only, in the future, the Holy of Holies will function in the way G-d always wanted it to, not in the stilted, broken way it functioned in ancient Israel. The Holy of Holies is the place where G-d dwelt among the Jews. But no one was allowed to enter His presence due to their sins. Only once a year could the High Priest briefly enter this space to perform a ritual. But at this point, G-d will have completed His plan to restore humanity, and all people will be welcome to come into His presence and spend time with Him. In the words of Jeremiah: "'And they shall not teach again, each man his

---

[593] Zech. 12:10.

neighbor and each man his brother, saying, "Know the L-rd," for they shall all know Me, from the least of them to the greatest of them,' declares the L-rd, 'for I will forgive their iniquity, and their sin I will remember no more.'"[594]

Our state of moral imperfection, which bars us from G-d's presence, will be dealt with by G-d when He transforms us per Goal 4. Likewise, the issue of our moral guilt, which separates us from G-d, was taken care of by the Messiah when He completed the third goal. Therefore, G-d will be free to have a relationship with us as He has always desired.

All our lives G-d has had His eye on each of us. In the words of David in Psalm 139:

> O L-rd, Thou hast searched me and known *me*. Thou dost know when I sit down and when I rise up; Thou dost understand my thought from afar. Thou dost scrutinize my path and my lying down, and art intimately acquainted with all my ways. Even before there is a word on my tongue, behold, O L-rd, Thou dost know it all. Thou hast enclosed me behind and before, and laid Thy hand upon me. *Such* knowledge is too wonderful for me; it is *too* high, I cannot attain to it....
>
> How precious also are Thy thoughts to me, O G-d! How vast is the sum of them! If I should count them, they would outnumber the sand. When I awake, I am still with Thee.[595]

G-d knows everything about us. He knows exactly who we are.

But we cannot see Him. Indeed, we forget about Him. What is more, we have been told lies about G-d, and we are scared of Him. But at the end of time, those of us who have a heart for

---

[594] Jer. 31:34 (33.)
[595] Ps. 139:1-6, 17-18.

G-d will be with Him. Then we will know the truth, and we will love Him fully.

The prophet Zephaniah has prophesied of the days when G-d will live amongst His people:

> The L-rd has taken away *His* judgments against you, He has cleared away your enemies. The King of Israel, the L-rd, is in your midst; You will fear disaster no more. In that day it will be said to Jerusalem: "Do not be afraid, O Zion; Do not let your hands fall limp. The L-rd your G-d is in your midst, a victorious warrior. He will exult over you with joy, He will be quiet in His love, He will rejoice over you with shouts of joy."[596]

How astonishing. G-d will be with us. We will see G-d experience joy, and we will personally receive His gentle love.

Incomprehensibly, today we have cast G-d out of our midst. He is not welcome in our society. In the day that G-d completes His goals, we will never want to leave His presence.

*   *   *   *   *

Human beings are an amazing part of G-d's creation. Humans have climbed Mt. Everest and swum the English Channel. We have even figured out how to split the nuclei of radioactive elements in order to harness nuclear energy.

But we cannot stop fighting wars or harness our mouths.

Praise G-d He has a plan to rescue us, and it is glorious.

One of the surprising features of G-d's plan is that He uses us to play a part in it. First He used the Jews, now He is working with Christians, and soon He will return to working with the Jews again. As His people, we are the objects of His love, and our role is to be witnesses of His goodness to the rest of the world.

---

[596] Zeph. 3:15-17.

As we saw in this chapter, the six goals of His plan are wondrous. They are G-d-sized goals that are beyond us. For example, it is inherently obvious that we are incapable of making atonement for iniquity or bringing in everlasting righteousness. Indeed, the context of Daniel Chapter 9 is Jewish sin and inadequacy as Daniel is appealing to G-d for the deliverance of the Jews on the basis of His grace. In the words of Isaiah, "all of us have become like one who is unclean, and all our righteous deeds are like a filthy garment."[597] Even our good deeds are tainted by our unrighteousness. This is a harsh statement, but Isaiah wants us to realize that this is who we really are.

Only G-d could accomplish these magnificent goals. Therefore, His plan itself is evidence for Jesus being the Messiah.

---

[597] Isa. 64:6a.

18

THE MAGNIFICENT PLAN OF G-D

Adam and Eve rebelled in the Garden of Eden and were removed from G-d's presence. They were sent out into the world to have children. We have been rebelling ever since. Nonetheless, G-d is so good that He initiated a rescue plan to save us from our sins.

In Chapter 11 we discussed how G-d's long-term plan is a two-stage plan. But in reality, it has four stages. The two we discussed in that chapter are the two longer, human-assisted stages. The other two are brief stages in which the Messiah comes to earth and performs His two roles as the atoning sacrifice and the conquering king.

The first visit by the Messiah came in the middle of the two longer stages. During that visit, Jesus' public ministry was only three to three and a half years long. He accomplished a number of tasks in that brief period, but by far, the main one was to die as a sacrifice for our sins. Indeed, it all boils down to what happened to Jesus on the cross. As He hung there without His clothes on, His blood dripped down the wood. His nerves fell victim to the cruel form of execution, and His body spasmed in pain. The flesh around the holes in His hands and feet proceeded to slowly rip open as He kept repositioning Himself to try to breathe properly. At some point, gravity overcame His skeletal muscle, and His bones released from their sockets. Once He had suffered enough to pay the price for the guilty, He gave up His life, and the physical pain and emotional distress were over.[598]

Jesus will return to perform His second role at the end of history. The fourth stage will be brief as well. Jesus will come in all His glory to put an end to the oppression wrought by sinful human governments and save us from this broken world.

The ultimate goal of G-d's rescue plan is to restore humanity to the life Adam and Eve knew in Eden when they were unified with G-d. Of course, not everyone is interested in G-d's offer of salvation. His desire is for everyone to receive His forgiveness, but He does not force it on those who are not interested.[599] Those who decline it will not be reunited with G-d but will spend eternity in a state of hell, or separation from G-d.

In the previous chapter, we discussed Daniel 9:24. This verse prophesies the outcomes G-d will achieve at the conclusion of His rescue plan. Here they are again:

> "Seventy weeks have been decreed for your people and your holy city, to finish the transgression, to make an end of sin, to make atonement for iniquity, to bring in everlasting righteousness, to seal up vision and prophecy, and to anoint the most holy *place*...."

In the words of Jesus' disciple John, "Come, L-rd Jesus."[600]

* * * * *

---

[598] Lk. 23:33-49; Jn. 19:28-30.
[599] Isa. 55:6-7; Jn. 1:12; Rev. 3:20.
[600] Rev. 22:20.

In terms of the rescue plan itself, the glaring question is, why did G-d choose people to play a role in His plan? After all, both the Jews and the Christians failed spectacularly in their missions.

Perhaps part of the answer is that we are arrogant, and we need to fail so that we will stop talking and instead listen to what G-d is saying. One of the pitfalls for G-d's people is that we are prone to becoming self-righteous. This has been the case for both Jews and Christians. But when you examine our histories, how foolish is that? G-d wants us to see clearly. It is not that He wants us to wallow in our shame, but He does want us to see our need for forgiveness.

Judah was one of Jacob's 12 sons. Just before Jacob passed away, he spoke prophetically about the futures of the tribes that would come forth from each of his sons. When he came to Judah, he said this:

> "Judah, your brothers shall praise you; your hand shall be on the neck of your enemies; your father's sons shall bow down to you. Judah is a lion's whelp; from the prey, my son, you have gone up. He couches, he lies down as a lion, and as a lion, who dares rouse him up? The scepter shall not depart from Judah, nor the ruler's staff from between his feet, until Shiloh comes...."[601]

We studied this prophecy in Volume 2. In these verses, G-d prophesied that the Jewish kings would come through the line of Judah, including the Messiah. As the centuries unfolded, so they did. What is interesting is that G-d would choose Judah, of all people, to be the ancestor of the Messiah. Judah grew as a person. We can see this when he pleaded to go to prison in place of his youngest brother in order to fulfill his promise to his father.[602] But earlier in his life, he disobeyed G-d and married a

---

[601] Gen. 49:8-10.
[602] Gen. 44:14-34.

Canaanite woman.[603] After his wife died, he slept with a prostitute. Except, she wasn't a prostitute; she was his bereaved daughter-in-law in disguise.[604]

Furthermore, in Genesis, we learn that Judah's oldest son was "evil" and that his second son did something that was "displeasing in the sight of the L-rd."[605] So, why would G-d bestow on Judah the honor of having his descendants be the kings of Israel? Could it be so the Jews would know that their ancestors were not saints, but sinners like everyone else?

Or, how about Rahab? She was a Canaanite prostitute. But she believed in G-d, and she placed her faith in Him.[606] She wound up marrying Salmon, a Judahite. Her great-grandson was Jesse, the father of David.[607] Of course, G-d promised David that through him would come the Messiah.[608] The point is that the Jews had no call to be proud. They were not chosen by G-d because their ancestors were especially righteous. Rather, G-d chooses people to use in His plan based on their faith. Rahab was not Jewish, and she was a prostitute, but she had faith. The lesson is that none of us are special, and none of us are righteous. We all need forgiveness. We need to be humble and look to G-d for salvation.

Ultimately, our mission is to bear testimony of the G-d of the Jews. He is the one true G-d, and He is a G-d of love. Since we are all sinners, seeing clearly gives us the humility we need to present the message of G-d's love to people with compassion instead of contempt. Isaiah was a very godly man, but when he found himself in the presence of G-d, he immediately knew he did not belong there because of his sins. In his words: "Woe to me, for I am ruined! Because I am a man of unclean lips, and I live among a people of unclean lips; for my eyes have seen the

---

[603] Gen. 38:1-5.

[604] Gen. 38:12-16.

[605] Gen. 38:6-10.

[606] Josh. 2:1-21; 6:17-25.

[607] Mt. 1:4-5.

[608] Ps. 89:34-36 (35-37;) Isa. 9:6-7 (5-6;) Jer. 23:5-6.

King, the L-rd of hosts."[609] From that point on, Isaiah was able to present all of the warnings G-d gave him with humility as opposed to arrogance. So too with Christians today, we need to be humble when we tell people about Jesus. This makes it easier for them to hear our message instead of being put off by our arrogance.

We see an example of this in John 4. In that event, Jesus had a dialogue with a Samaritan woman, who was a social outcast because of her loose moral lifestyle. In the course of their conversation, He convinced her that He was the Messiah, and she placed her faith in Him. The idea of G-d accepting her was very attractive to her because she had been rejected by her community. Despite her rejection, her first instinct was to tell the people in her community this great news:

> So the woman left her waterpot, and went into the city and said to the men, "Come, see a man who told me all the things that I *have* done; this is not the Christ, is it?" They went out of the city, and were coming to Him....
>
> From that city many of the Samaritans believed in Him because of the word of the woman who testified, "He told me all the things that I *have* done." So when the Samaritans came to Jesus, they were asking Him to stay with them; and He stayed there two days. Many more believed because of His word; and they were saying to the woman, "It is no longer because of what you said that we believe, for we have heard for ourselves and know that this One is indeed the Savior of the world."[610]

When we approach people as forgiven sinners, they will listen. This is one reason G-d has chosen to use us in His plan.

---

[609] Isa. 6:5.
[610] Jn. 4:28-30; 39-42.

We have street credibility, and G-d is able to use us to reach the lost.

Another reason He uses us is because He loves us, and He wants to give us a fulfilling role to play. Here is an example from the apostles' lives of how life-giving it is to be used by G-d to do His will:

> When they had brought them, they stood them before the Council. The high priest questioned them, saying, "We gave you strict orders not to continue teaching in this name, and yet, you have filled Jerusalem with your teaching and intend to bring this man's blood upon us." But Peter and the apostles answered, "We must obey G-d rather than men. The G-d of our fathers raised up Jesus, whom you had put to death by hanging Him on a cross. He is the one whom G-d exalted to His right hand as a Prince and a Savior, to grant repentance to Israel, and forgiveness of sins. And we are witnesses of these things; and *so is* the Holy Spirit, whom G-d has given to those who obey Him."
>
> ...after calling the apostles in, they flogged them and ordered them not to speak in the name of Jesus, and *then* released them. So they went on their way from the presence of the Council, rejoicing that they had been considered worthy to suffer shame for *His* name. And every day, in the temple and from house to house, they kept right on teaching and preaching Jesus *as* the Christ.[611]

It was very important for the apostles to play their roles as G-d's representatives in the days following Jesus' resurrection

---

[611] Acts 5:27-32, 40b-42.

and ascension. Even getting beaten unjustly paled in comparison to the honor of representing Jesus.

It would be natural to think that only the heavy hitters, or only the most important Christians, get to play roles like the ones these men played. But that was not the case in the first century. Only a few were apostles, but they all had an important role to play, and the movement grew tremendously because of that. In Ephesians, Paul wrote,

> For we are His workmanship, created in Christ Jesus for good works, which G-d prepared beforehand so that we would walk in them.[612]

Indeed, G-d has prepared important works for each Christian to perform. In John 10, Jesus said,

> "...I came that they may have life, and have it abundantly."[613]

Jesus came to secure our eternal destinies, to heal our wounds, and to bless us for the remainder of our lives on earth. There is nothing more fulfilling than being used by Jesus to play a part in His mission, for the fruit of our labors for Jesus will last into eternity.

Despite all of the failure in Christian history, we can succeed in following Jesus. In the book of Philippians, Paul wrote:

> Not that I have already obtained it or have already become perfect, but I press on so that I may lay hold of that for which also I was laid hold of by Christ Jesus. Brethren, I do not regard myself as having laid hold of it yet; but one thing I do: forgetting what lies behind and reaching forward to what lies ahead, I press on

---

[612] Eph. 2:10.
[613] Jn. 10:10b.

> toward the goal for the prize of the upward call
> of G-d in Christ Jesus.[614]

and,

> I can do all things through Him who strengthens
> me.[615]

In the first set of verses, we see that Paul still sinned. So, we are not alone. Yet, he did not let that paralyze him as he pressed on in his Christian life. In the second passage, he shares with us that he drew on the strength and assistance of the Holy Spirit to carry out his ministry. The Holy Spirit is accessible to us too.[616]

Living the Christian life the way Paul and the Christians in the first century did has always been important. Unfortunately, as we saw earlier in this book, most Christians throughout history have not lived this way. But it may be even more important to live this way now than ever before. In His prophetic speech about the end of time, Jesus said,

> This gospel of the kingdom shall be preached
> in the whole world as a testimony to all the
> nations, and then the end will come.[617]

In this verse, Jesus is telling us that when the gospel message is being presented to every people group on earth such that everyone has an opportunity to hear about Jesus, then His return will come soon. Each Christian has a role, and the Church as a whole has a mission too, and this is it: to take the gospel message to the farthest corners of the earth. We are getting close to completing this mission, and we cannot let off the gas now.

---

[614] Phil. 3:12-14.
[615] Phil. 4:13.
[616] Jn. 14:16-27; 16:5-15; 1 Cor. 12:4-11; Acts 10:34-47.
[617] Mt. 24:14.

G-d has brought about a revival in American Christianity over the last 50 years. New churches based on the church model from the first century have sprung up across America, and a movement is underway today. In addition, mission agencies are focused on Jesus' goal for the Church, and they are working diligently towards its completion.[618] Today, quietly, Christianity is spreading all over the world. Unbeknownst to television news channels, which are focused on things like politics, Christianity is growing rapidly in places like China and the Muslim world. This is a result of G-d blessing the efforts of Christians, and it is also due to G-d Himself sprinting across the globe to reach every person whose heart is open to Him. Indeed, there will be a magnificent harvest of souls to meet and spend time with in eternity from every people group on earth:

> After these things I looked, and behold, a great multitude which no one could count, from every nation and *all* tribes and peoples and tongues, standing before the throne and before the Lamb, clothed in white robes, and palm branches *were* in their hands; and they cry out with a loud voice, saying, "Salvation to our G-d who sits on the throne, and to the Lamb." And all the angels were standing around the throne and *around* the elders and the four living creatures; and they fell on their faces before the throne and worshiped G-d, saying, "Amen, blessing and glory and wisdom and thanksgiving and honor and power and might, *be* to our G-d forever and ever. Amen."[619]

---

[618] Cf. Chapter 14 for details.

[619] Rev. 7:9-12. (This multitude of Gentiles in Revelation 7 will come from the harvest of souls occurring during the Great Tribulation. The total number of Gentiles from around the globe who will be with G-d in eternity will be far greater.)

The point for Christians today is that we can and we must play our part in G-d's plan. Let us not delay G-d's plan as the Jews coming out of Egypt did when they said no to Him.[620] On that occasion, G-d waited patiently for 40 years for the next generation to arise, trust Him, and cross the Jordan River into the Promised Land.

*   *   *   *   *

What if you are Jewish—what is G-d calling you to do today?

Fortunately, the answer to that question is readily available in the Tanakh. The Tanakh is G-d's instruction manual on how to live. Unlike the poorly written, confusing instruction manuals that come with the products we buy today, the Tanakh is understandable.

G-d emphasizes certain things in the Tanakh. If you emphasize them in your life, you will know peace.

One thing the Tanakh emphasizes is to approach G-d in the way that Abraham, Moses, and David did. Namely, have faith in Him and welcome Him into your life. As per Abraham's example, believe G-d and follow His direction for you, for G-d is good. Like Moses, get to know G-d and enjoy a relationship with Him. In David's case, he wrote approximately half of the Psalms. Read them, and then write your own Psalm to G-d.

Another emphasis in the Tanakh is the Law. You should follow the Law and show the world the correct way to live. As the Prophet Micah wrote:

> He has told you, O man, what is good; and what
> does the L-rd require of you but to do justice,
> to love kindness, and to walk humbly with your
> G-d?.[621]

Of course, you will not be perfect. No one is. In the Tanakh, G-d is asking you to obey Him from your heart, to lead a godly

---

[620] Num. 13:1-14:38.
[621] Mic. 6:8.

life, and to be kind to others. He is not asking you to try to achieve moral perfection, which brings us to a third emphasis. This emphasis, which runs like a heartbeat throughout the Tanakh, is G-d's rescue plan for humanity. We see it in the ceremonial portion of the Law in the Torah, and we see it in the messianic prophecies that are present in both the Nevi'im and the Ketuvim. The prophets foretold that a savior would come who would pay the price of atonement for the sins of the world. According to the Tanakh, we are all in need of a savior. In the words of Solomon:

> Indeed, there is not a righteous man on earth who continually does good and who never sins.[622]

Surely, this subject of our unrighteousness and our unfitness to come into the presence of a holy G-d is a major theme in the Tanakh. Pay attention to it as you read through the Tanakh. The language concerning the seriousness of our sins is stark, and it is heart wrenching when the subject is the ordeal that the Messiah would go through on our behalf. In the words of David and Isaiah,

> I am poured out like water, and all my bones are out of joint; my heart is like wax; it is melted within me. My strength is dried up like a potsherd, and my tongue clings to my jaws; and Thou dost lay me in the dust of death.[623]

and,

> Just as many were astonished at you, *My people*, so His appearance was marred more than any man, and His form more than the

---

[622] Eccl. 7:20.
[623] Ps. 22:14-15.

sons of men. Thus He will sprinkle many nations, . . .[624]

Could Jesus be the Messiah? I recommend you read the New Testament and consider Him. Who was Jesus? He was your ancestor, and He was a man of peace. He followed the Written Law,[625] and He died as a martyr. Then His body went missing. The people who knew Him best, His disciples, loved Him. They were just working-class Jewish people. Several were fishermen, and one was even a traitor to the Jews, a despised tax collector for the Romans. But it was this group of men who started what is today the world's largest religion. Along with Paul, they wrote the New Testament. Finally, they went to their deaths rather than recant their testimonies that Jesus rose from the dead.

None of these statements are in dispute. Jesus is worthy of being considered, as opposed to being dismissed out of hand. Jewish people in Jesus' day wrestled with this same question: who was He? At one point, Jesus asked His disciples who people thought He was:

> Now when Jesus came into the district of Caesarea Philippi, He was asking His disciples, "Who do people say that the Son of Man is?" And they said, "Some *say* John the Baptist; and others, Elijah; but still others, Jeremiah, or one of the prophets." He said to them, "But who do you say that I am?" Simon Peter answered, "You are the Christ, the Son of the living G-d." And Jesus said to him, "Blessed are you, Simon Barjona, because flesh and blood did not reveal *this* to you, but My Father who is in heaven."[626]

---

[624] Isa. 52:14-15a.

[625] Mt. 5:17-20.

[626] Mt. 16:13-17.

Dear reader, who do you say that Jesus was? Perhaps you are not sure. If you want to know, you should pray to G-d to show you. He is more than capable of doing this.

TO BE CONTINUED . . .

INDEX

Aaron, 43
Abolition, 213
Abolitionist, 213
Abraham or Abram, iv, ix, 15, 18, 20-28, 31, 32, 38, 39, 46, 64, 66, 84, 111, 133, 134, 145, 148, 149, 159, 187, 223-226, 237, 263, 282
Adam, 5-13, 93, 94, 106, 122, 233, 248, 252, 273, 274
Age of Exploration, 206, 220
Ahab, 61, 62, 64, 126
Ahaz, 67, 68
Amorite(s), 24, 35
Anglican Church, 213
Antichrist, 234, 241, 242, 245-253, 259, 260
Antiochus IV Epiphanes, 88, 90, 241, 242, 243, 245, 246, 254, 259, 260
Anti-Semitism, 128, 130, 230, 237
Anti-Semitic, 207
Apostle(s), 17, 39, 113, 131, 147, 151, 157, 159, 160, 165, 166, 171, 174, 176, 179, 190, 191, 201, 238, 278, 279
Archbishop(s), 181
Ark of the Covenant, 265
Asherah, 60, 62, 65
Assyria, 65, 224
Assyrian(s), 60, 65, 137
Assyrian Empire, 65
Augustine, 175, 188, 192

Baal(s), 33, 51, 61-64, 66, 124
Babylon, 70, 71, 74
Babylonia, 73, 224, 225
Babylonian(s), 73, 76, 89, 97, 103, 119, 266
Babylonian Empire, 248
Babylonian Exile or Captivity, ix, 33, 50, 77, 79, 104, 125, 225, 256, 258, 268
    Return from Exile, 87, 89
Billy Graham, 213, 214
Bishop(s), 127, 176-179, 181, 188, 191, 195, 212, 213
Bull (see Papal Bull)

Canaan, 32, 34, 223, 224
Canaanite(s), 24, 29, 31, 32, 56, 62, 64, 276
Cardinal Richelieu, 183
Cathari, 190
Catholic(s), 128-130, 166, 174, 177, 179, 180, 183, 184, 186, 189, 191, 195-199, 201-204, 210, 217, 235, 260
Catholic Church, xi, 166, 167, 173, 174, 176, 178, 181, 183, 184, 186, 194-196, 199-203, 207, 210-212, 214, 217, 236
Catholicism, 177, 198, 201-203, 207, 235
Charlemagne, 180, 181
Child Sacrifice, 34, 39, 70

Church Fathers, 175
Clergy/Laity, 156, 172, 176, 215
Coming(s) of the Messiah, xiv, 142
   First Coming, 9, 10, 85, 87, 144, 264
      Servant, 12, 26, 27, 46, 143-145, 150, 151
   Second Coming, 255, 269
      King, 110, 186, 215, 271
Constantine, 179
Constantinople, 173
Covenant(s), 24, 51, 84, 132, 239, 249, 250, 259
   Abrahamic Covenant, 22, 24, 25, 145
   Mosaic Covenant, 30, 45, 51, 65, 70, 74, 75, 149, 226, 257, 262
   New Covenant, 231, 233, 262
Crusade(s), 128, 184, 185, 188-190
Crusaders, 129, 185, 188, 189
Cyrus, 89, 149

Daniel, ix, xiv, 37, 76, 77, 120, 121, 125, 220, 227, 234, 235, 241, 242, 245-249, 251, 252, 256, 258-261, 263, 265, 272, 274
David, 39, 42, 43, 47, 53, 54, 56, 58, 59, 67-69, 82, 86, 101, 105, 107, 110, 125, 231, 249, 252, 264, 269, 270, 276, 282, 283
Deacons, 176

Diaspora, 125, 129, 131, 226, 228, 235, 236
   Return or Regathering from Diaspora, ix, 131, 150, 223, 224, 228, 229, 231, 233, 252
Disciple(s), 8, 84, 87, 100-102, 104, 106, 107, 111-113, 115, 116, 118, 123, 125, 147, 151, 153-155, 159, 167-169, 237, 265, 274, 284
Discipleship, 168

Eastern Orthodox Church, 173
Egypt, 24, 32-37, 50, 51, 56, 59, 72, 73, 89, 92, 185, 223, 224, 230, 242, 243, 245, 262, 282
Egyptian(s), 32, 90, 260
Elder(s) (church), 176, 178
Elijah, 61-64, 75, 85, 123, 124, 284
Encyclical,
   Maximum Illud, 217
   Mit Brennender Sorge, 203
Ephesus, 161, 162
Episcopal, 212
Esau, 133, 133
Ethne, 218
Evangelical, 215, 220
Evangelicals, 215
Evangelism, 168
Evangelize, 161, 163, 217, 218, 221, 223
Eve, 3, 5-7, 9, 11-13, 93, 94, 122, 159, 248, 252, 268, 273, 274
Ex Cathedra, 207
Explorers, 202
Ezekiel, 226-229, 232, 249

Galileo, 207
Gemara, 21, 96
Gnosticism, 190
Gnostics, 190
Gospel, 18, 130, 146, 147, 157, 158, 162, 163, 172, 184, 194, 200-202, 219-221
Great Commission, 167, 176, 188, 201, 217, 221
Great Tribulation, 146, 238, 247, 251, 281
Greece, 161
Greek(s), 87, 88, 90, 145, 154, 158, 171, 173, 177, 178, 218, 245, 260, 261
Greek Empire, 87, 246

Habsburg(s), 183
Hanukkah, 88
Heresy, 165, 166, 175, 181, 190, 192
Heretic(s), 174, 190-196
Heretical, 195, 212
Hesed, 44
Hierarchical, 174, 175, 201
Hierarchy, 130, 175
High Priest(s), 101, 107, 264, 265, 269, 278
Hitler, 210, 230, 241, 246
Holocaust, 135, 136, 185, 237
Holy of Holies, 75, 111, 264, 269
Holy Spirit, 7, 85, 111, 132, 146, 152, 155, 158, 159, 162, 163, 165, 167-171, 176, 194, 217, 219, 226, 228, 232, 239, 269, 278, 280

Idol(s), 56, 60, 66, 75, 79, 119, 161, 232, 244
Idolatry, 52, 58, 67, 69, 131

Indulgence(s), 199, 200
Inquisition, 184, 185, 190, 191, 193-195, 235
Inquisitor(s), 190, 194-197
Isaac, 22, 25-27, 38, 39, 64, 133, 134, 224, 225, 263
Isaiah, 12, 26-28, 46, 70, 79, 85, 103, 110, 113, 143-146, 233, 238, 240, 264, 272, 276, 277, 283

Jacob, 12, 22, 27, 32, 33, 84, 132-134, 143, 144, 150, 151, 223-226, 233, 242, 260, 275
Jeremiah, 70, 72, 73, 103, 110, 119, 123, 225, 231, 232, 256, 258, 260, 262, 265, 267-269, 284
Jeroboam, 56-61
Jezebel, 61, 62, 64, 124
John the Baptist, 45, 87, 88, 102, 104, 108, 113, 114, 125, 286
John, the Disciple, 111-113, 116, 125, 165, 237, 241, 247, 274, 277, 279
Jonah, 126, 127, 137-139, 142
Josephus, 87, 88, 90, 151, 242, 244, 245, 255
Joshua, 34, 35, 37, 51, 75, 224
Judah (Son of Jacob), 275, 276
Judah (Tribe or Kingdom), 58, 59, 61, 66-73, 76, 110, 187, 262, 266
Judas (the disciple), 8, 155
Judas Maccabaeus, 88

Law, the, ix, xiii, 28, 30-41, 43, 45-51, 53, 59, 60, 66, 69, 70, 74, 75, 81, 82, 88, 93, 94, 102-105, 112, 119, 123, 132, 149, 216, 220, 231, 243, 244, 260, 282, 283
  Mosaic Law, 81, 121
  Written Law, 284
Liturgical, 167, 173, 177

Macedonia, 161, 162
Malachi, ix, 79-82, 84-87, 225, 267
Malleus Maleficarum, 196, 197
Martin Luther, 130, 131, 200, 201
Megachurches, 215, 217, 220
Messianic Judaism, 220
Mishnah (see Oral Law or Mishnah)
Mission Agencies, 147, 219, 281
Missionaries, 147, 149, 152, 158, 163, 164, 211, 215-219, 221, 222
Mission(s) (modern foreign), 202, 206, 214, 215, 217-219, 221, 280, 281
Molech, 56
Monk, 200
Moses, ix, 21, 30-32, 34, 35, 38, 39, 41, 43-46, 50, 58, 74, 82, 92, 94, 96, 112, 132, 154, 224, 282
Mother Teresa, 211

Nadab and Abihu, 264
Nebuchadnezzar, 70, 71, 76, 149
Nero, 163, 164

Nineveh, 126, 137-139
Ninevites, 126, 137, 138
Noah, 14, 17, 22, 259

Olivet Discourse, xiii, 19, 218
Oral Law or Mishnah, 21, 95

Papacy, 178, 180, 182-184
Papal Bull, 173, 193-195, 197
  Ad Extirpanda, 192
  Summis Desiderantes, 195
Papal States, 181-183, 186
Passover, 59, 70, 154-156, 224, 263
Paul or Saul, 17, 39, 40, 84, 113, 117, 131-134, 145, 147, 157, 158, 160-165, 168, 172, 191, 213, 216, 238, 239, 248, 279, 280, 284
Pedophile, 248
Pedophiliac, 210
Penance, 193, 199
Pentecost, 59, 154, 156, 170, 178
People Group(s), 18, 19, 147, 215, 218, 219, 280, 281
  Reached People Group, 219, 221
  Unreached People Group(s), 147, 218, 219, 221
Persecute(d), 210, 222, 247, 252, 254
Persecution, 127, 129, 131, 157, 158, 164, 165, 174, 179, 222, 235, 236, 246, 254

Peter or Simon, 107, 115, 123, 124, 155, 158-160, 164, 165, 177, 178, 188, 235, 265, 278, 284

Pharaoh Who Contended with G-d and Moses, 58, 89, 92

Pharisee(s), 48, 81-83, 94, 95, 100-106, 108,157

Pontius Pilate, 90, 186, 187

Pope(s), v, 173, 174, 176-181, 183-186, 188, 190, 191, 194, 196, 200, 202, 207
  Benedict XV, 217
  Hadrian I, 180
  Innocent III, 191, 235, 236
  Innocent IV, 191-194
  Innocent VIII, 195, 197
  John XII, 181, 182
  Leo III, 180
  Leo IX, 173, 180, 181, 202
  Leo X, 200
  Paul IV, 128
  Pius XI, 203
  Pius XII, 207-210
  Urban II, 185, 188
  Urban VIII, 182-184

Priest(s) (Catholic), 172, 176, 177, 181, 200, 208, 210

Priest(s) (Jesus), 172, 177

Priest(s) (Jewish), 33, 59, 60, 68, 80-83, 105, 107, 172, 186, 238, 264-266, 269, 278

Prodigal Son, 17, 114

Protestant(s), 130, 183, 184, 201, 202, 207, 212-214, 217, 235

Protestantism, 183, 199, 201

Purgatory, 199

Rabbinic Judaism, 104, 220

Rack, 195

Rahab, 29, 149, 276

Reformation, 130, 199, 201

Rehoboam, 56-59

Renaissance, 201, 205

Revived Roman Empire, 246, 247, 259

Roman(s), 31, 84, 90, 113, 120, 121, 125, 131-134, 142, 158, 160, 163, 164, 175, 176, 180, 182, 186, 222, 229, 234, 243, 245, 247, 248, 258-260, 263, 284

Roman Empire, 89, 113, 158, 160, 176, 179, 182, 191, 245

Rome, 86, 127, 163, 164, 176, 178, 181, 192, 203, 217, 224, 247

Sabbath, ix, 29, 30, 82, 91-95, 97, 98, 100-102, 104, 105, 107, 108, 251, 260

Sacraments, 177, 181, 192, 200

Sages, 81, 95-97, 121

Saladin, 185

Samaria, 61, 62, 146, 151, 157, 158

Samaritan(s), 65, 114, 277

Sarah, 25

Saul (First Jewish king), 52, 60, 252

Shavuot (Feast of Weeks), 154-157

Shema, 112

Simoniac, 181

Simony, 180, 181

Singer, Tovia, v, 40, 41, 44-46, 131, 144, 268

Six-Day War, 231

Solomon, 38, 54, 55-57, 126, 149, 283
Strappado, 195
Sukkot (Feast of Booths), 154
Synod(s), 180, 181, 191

Talmud(s), 81, 95-98, 130
Talmudic, 47
Temple, 55, 59, 69, 83, 84, 86, 88, 132, 149, 161, 234, 243-245, 248-250, 258, 260, 278
Terah, 18, 20, 21
Torah, 38, 40, 41, 96, 98, 283
Torture(s), 191-199
Torture Chambers, 194

Trinity, 112, 175, 269
Turkey, 160, 161, 165, 236

UN, 231

Vatican II, 207

War (War of Independence), 231
Witch Hunting, 185, 195, 197, 201

Yad Vashem, 135, 136, 229, 231

Zechariah, 226, 269

Thank you for reading my book!

The final volume of this series, **The Tanakh**, will be out
at Christmas time, 2026.

For more information, go to:
amazon.com or https://lovingkindnessofadonai.com